BLACKS AND THE POLITICS OF HATE

A New Look At the Issue of Race As We Move Forward Into the 21st. Century

To: mark

albert

ALBERT L. JAMES

Library and Archives Canada Cataloguing in Publication

Cataloguing data available through Library and Archives Canada

ISBN 978-1-926582-29-0

CONTENTS

Dedication

This book is dedicated to people everywhere who are presently working to make the lives of others better. It is dedicated also to the memories of those who have passed on, but who had given of their time, effort, and even their lives to help those who were held in bondage and enslavement.

Foreword:

According to Webster's Dictionary the word politics have two meanings — "the art or science of government," and "the total complex of relationships between peoples living in society." It is the latter definition that is attached to the title of this book. While the main thrust will be on the complexities of relationships between two groups of people – the Whites and Blacks, and mainly in North America — the same elements of relationships between Blacks and other racial groups all over the world will also be looked at.

While some people from the White race can be accused of strong inhuman treatment of Blacks, and can be held responsible for some of our misery, it should be also made clear that without the help of members of that race there would have been very few successful Black people in the Western application of the word today. This is especially true of Blacks in the United States. From what I gather, there are no outstandingly successful Blacks in that country who did not have somebody White in their corner at some point, or somewhere. If it is education there has been a White teacher, in sports a White coach or manager. Even in entertainment the same thing can be said. Where there was Cassius Clay (Muhammad Ali) there was Angello Dundee. Oprah Winfrey was helped to the exalted position of probably the richest Black woman in the world by Roger M. King, and Dr. Benjamin Carson would probably not have made it to the world-reknowned Neurosurgeon that he is without the help of William Jaeck. And there are many other cases. So, while much of the evil perpetrated against Blacks will be highlighted, the book will also encourage appreciation and gratitude for the good that some of the same people have done for Blacks and how we have benefited from them.

The book will also discuss the detrimental aspects of the behaviour of Blacks where that exists. It is my considered opinion that our negative behaviour is quite responsible for some of the widespread and unfavourable opinions and dislike for us as a race in some places. This being near universal, Blacks will be encouraged to take full responsibility for our own actions, respect ourselves and others, and seek ways to improve our lives instead of always blaming our poverty and lack of achievement on other people, and our unfavourable situations.

How This Book Came About.

Luke is a former casual worker of mine. His brother once told me that he stops talking only when he is asleep. And indeed, around me his tongue was constantly engaged. We were having a conversation one evening as I was driving him home from work when the topic turned to the problems of Blacks in Canada and elsewhere, focusing on the attitudes of others toward us and what we might have done to deserve the unfavourable reputation that we have acquired. We got into discussing how we might change the way we are seen and what might be the cause why some of us behave the way we do. Luke was not comfortable with the idea that we should be held responsible for any antisocial behaviour, and somewhat insisted that we were hated without just cause in all cases and at all times. I tried to present a counter-argument to this idea but was unable to change his mind. At the time, I was writing a book on an unrelated topic, and he suggested that when I was through writing that book I should write one on "Why Black People Are Hated". I thought about his suggestion for a while and then told him I would write it if I could find the time. I realized it would be a monumental task and thought if it was ever written and published that it would generate a lot of controversy as well as making me unpopular, and probably it still wouldn't solve any of our socio-economic problems.

Being Black, and having been personally confronted with what I consider racial bias in five countries and on three continents, I realize that racism is an international problem. I have had these challenges in Canada and the United States in North America, in South Korea , and the Philippines in Asia, as well as in South Africa on the continent of Africa. I have experienced racially in-tolerant behaviours from people in almost every walk of life and from every race of men including Blacks. Some of these confrontations were more un-comfortable than others. I have also read and heard of conditions of racial disparities in places like Brazil, Japan, India, England, France, and Australia, just to name a few of these places. A book written on the subject of race re-lations should cover the problems not just in North America but worldwide, even though here is where most of the books would in all likelihood be read and where the material would be considered most relevant. I thought too that Blacks may hate it if I got objective and cite some of our own bad behaviours as reasons for us being hated in some instances.

My thought issues led me to the thinking that such a book might even be considered irrelevant in this time of "racial tolerance,". I almost concluded that it might be outdated even before it went to print. I decided that I would risk it and write the book anyway and to title it *Blacks and the Politics of Hate*.

Thanks to Luke for making the suggestion.

A Note from the Author

Many people probably believe that the Black race is in disarray in many parts of the world. From prosperous America to the continent of Africa we hear and see examples of the woes of the lives of of Blacks. We seem mired in confusion, crime, social turmoil, poverty, ineptitude, and despotic regimes with leaders who care only for themselves. Some of our surroundings, even in places like Canada and America, continue to be some of the worst and our civic pride is, quite sadly, mostly lacking.

Mostly everywhere, we are unhappy and unsatisfied with our lives and what we see as our future and that of our children. Some of us feel that much of the White world laughs at us and quietly wishes for our extinction. Indeed, some among us think that it has gone beyond wishing, pointing to AIDS in Africa among the Black population as undeniable proof that those who want to destroy us have already began to do so by spreading this deadly disease which they claim members of the White race has initiated. This they think even though there is no substantive proof to the allegation. Those they think act as if they are the originators of the Black race and the arbiters of our destiny, with the right to do to us as they wish. And though we are unhappy about our situation: we see our powerlessness to make any political, economic, social, or military improvements and wonder what will keep us from complete irrelevance. We think this even though America, the world's greatest nation, has just elected a mixed-race Black man as president of that country. Indeed this one lone man though educated, intelligent, very functional, and efficient, and someone Blacks can all be proud of, and whose accomplishment we may admire -may do very little to erase all the negative stereotypes of the past.

This book will address some very thorny social, spiritual, and economic issues as they affect Blacks, and will present probable reasons for the chaos among us. While it will seek to place much of the blame on others, mainly because of slavery and other aspects of disenfranchisement -even blaming our criminal bent on the experiences of the past. It will also call us to take full responsibility for our own actions and dispel the "earned" negative stereotypes with which, rightly or wrongly, we have come to be associated.

Throughout this book, two aspects of Black life will be looked at, even when such is indirectly referenced. One will be historical with its record of hate and malignancy toward the Black race. The other will be the failure of most Blacks to make responsible decisions, both from an individual and corporate perspective, and to take advantage of present opportunities to make our lives better in numbers large enough to make a positive impact on ourselves and others. I will also look at the almost total impotence of the leaders of Black nations everywhere to effect good and exemplary leadership. This I will look at even on the continent of Africa where, of all places, Blacks should be able to see some inspiration in their leaders. I will nonetheless endeavour to point out anything worthwhile that any Black leader may have accomplished where that may be, even though such might just have created a political or philosophical impact. Most Blacks should readily agree that none of us have grown any national economies worthy of note, created many jobs for our people, or have developed any enterprises of international stature. But please forgive me if after searching through the haystack I cannot come up with any needles.

What Readers Will Find In This Book.

This book is written as a frank discussion about aspects of racial disparity in our social interactions as shown by our disposition to hate, and treat others poorly because of preconceived ideas and upbringing, and because some have decided that they are inherently superior to others because of color or race, or because of skills they have acquired, talents they have developed, and their achievements. It is a hard hitting book on the issue of race, and some of its contents may be very upsetting to some. To discuss openly and frankly the subject of racial intolerance may seem a topic of no interest to sensitive readers, and a frank and open discussion may even be misunderstood or discouraged. I believe that some progress is being made as we see some governments and business enterprises make changes to accommodate Blacks, and where Blacks are now more visibly seen in politics and so on. This is further helped by the arrival of the Internet, and television programs like those of Jerry Springer, the Opera Winfrey Show, Divorce Court, and others of the kind that tell us ever so succinctly of similarities between races in our morals, behaviour, and abilities. But a lot of inequities still do exist among racial groups here in North America, as well as in other parts of the world, and I wonder if we will ever have a society free from this virus? Though racism exists here in North America, we are nonetheless afraid even to refer to individuals as Black or White, just so we can be quiet about, and therefore ignore a very important element so essential to our existence.

People all over the world are still unable to see beyond skin colour and the negative historical stereotypes that have hindered the progress of some and have inflicted intentional and purposeful malice, both social and emotional, on the weaker members of society. Many behaviour patterns still show the unwillingness to make changes that will benefit everyone. In North America, new comers are often given opportunities that historically have been denied to Blacks who have been a part, albeit an unwanted part- of the fabric of the nations for hundreds of years. They bent their backs to labour for the up-building of a society, especially that of America, which has never expressed any real gratitude to the Black people, even though immense profits have accrued to those who took advantage of their efforts.

The same observations can be made of some other countries where Blacks have lived through centuries of slavery and even now live in obscurity, and are almost without representation in government and private industry. In Brazil, for example, even though Blacks comprise almost half the population and were slaves there for more than three hundred years, they continue to live the most wretched and oppressed existence of Blacks anywhere in the Western Hemisphere. Entrenched ethnic hatred with its accompanying evils can also be a topic of discussion for the sub-continent of India where it's Blacks- the Untouchables or the *Dalits*—are the most oppressed people on planet Earth today. We also have the former Iron Curtain, the Middle and Far East, where Blacks are looked upon with much suspicion and hate. In some of these places, there have been allegations of Black residents being beaten so badly they end up disabled, all because of racial prejudice.

In places like America, and even Brazil and South Africa, we can and should give credit to members of the White race for transforming what was essentially wildernesses into the urban infrastructure that exists today. But let us not forget that Blacks contributed their sweat and muscles to complement the efforts of the others.

In twenty-first century America, most inner city Black schools are the stuff of legend when it comes to chronic under-funding, decrepit walls, broken down washrooms, and the poor quality of the education they offer. Living with such inequities from an early age, Blacks sometimes become traumatized by the unfairness and turn to unsociable behaviour, which in many cases leads to criminal acts. It is cited by statistics which will be penned later in this book that many thousands of young Black American males languish in jails, sometimes without formal charges or convictions. Blacks are labeled as criminals from the time they are born and are treated as such until they die. Since no one is really "born" a criminal, maybe in many instances society bears the awful responsibility of making them what they have become. A lot of them seem not to "disappoint" the society in which they live in regards to crime because criminal behaviour is "expected" of Black people. Will the society in which they live ever wake up and realize that if they were expected to become professionals and make positive contributions to society, and were fed those expectations from the earliest years, they would rise to the challenge also? Or does our sadistic, banal society need an underclass to shore up the superiority of the rest? People who know that hatred is levelled at them almost from the very first moment they are exposed to an unfriendly society are barely ever able to make good in life when that continues.

Why does society, especially in America build so many jails aimed at Blacks instead of building better schools and places where affected Blacks can get the help and counsel they need to avoid jails in the first place? Why do social scientists excuse the negative behaviours of other races, claiming it is caused by unfavourable mental conditioning and upbringing, but despise Blacks who have had more than their fair share of such conditions? Black communities become the playground of unseen, White drug lords who victimize them by choosing members of those communities to sell their products for them. Gullible, unsuspecting Blacks are seen only as a source of income by these "suppliers of poison," who are usually the importers of the drugs flowing into these neighbourhoods. We know this because most Blacks don't have the ability to effect the network of contacts it takes to accomplish that on their own, or they import on such a small scale that it hardly makes a dent in the illegal drug supply. If enough evidence to convince could be uncovered, The Iran-Contra Affair of some years ago in the United States may then show what even governments will do to make money for their illicit schemes at the expense and well-being of Blacks by aiding and abetting the free flow of drugs into their neighbourhoods.

Blacks should wake up and stop behaving like losers, whether such is intentionally or unintentionally brought on them by circumstances over which they think they have no control. They must also expunge the cycle of self-hate and self-destruction that now pervades the race and change their focus and lifestyle if they are to have success in life. Blacks should never be content to live the stereotype but should instead be willing to educate and improve ourselves in numbers large enough to make strong, favourable impressions both on society at large and on our own people. We should see that without radical changes in and about our own selves, we will all self destruct. Even so many Black entertainment initiatives fail the test of uprightness, both from a moral and a civil perspective, especially those that glorify hating others and encourage anarchy among the young. Why can't we turn our energies into positive stimuli for the benefit of our race and society and become better role models? Why are we so willing to support the business initiatives of others but are so inclined to ignore the ones our people are involved in? Why are we killing and robbing our own people and others on such a large scale? Why are most of us such purveyors of poverty from one generation to the next?

Shouldn't successful Blacks make a concerted effort to improve the situation of other Blacks, in the way that the people of other races support their own? Why do Blacks continue to behave like little helpless children looking up to other people to hold our hands and guide us as if we can never take on the responsibility of growing up? When will we stop childishly expecting approval from others and grow up to be mature and responsible individuals on our own? The sooner we do this the sooner we will come of age and show the self confidence and self assertiveness the other races have attained to, and make our lives better. Is it because we think others are better than we are that we still spend vital energy and unredeemable time looking up to them even when we don't emulate their achievements? When will we stop hating ourselves and others, and when will we stop blaming everyone else except ourselves for our failures?

I hope this book contains some reflection for everyone who reads it, and will speak to the very hearts of those who see themselves in its pages. I hope too that we will all make an honest effort to eradicate the social evils that mostly all of us have contributed to either by our negative attitudes, our neglect of duty, our failure to act, or our hatred for others.

Introduction:

Like most children, growing up my life had its little problems and headaches. Sibling rivalry was fairly intense between me and my younger brother mainly, but also on and off with my older sister and an older brother as well. With chores and little responsibilities, my life was certainly not what I would call a bed of roses. Along with these other growing pains, I was always scared of the ever-ready whip of a disciplinarian mother, and would cower in what to me was the awful presence of a princely and very over-powering father. Though I feared both my parents to some degree, I also admired, loved, and respected them and always had my eyes fixed on my father whenever he was around; proud that I had such a handsome, strong, hardworking man as my father. He, however, seemed to have taken some dislike of me from a very early age; a dislike I could not understand and found somewhat bewildering.

It disturbed me to the point that one day I decided to discuss it with my mother. In spite of her disciplinarian traits, she was someone I could tell almost anything, even discussing my crushes on neighbourhood girls with her. I spoke about my father's dislike of me to her, but on answers she was somewhat ambivalent. I gathered however, that my father did not like me too much because he thought that I favoured my maternal grandfather. My maternal grandfather had his roots partly in England and partly in Africa. He though, was very light-skinned and except for his kinky hair, his African roots were not very obvious. My mother took his skin colour completely, as opposed to that of her mother who was dark brown. She had siblings who were like him in colour, some like her mother, and others coloured in between them both. My paternal grandfather was from the sub-continent of India, and my paternal grandmother was a descendant of African slaves. My father's skin tone sat directly between those of his father and his mother, but his hair was the hair of an African. I too, am directly between the colour of my mother and the colour of my father. I was therefore shocked to hear that my father thought that I favour my maternal grandfather.

On further investigation, I discovered that my father's problem was not about my skin colour but about two other traits of mine—one physical and the other to do with character. The character trait was my outspokenness, and the physical trait was the fact that my forehead was "formed high" as we say in Jamaica, somewhat like that of my maternal grandfather. Though I loved my father very much and defended him with great energy when the neighbourhood boys criticized him, and would not change him for anything in the world, I secretly wished that I were as fair as my mother and my two younger brothers who inherited her complexion. I had no idea where this wish came from, and I'm glad my father never knew how I felt because I never discussed that with anyone else.

Two of my most obsessive pre-occupations as a child were admiration for beautiful women , and admiration for people who had light-coloured skins. I have grown to overcome the skin colour issue, but I still love beauty. Back then, to my mind, the fairer skin was more desirable, and light-skinned people in general seemed more pleasing to the eye. Looking back now, I wonder if this is because of my mother, the first woman I ever saw. Where I grew up, there were a lot of mixed race people, including my family and countless others. I have relatives with varying eye colours, different types of hair, and varying shades of skin. In my immediate family, there are three distinct shades of skin colour. I began to question myself about my pre-occupation with skin color and external beauty.

From an early age I was an avid reader and went through every bit of paper I could find that had words on it. No book would get past me without being read or perused briefly if time and circumstance prevented a complete read, and I had trouble falling asleep if I couldn't read for a while first. I have a large scar on my left forearm to prove that statement. As children, we had to take time out from school to help my father in the fields when it was "sugar cane time". At the end of each day of field work, I was so tired that I had no energy to read. When the reaping was finally over, I took up my book with a vengeance. About a week after all that hard work, I fell asleep one night with an open wick lamp with me in bed as well as a book. The lamp tilted and the bed sheet caught fire, but luckily only a spot on my forearm was burned. Thanks to my mother who through Divine influence, I believed, had been urged home from Prayer Meeting early that Wednesday evening. She got the flames out in time to save me from what could have been certain death or at least extensive injury. In the process she might have done the same for my sleeping siblings also. Our house then was made of wood and could have fired up like a tinder box in the summer heat of Jamaica.

It's possible that my admiration for fair skin was due in part to the images and pictures I found on the pages of some of the books I read. The people were usually White, and if they were any other colour, the reference was rarely admirable. We had no television sets where I grew up because we had no electricity, but every once in a while a traveling movie company would pass through the area, loudspeakers blaring, announcing that a film would be shown on big screen at the village square or on the elementary school grounds. The proprietors would have their own portable generators to give them the electricity they needed. Our hearts would beat with excitement and my siblings and I, as well as the other neighbourhood children, would beg our parents to give us the equivalent of the six cents that we would need to pay to see the movies. Even though they were shown under open sky we were obliged to pay for the view.

The amount we paid may seem small today but to our parents finding it was a challenge at times. But if they had any little extra cash and there had been no recent behaviour problems, they would give us the money. Many adults would go to these movies also. The movies were always American Westerns with White stars like Roy Rogers and Broderick Crawford. And even though they were White, these actors were our heroes. Because the jury was still out in our minds about the "reality" of movies, we trembled in fear and apprehension when we saw Indians approaching to attack them. We did not want any of them to get hurt, and were very happy when they "killed" the Indians.

Little did we dream that because we were Black, most or all of those actors would probably have disliked us had they ever set their eyes on us, and that our concern should have been for the Indians who in part shared our lot so far as privilege, status, and social acceptance were concerned. We did not see any Blacks in those movies. I did not see many Blacks in those books I read, and those that did appear were shown in pretty negative ways. Blacks did not seem to matter, and as a child I grew up with a strange mindset in regards to my view of Black people, including that of myself.

Thankfully, I also grew up with sympathy for the disadvantaged and the underdog. In school, I learned about the History of the West Indies. I learned of the British fighting with the Maroons in the Cockpit Mountains of Jamaica. One History teacher, a light-skinned relative of mine, told of the Maroons, a very strong and stubborn group of run-a-way African slaves with weapons stolen from raiding White plantations, who would defeat and chase off groups of pristinely trained British soldiers, then called Redcoats one after the other. The remaining Redcoats usually ran for their lives like rabbits down the mountain trails they came up. This happened many times, frustrating the Redcoats who could never figure out the fighting plans of the Maroons. I guess they did not apply the principle of military infiltration back then. My teacher was clearly on the side of the Maroons, and it began to dawn on me that the people I had rarely seen in the books and never in the movies, had some relevance and worth after all. I did not fully understand her glee, however, because she was part White herself, and I thought that she should have been balanced in her reaction. But maybe she was educated enough to know that the different skin tones among us did not matter, and that we were all considered Black in spite of that, without any recognition of our blood relationship to the White race. In any case, she was totally happy that her Black countrymen won victories over their hated White enemies, and over time most or all of us in these classes came to share her enthusiasm for the victories the Maroons gained over the British Redcoats.

While Scripture recognizes only one race—the human race -social scientists and anthropologists now believe that we have four distinct races: Caucasoid, Negroid, Mongoloid, and Austroloid. The definition of Negroid, includes broad-nosed and broad-mouthed characteristics along with Black skin and short, kinky hair for the people thus classified. The Caucasoid definition includes aquiline nose, tall stature, and straight or wavy hair. Though loosely referred to as White, there are dark skinned people who are Caucasians. Mongoloid includes yellow skin with epicanthic folds or slanted eyes, straight black hair, and relatively small stature. The definition of Austroloid is dark skin, curly hair, large teeth and jaws. Austroloids are mostly found in Australia and New Zealand. This is a fairly recent classification.

I am of mixed blood, and this is true of a lot of Jamaicans as well as many others in the world. As such, I assume a tremendous responsibility. I have to love and respect the different racial ancestries from which I descended. Legally speaking, I am a Black man and mostly proud of that. But I have the blood of the Caucasian coursing through my veins as well, and from two angles. My maternal grandmother was a mix of Black, Jewish, and Oriental. Adding to that, I am presently married to a part-Mongoloid woman, and have a Mongoloid-looking son as well as a daughter whose racial mixture is evident although not quite as obvious as that of her younger brother from this relationship. I also have two older children from a previous relationship with a Trinidadian woman of East Indian extraction. These children look more like Indians than like Blacks. I say my wife is part-Mongoloid because she also is the product of a mixed marriage. Her mother is Chinese and her father is Spanish. Her features are more Mongoloid than Caucasoid. Because of the foregoing, and even though it has not done me any tangible good, I can say that I have the United Nations sewn up in my back pocket, in a manner of speaking. Therefore, logically, I should not, and does not hate any racial group. Despite the fact that I may have no relevance to a lot of Whites, Indians, Orientals, and even Blacks, I am very proud of my ancestral roots and will never deny my ties to any part of it. Intrinsically it is what defines me, and though in this book I will not pull any punches about the things I see as necessary to say, I will not ever again succumb to the temptation to hate or degrade any part of my ancestry.

Why is the preceding paragraph necessary?

The above is necessary because this book will address some very controversial issues, with you the reader, seeing things from the perspective of me, the author. I will appear to step on many toes as I will candidly express my opinions. I am known for calling a spade a spade. And in writing this book I will be no different. I expect to be disliked by people from all racial groups if this book is ever published and circulated. If you, the reader, develop these feelings of dislike toward me, please bear in mind that the sentiments expressed are those of someone who presently hates no one in particular seeing that racially I am tied to them all, and also because I am a person who tries to love everybody.

While I admire people of achievement no matter their colour I particularly admire the progress and capacity of White Caucasians, and hold them in high regard for their genius, their achievements, their technological abilities, their advancement in the arts and sciences, and all the good they have brought to the human species all over the world through their positive accomplishments. Even so, I will be expressing strong feelings against some very bad things that they have done to Blacks. I see these expressions as fair and truthful, and not as an attack on White people. Neither should anything I say against any other racial group, including Blacks, which I consider factual or historical to be considered an attack on them. I am not prone to political correctness as I believe that sometimes it muzzles freedom of speech. I do not agree however, that free speech should be used to incite hatred, disrespect of anyone, or disobedience to the just and reasonable laws of society. I will also express very strong opinions on things that the Black race specifically has failed to do. This does not mean that I love them any less. It is just that my conscience does not allow me to be other than candid. I will appear to readers at times to be speaking through both sides of my mouth, but I say I am looking objectively at both sides of the coin, keeping in mind that I see both sides of the coin as valid.

I will accept all comments and negative criticisms from those who wish to make them. Being Black and living on this side of the racial divide, I have always had more than enough hate pointing in my direction anyway by people from all walks of life that don't even know me, so I am used to it, and although I don't feel like a victim, I conclude that some hate me because of what they perceive my shade of skin represents. On a lighter note, some people really desire to have my nice, brown, copper-toned skin and have told me so. No one needs to be afraid of me because of this book. I have always been as sweet as sugar and as harmless as a day-old lamb, and what I have penned has not altered my disposition in any way.

I also believe that there are people who will welcome a frank discussion about racial issues, knowing that they will not go away and that we need to find a sensible way to work with them. Since the end of slavery and long before, there has existed the hope that the next generation will be practioners of improved race relations. But what we see instead are sons practising the same sins as their fathers, and the problems continue to exist and seem unready to go away any time soon. Society hides its collective head in the sand hopes that racial issues will disappear if we refuse to acknowledge them. A frank discussion of issues in print, especially those that affect our lives as much as race does, will be helpful to most.

Finally, it is my strong desire to see some real and lasting progress in Black societies and neighbourhoods, from ultra-modern America where so many Blacks still live in the quagmire of ignorance and abject poverty all over that country, sometimes because of their own lethargy and sometimes because of what society has placed upon them, to the land of Africa, where Blacks even on their own indigenous continent are still mired in political chaos, Black-imposed slavery, demon worship, cannibalism, poverty, militia rape of defenceless women and young girls even to the point of permanent physical injury and sometimes even death, and genocide. I hope some Africans will read this book and get angry enough with themselves and their contemporaries to make some positive changes for the benefit of themselves and their continent. The improvement of the Black race has been one of my most cherished hopes from the earliest years of my childhood when I first began to realize the plight and challenges of being Black. I hope I live long enough to see my desire become reality.

CHAPTER ONE
In The Beginning

This chapter looks at the probable origin of the races. It discusses the possible origin of the concept of one race being superior to the other based on skin colour, the probable reasons for people living in areas as determined by colour, the Black man's early diaspora, his contribution to the global society, and his subsequent fall from grace.

One of the first books I read was the Bible. It was the most relevant book around my house and so naturally was the primary source of spiritual edification. Along with its revelation about the Creator and His will for me and us, it brought up other issues also. The next most influential book was our Church Hymnal. My mother guarded them both with pride and utmost care. She made sure that as soon as either wore out, that they were immediately replaced. I loved reading the Bible and would read it as much as time and opportunity allowed. One of the most conspicious stories in the Bible, and the most important from the perspective of this book, is that of Noah's drunkenness after the flood. The Bible states that Noah cursed Canaan and banished him to a life of servanthood to his brothers because his father Ham had laughed at Noah's uncovered "tutus" (one of the words Jamaicans use for penis). Canaan was the son of Ham, and as I read the story of the geographical area of Ham's descendants, I concluded that he was the father of the Black people.

That story puzzled and confounded me, and it also made me very angry at Noah for placing that curse upon his grandson Canaan. Did this now mean that I, a member of the Hamitic race by genetic ancestry at least in part, was now destined to be a servant for the rest of my life to the descendants of Canaan's uncles, Shem and Japheth? It was a dilemma for me every time I thought about it. But I reasoned that with the blood of the African, I also had the blood of the European, the Indian, and the Oriental coursing through my veins in varying degrees. At the time I did not consider the Indian man from South West Asia to be Black, but I did not realize that along with the European he was also a Caucasian. I concluded that at least my destiny should be a combination of mastery and servanthood. I preferred mastery. And indeed I have been the servant/employee of Japhet and Shem, and as well as the employer of sons of Shem, Japheth, as well as sons of Ham. I wondered agitatedly why God would allow the curse from Noah to take effect. After all, he was partly to blame for being drunk. And it was apparent that it was Ham's first time doing something of the kind. Should he not have been dealt with it a little more kindly - a dog being entitled to its first bite? In any case, Noah must have taken the sighting of his naked penis by his son very seriously. If he had not he would not have issued such a curse on Canaan.

A lot of Black and White people who I have spoken to about this story are really convinced that this curse is the reason for the plight of Blacks and take the conclusion very, very seriously. All of them seem to think that the effect of this curse will last forever, and all of them think that it was/is totally unconditional. Are they correct? I will address this a bit later in the book. Further reading of the Bible indicates that one time when Miriam and Aaron, Moses' older siblings, had nothing better to do with themselves, they started bothering him about the Ethiopian (Black) woman he had married. This distressed me very much. Where did they get the idea that they should complain about his Black wife? Did they think that she was inferior to them because of her colour? The fact that the Lord dealt severely with them did not assuage my consternation to complete satisfaction because by my time, it seemed firmly entrenched in the minds of humans that members of the Black race were inferior to everyone else just because they had a different skin tone, different hair, as well as other physical differences.

Later in the Bible, I read that the Lord sent a message through one of His prophets to Israel pointing out to them that without His help it was impossible for them to change from bad to good just as it was impossible for the Ethiopian to change his (Black) skin. Also, I read that the Israelites defeated the Ethiopians who had come to fight them with a much larger army. I sort of hated the fact that the Ethiopians lost. Reading these negative stories about the Black race, even in the Bible, made me worry that not even God cared for Blacks. I spoke to an elder of my church about it who I thought would have the answer, but he did not and I became even more bewildered.

There was a time after the re-population of the Earth began when the Black man was apparently worshipped as a god. It happened at the time of Nimrod, the mighty hunter who it is reported, was Black. He was adored and worshipped for his great strength and skill as a hunter. I did not see how just being an ordinary hunter made anyone mighty, so I concluded that he and his companions must have done more than just "hunting," as I understood it at the time. They may have been involved in some kind of sports hunting of wild and ferocious animals. Nimrod became the first sun-god, after he was allegedly killed by Shem who was still alive at the time, and who dismembered his body and sent it over all the then known world as a sign of what would happen to those who did like what he did. His sister, Semiramis (some say his mother), who apparently had been his wife, was able to gather up all the pieces and made him a god to the secret cult they had formed. She was later worshipped as a goddess. They were the first two recorded people to be worshipped as god and goddess after the flood. She undoubtedly was also Black. Down through the ages, different nations have worshipped some kind of Black gods and Black goddesses. Baal, whom the Canaanites and the apostatizing Israelites worshiped, was Black. The Amorites who, it is reported, were White-skinned, blue-eyed, and had partly reddish hair, also worshipped Baal. (Notice that the Amorites were called Canaanites — descendants of Canaan who Noah cursed). The Hindus still worship a Black god, and when I was in the Philippines some years ago, I saw a Black doll at a shrine that the adherents held in great adoration, worshipping it and rubbing it on their faces and holding it to their bodies when they were able to get their hands on it. It seems back then that along with being worshipped, the descendants of Ham were also the first to accept or lead out in the worship of a god other that the Mighty Creator. This will be an important point to keep in mind as you go through this book because it will be addressed later in more detail.

In spite of all those details, negative thoughts about the Black race bothered me till I migrated to Canada. Imagine my further worries when I heard that some of the White people in the church denomination to which I belong had their own theory about the origin of the Black race. According to them, the prophetess, one of the human instruments through whom God set up this church, had something to say about the antediluvian or pre-Flood manipulation of the created species resulting in amalgamation, producing creatures that God did not create. This resulted in animals like the mule, or the Rottweiler and some other species of animals. And though it was never addressed publicly, the thought was that it was the combining of a human with apes that produced the Black race. In their malicious rush to degrade Blacks, they have forgotten that all the confused species that God did not create died in the Flood, a point that the prophetess made, and one which I myself did not know of until just a few years ago. This was something they should have known, however, because they consider themselves experts in such fields. They had ignored the fact that only eight people were saved in the Ark, and that therefore all people now living came from them. However, it is not totally unlikely that they think amalgamation had again taken place since the Flood. They base their arguments on the physical appearance of some of the members of the Black race.

This theory was taken so seriously by them that they thought any marriage between a White and a Black person was a sin. When I just got to Canada, I met a young mixed-race woman from Trinidad who had three of the most beautiful children I ever saw. She had been married to a White fellow of the same religion, but it is alleged that there were those among the church leaders back then who convinced him that his marriage was a sin in the eyes of God. The result of that overview was the abandonment of his very beautiful wife, and his three small children, all under ten years old at the time, leaving them to fend for themselves. I have wondered ever since hearing that about which act was the sin in this instance and who had committed it. It is apparent that the woman's genitals and other natural properties were like that of any White woman and had given him so much pleasure that he indulged himself enough times to produce three fully human offspring with very pronounced White features. They had no resemblance, obvious or apparent, to any lower form of animals to me or anyone else who saw them.

In any case, my mind began searching for logical reasons why these White people came to those conclusions, and because they linked us more to the apes, thinking that those creatures were the most likely ones which were amalgamated with humans, I started seeing what I thought were similarities between the apes and some Black people I looked at. Anyway, monkeys in other parts of the world seem to take on the features of the indigenous people also just like a pet sometimes seems to look like its owner. If you do not agree with the above statement, take a look at monkeys from South and North East Asia next time you get a chance. You will certainly think that they seem to resemble the inhabitants of those countries sometimes.

I looked at Mongoloids and saw that aside from the skin colour and hair some of them shared some physical features with us, the Blacks. Some Blacks were beautiful and pleasing to the eye and I wondered how to tell the difference. I wondered also if being mixed racially would lessen the curse or the severity of the impact of the theory these people came up with. Then also, I could not understand why Blacks have kinky hair when neither the human nor the ape from which they came had that kind of hair? And why had they not taken on the more handsome features of the human combination as opposed to that of the apes?

These preoccupations created a huge problem for me and brought about tremendous amounts of mental stress as I struggled to find answers to the questions and conclusions they left in my head. I admired the beautiful White women I saw and thought of marriage to one of them, but was afraid of their mindset about committing this "sin" as these church members called it. There were few people to talk with about these things on my mind, and the one or two to whom I could speak had no answers to give. They were just as confounded as I was, and most had no such pre-occupations at all.

Stories abound in the Bible of people whose illustrious lives filled the world with inspiration, but where were we? Jethro was the father of Moses' wife. If she was called Black, then he must have been Black as well. He did a good thing for Moses. But he was also called a Midianite, and we know what they became and what happened to them later. I read that an Ethiopian saved the life of the prophet Jeremiah, and that Phillip the Evangelist was sent by the Holy Spirit to give the Gospel to the Ethiopian (Black) eunuch. But some people think that this Ethiopian eunuch was a Jew, and therefore a Caucasian, who was employed by the queen of the Ethiopians. And the overwhelming weight of evidence was unfavourable in my now defensive mind, toward the Blacks - the mind that was also now becoming sympathetic to the plight of members of the Black race.

I wanted to go way back in time to inquire about why the Blacks became a hated race. I wanted to discover the reasons for other races getting it into their minds that the fairer the skin the better one was. I wanted to find out who or what told us what was beautiful and what was not. I wanted to know where the concept of human inferiority and superiority come from. Were there other beings greater than us humans who were able to plant bad ideas into our minds to make us think and develop attitudes which disrupt normal human behaviour, and put in perpetual misery whole generations of the Black race?

Growing up, my older sister and I were so pre-occupied with the skin colour issue that we would sometimes compare even our own skin tones. As far as I can recall, only she and I in our immediate family had such pre-occupations. My other siblings did not seem to give the matter a single thought and certainly never talked about it. And then, as well, for me, everyone had to be beautiful. Whether it was a man or woman, boy or girl, dark skin or fair skin, beauty was a big issue. It became such a problem that if I considered someone ugly, he or she had no relevance to me at all. I would not play with what I considered an ugly child, and I avoided talking to people who I considered ugly whenever I could, though I am not so handsome myself. Even now, I will spend hours on end looking at a beautiful person, usually a woman. As I grew up, much of my mental energy was absorbed in the pre-occupation of these two issues – skin colour and beauty.

Now, my first physical person-to-person contact with a real White individual came one day when my older brother and I were running an errand for our father. We were sent to a village about three miles from where we lived. This village was situated in a deep valley separating the mountaintop on which we lived from another that we could look across at. The village was called Gold Mine. This place was so called because a group of White foreigners had at one time been digging for gold in the area after finding what they thought was a vein of gold somewhere there. They left a couple of yellow Land Rovers, which are probably there to this day although they must be completely rusted out by now. I remember my brother, whenever he passed that way, spending time turning the steering wheel, tooting the soundless horn, and making car noises as he pretended to drive. I was always too much of a coward to do that, but I enjoyed sitting on the passenger side of the vehicles. He was going to do the same this time also.

As we neared the place, we saw two young White men coming toward us. They were very blonde with blue eyes, very scared, and to us, very scary looking. They also looked completely lost. We were very afraid even though it was our domain. What on earth were they doing in this remote area of Jamaica, let alone in this deep Gold Mine gorge! We tried speaking to them, but they seemed in a mighty hurry to get away from the place and into familiar territory. By then, I had learned a bit about White Americans from the few gentlemen who had gone from our area to do seasonal farm work there. We thought that these men could only have been Americans. I was about six or seven years old at the time, but wanted them to feel safe. They were at least sixteen miles from "civilization" in the direction where they were going, and going on foot would not get them there anytime soon. We wondered if they had come to retrieve the Land Rovers but found the engines unable to start.

Seeing other White people came when some visiting missionary from America would visit our church, or occasionally when our own occasional Jamaican White pastors would come to visit us. It was not their skins that awed me so much because in my village were lots of fair-skinned people, my mother and two brothers among them. It was their hair and eyes and their totally different mannerisms. The head elder from my local church had been on one of those farm working expeditions and made an acquaintance with a White woman from America. From time to time, she would take her vacation in Jamaica and spend time with his family. I would ask all I could about her from one of his adopted boys. They mentioned one time how she had kissed them goodbye and how cool it was to be kissed her thin lips. I envied them and wished I could have been there to have that experience. Whenever she came to our church, everyone seemed to sit as far away from her as they could. Sometimes she seemed to have the long wooden pew all by herself. It was not because they hated her. They were just shy and not sure what to do. The elder did not seem too interested in sharing her company with any other member of the church family and very little acquaintance was ever made with her by anyone other than his family. I obtained her American address and wrote to her asking her to take me to her country. She never replied to me but instead wrote to the elder and told him of my request. The elder was not very happy with me for doing that, and I was very embarrassed about the whole thing. She only came back once after that. I believe she was not in a position to help, it being the Sixties, she probably knew she would be making herself a social outcast having a Black kid living with her in Florida where she came from.

When I was seventeen years old, I started a teaching job at the Primary school in my district. On one occasion, three White foreign Peace Corps members came to our school to look around and observe us. They seemed distant and detached from us and maybe even scared. We were all normal, beautiful people. The community that I grew up in, had some of the most beautiful, intelligent, and civil people I ever came across anywhere. We came in all hues and colours. We were well dressed and most of our older folks were avid readers of the newspapers, discussed politics, listened to their radios, read the Bible, and knew about the world, etc, and I saw no reason for anyone to be afraid of or to look down on us. They left after a very short time having only spoken to one of our staff. I thought to myself that they could have learned something about us by meeting some of us and asking us questions about ourselves. I did not have the same kind feeling for them as I had for the two young men in Gold Mine. By then also, I had become a little more knowledgeable about what was happening in the world relative to racial issues, and what I thought of as the evil designs Whites had for Blacks. By then I was also quite suspicious of anyone who was White and especially a foreigner. I don't necessarily have the same depth of feelings now.

The very first time I had a person-to-person conversation with a White Caucasian was on a visit to the city of Old Harbour. It was on one of my monthly trips I took as a teacher to change my paycheque at one of the banks there. On this occasion, I went to a variety store to buy something to eat. The ever-popular Jamaican patty was the purchase of choice, and I got me a cream soda to drink as well. As I came out of the store, a tall, one-eyed, White Jamaican man approached and started a conversation with me. Ever curious to learn about new people, and because he reminded me a bit of my maternal grandfather, I stopped to speak with him. He engaged me in a very animated conversation and spoke to me as if he had known me all his life going into personal details about himself. I listened quietly not knowing quite what to say except for nodding my head and expressing the soft guttural tones of "ah ah" and "uh uh." At length, he asked me to get him something to eat, something like what I had. I went back inside the store and bought two patties and a drink for him. Such a thing I was always happy to do, but in this case I was taken aback that a member of the White race would "condescend" to ask me to buy him something to eat. Except for the Gold Mine incident, every other time when I saw them, they always seemed to be the ones who had what they wanted.

He never thanked me for the purchase, but I was not offended by that. When I was growing up in Jamaica, I would be lucky if as a young person I would ever get one older than I to say please or thank you. We the younger ones understood that to mean that we were subservient to them, and that they did not have to use those courtesies if they didn't want to. Such things as gender, skin colour, even if they were strangers, were not factors to consider. We respected and obeyed everyone and anyone older than ourselves. We continued talking for a while, and then I had to say goodbye to him to get on to other things that I had gone to the city to accomplish. All through that encounter the colour of my skin seemed completely insignificant to him. I was quite impressed by that and still remembers his serene and benign face to this very day.

As I began my search for answers about the inequities of being Black, I was taken here, there, and everywhere for answers to the unspoken questions I had in my mind. All my teachers, all the policemen, lawyers, judges, doctors, nurses, and most of the politicians were Black in the general sense. I say in the general sense, because here on this side of North America, the skin colour is defined quite differently from the one we used. In Jamaica, a Black person was someone whose skin colour was close to coal black. We then said dark, meaning not quite so black, brown, the classification that I would come under, fair, which was a notch or two up from my shade, or "malatta," a perverted Jamaican word for Mulatto. This was the classification that my mother and two brothers would come under. Sometimes we would use the word to mean a half-breed, to most Jamaicans a half-White, half-Black person. Some places in the West Indies and Asia define that as a mix between any two races. In America, which seem to set the standard for these things in North America, the legal definition of Black is someone with sub-Saharan African blood. No matter how many generations removed, even if that person is blonde and blue-eyed, with a skin as white as milk, as long as he or she had a Black ancestor - some great, great, great, great, great grand-something, if the White society finds out, he or she is considered legally Black.

Even though the Jamaican professionals mentioned previously were mainly Black, none of them had businesses, enterprises, or corporations that I knew of. In and around my district, the shopkeepers were Black, but it was almost always some other race of persons coming around to sell breads, cookies, other confectioneries, and staples such as sugar, flour, and rice. I began to wonder why we did not have large businesses. Since living in Canada I have met other Jamaicans with a different experience, but as I grew up my mind and outlook were shaped by the events and realities around me. To this day, when I hear of a Jamaican businessman who is successful on a large scale, I ask the question : "Is he Black?" Many times I am given a resounding "Yes!". I am beginning to believe it. The people who seemed to me to have had the commercial successes were obviously the Whites, the Chinese, Syrians, Indians, and others. The corporations were owned by the Whites as well. The Blacks seemed to have been the teachers, nurses, and so on. All this was of general consensus in my mind.

Another concern I had at the time was of our not having much flat, fertile land to grow crops, and why we mostly lived in the hills or cities. The head elder of my church had the answer for that. He said that generations back, when Black people were finally emancipated from slavery, they were very scared of being enslaved again, so they took to the hills for safety and would not come down even when entreated fervently to do so. He did not have an answer for why they lived in the cities. I was not very happy with his answer because though it may have been true, he had some kind of sneer in his voice, and he had previously made statements that were somewhat derogatory in my mind towards Blacks even though he was one of us. Had the term Oreo been in use in those days, I would have concluded that it was a good description of him. To make him even a bit more incendiary in my mind, he was a part of the upper crust in my area and that kind of made him keep his nose in the air. I, therefore, had to take his answer with a grain of salt. Incidentally, by the time you finish reading this book, you might also think of me as an

Oreo. Anyway, I can live with that, but I assure you that I am only trying to be objective and look at both sides of the issue.

When I was a teacher, we sometimes went on day trips to various parts of our Island. My church group did this too. Teachers were required to take their students on what we called Outings. We went to places like Dunn's River Falls on the north coast, the Prime Minister's residence, the Governor General's residence, the Zoological Botanical Gardens, and the Airport in Kingston. We invariably came across White folks on those trips. I believe some of them were local Jamaicans, but a lot of them were foreign tourists. Sometimes I would engage them in conversations about their countries and lives.

Some were shy and merely mumbled, there were others who simply tolerated me in conversation or would not speak to me at all. Then there were others who seemed not to mind talking to me or anyone else who would speak to them. On one of these trips, I met a man and his son in Ocho Rios. The boy was sitting on a reclining beach chair with pencil and paper in hand on which he was sketching something. I approached them and asked the father what his boy was doing. I was told that he was drawing the landscape of the area. He proudly told me that his son wanted to be an artist. I was shocked that a White person from abroad wanted his son to be an artist. When my older brother and I tried our hands at this sort of thing, and we were quite good: our parents would accuse us of idleness and totally discouraged us from the activity. Later on, I learned that artistic skills could be very valuable, even though it had never financially benefited neither me or my brother because we had not felt encouraged to develop that skill because of our parents' reaction.

CHAPTER TWO
Black African Early Diaspora

This chapter will discuss the diaspora of the Black man in the early days of three of the major nations of Asia. These are China, Japan and India. The chapter will detail the contributions of Blacks to these civilizations and how they were finally kicked out of them or relegated to the back seat of irrelevance. I will also look at Blacks in England, Brazil, Mexico, and in the Arab world from the early days of slavery till now.

Notwithstanding the general disrepute into which the Black race has fallen and the contempt in which we are sometimes held, it is believed by some that in the beginning Blacks were a positive influence all over the world from the Far East to the West, and that all other races came from the Black race. On a recent trip to South Africa, I visited a place referred to as the Cradle of Mankind from where it is believed that all the members of the human race descended. While I find that information of some interest, I really do not believe it. But that is another story.

Apart from Western countries, there are others which ignore the contribution of Blacks to their history and culture and continue to hold us in disregard for no other reason other than the fact of racism and information that they get from the Western media which reports mainly the bad things that Blacks do. This, they think, is the sum total of the Black experience and contribution, and even though none of these bad things may be happening in their countries, Blacks are feared and avoided by them as if we were a contagious disease. At the same time not everyone even in those countries can be found guilty of malice towards Blacks, even though they might not acknowledge us as having made any contributions to their culture, or of having been a part of their country. It is alleged that some of these nationals are aware of the Black influence in their culture, but avoid making too much of the information available. Though on a much smaller scale, sometimes, the hostility or misunderstanding of Blacks in these societies can be as harsh as it was and sometimes still is, in the Western societies. For example a female Black English teacher who taught in South Korea for a while tells of being propositioned on the streets for sexual favors, and when she refused to give herself, finds shock and disbelieve on the part of her would-be sex partners because of that. She claims to be always told by them that Black women from North

America are only interested in sex and that Blacks here live only in crime infested neighbourhoods and are only familiar with guns and violence. She claims also that some adult students refused to attend her classes because of the color of her skin. It should be intelligently concluded however, that they could not all be the same.

My purpose for inserting the concept of the Black presence in, and contributions to those countries is to assuage, if you will, the negative stereotype that Blacks have not done anything quite worthwhile in the past and that we have only been the dregs of society. Another reason is to get away from the idea that only Whites have treated Blacks harshly and have no respect for them. It may be said by some that European nations have done more to hurt the Black race than everybody else combined. However, they are not the only ones to despise us. Later on I will sum up attitudes and patterns of negative behaviour, and outline what I consider extreme lack of social and economic progress that Blacks themselves have failed to make using our own initiatives both in the past and in the present. For now, just let us concentrate on a few historical positives so far as Blacks are concerned.

Quite a lot will be said on the Black presence in South West Asia because, surprisingly, about 160 million "Black" people lives there today. This is undoubtedly the largest Black population residing in any country in the world outside of Africa. These people may not, however, be considered Black in the same way as Africoid Blacks. And to understand this concept of Blacks in South West Asia, it is necessary to gain a bit of knowledge relative to migration made by Africans many centuries ago. Some of that information will be covered as a pre-amble to discussing Blacks and their plight in that part of the world.

According to studies done and published for many decades now, Blacks from Africa have been in many of the countries of East and Southeast Asia. In the Far East as well as South East Asia, Blacks were and are still referred to as Negritoes. Some of them still racially homogenous continue to live today in the Philippines and parts of Indonesia, even though they seem to keep very much to themselves and do not mix with the general population. Some have been racially integrated into the mainstream of society because of mixed marriages. Japan is one of those places where Blacks are not usually seen in a favourable light. Yet, in recent years I have heard and read that a few of them have taken up residence there, most working as English teachers, and indeed I met one such person when I lived in the great state of Texas who had gone there to teach the English language. His report on things was generally positive. But there are others who have not such a glowing story on life for Blacks in that country. I understand that a lot of Black musicians go there to provide entertainment for the Japanese and I have met and spoken to one of them, Ernie Smith, a Jamaican Reggae star of a few years back.

Blacks in Japan

In the preparation for this book, I naturally had to do some research, and the Internet is one place I turned to for some information. One of the research sessions I undertook described what is considered "indisputable evidence" that Blacks have played an important role in the very early days of Japan's development until about the ninth century. To begin with what is called a "significant example" of past Black presence in Japan, a report in February of 1986 carried by the Associated Press stated that-the oldest Stone Age hut had been unearthed near Osaka. Archaeologists dated the hut to about 22,000 years ago and said it resembled the dugouts of African Bushmen, according to Wazuo Hirose of Osaka Prefecture of Education's cultural division. "Other homes, almost as old had been found before, but this discovery is significant because the shape is cleaner, better preserved and is more similar to the African dugouts," he said.

Anthropologist Ronald B. Dixon claims that in Japan the ancient Negrito element may still be discerned by characteristics visible there today. The earliest population of Japan was a blend of Proto-Austroloid and proto-Negroid types. Some claim that the Yellow Race came about as the result of interbreeding in a cold climate between members of the Black and White races. There are some who believe that the White race itself came from the Black race. The belief prevails in some minds that the people who populate the island of Japan today are descended from Blacks: that the first population of Japan was Black and gave to Japan its first language.

Of the Black people of early Japan, the most picturesque and singular figure was Sakanouye no Tamuramaro, a warrior symbolized in Japanese history as a "paragon of military virtues,", and a man who has captured the attention of some of the most distinguished scholars of twentieth century America. The first person to study Tamuramaro was Alexander Francis Chamberlain who lived from(1865- to 1914). He was an anthropologist born in England and taken to America as a child. In April of 1911, the *Journal of Race Development* published an essay by him entitled "The Contribution of the Negro to Human Civilization." While discussing the African presence in early Asia, he stated the following: "And we can cross the whole of Asia and find the Negro again, for when, in far-off Japan, the ancestors of the modern Japanese were making their way northward against the Ainu, the aborigines of that country, the leader of their armies was Sakanouye Tamuramaro, a famous general and a Negro." Lois Maillot Jones (1905-1998) in the November issue of the *Negro History Bulletin* pointed out that: "the probable number of Negroes who reached the shores of Asia may be estimated by the wide area over which they were found on that continent. Historians tell us that at one time the Indian Ocean and along the east coast as far away as Japan was the traverse of Blacks. There are many interesting stories told by those who reached that distant land, which at times they called Cipango.

In 1940, Joel Augustus Rogers, (1883-1966), who probably did more to popularize African history than any other scholar of the twentieth century, devoted several pages of the first volume of his *Sex and Race,* to the Black presence in early Japan. He cites the studies of a number of accomplished scholars and anthropologists, and even goes as far as to raise the question of "Were the first Japanese Negroes?" Rogers said: "There is a very evident Negro strain in a certain element of the Japanese population, particularly in the south. The Negro element in Japan is recognized by the Negroid aspect of certain inhabitants who have dark and often blackish skin, and frizzy or curly hair. The Negritos are the oldest race in the Far East. It has been proved that they once lived in Eastern and Southern China as well as in Japan where the Negrito element is still recognizable in the population."

Some Japanese names are also quite similar in sound and spelling to some sub-Saharan African names. As well in South Africa many of the accents of the various tribes are very similar in sound to those of people I have listened to in the Philippines and other parts of East Asia. It is conceivable that they could be languages with a common origin.

Tamuramaro himself was the most eminent Negro known to live in Japan. He was regarded as an outstanding military commander of the early Heian royal court (794-1185). It was during this time that the word *Samurai* was first used. The word really means "to be on guard" and applied especially to the soldiers who were on guard at the Imperial palace. In a sense, James Murdoch claims, Tamauramaro was the originator of what was subsequently to develop into the renowned Samurai class. He provided in his own person a worthy model for the professional warrior on which to fashion himself and his character, in battle, a veritable war god, in peace the gentleness of manly gentlemen, and the simplest and most unassuming of men. Throughout his career, he was rewarded for his services with high civil as well as military positions.

In 797, he was named the "barbarian-subduing generalissimo" (*Sei-i-tai-Shogun*). He was buried in the village of Kurisu, near Kyoto when he died, and it is believed his tomb is known under the name of *Shogun-zuka*. He is the founder of the famous temple Kiyomizu-dera and is the ancestor of the Tamura *daimo* of Mutsu. He was not only the first to bear the title of *Sei-i-tai-Shogun*, but he was also the first of the warrior statesmen of Japan. According to Dr. Diop, it is likely that it was because of Tamuramaro that the tantalizing and profound Japanese proverb was coined, "For a Samarurai to be brave he must have a bit of Black blood."

But in the Japan of today there is apparently much dislike of Blacks. Some Blacks report the open verbalization of hate toward them by Japanese people and some Japanese will admit that in their country, Blacks are highly discriminated against, even more so than by Caucasians. It is probably not fair however, to say that all Japanese are hateful of Blacks. And some Black people, who have lived there, tell of having met friendly and emotionally and mentally balanced Japanese people. This I have heard from at least four Blacks that have lived and worked there.

My view of the Japanese attitude toward foreigners comes from reading the history of World War II, and from one of their prime ministers, Nakasone, who governed in the late 1970s to early 1980. I remember him being a bit darker and taller that the average Japanese and now wonders if he thought that he had Black blood in his veins – something he most likely hated. Nakasone, demonstrated his dislike for Blacks to the point that it is reported that whenever a Japanese company was set up in North America while he was governing, he endeavoured to have that company set up in the suburbs so it would not attract any Black workers as they mostly live in the inner cities and were less likely to seek employment in the areas where those companies existed. In general however, the Japanese are probably indifferent to people of any other race or nationality. But as a general rule, people tend to express the worst of themselves toward those who are the weakest in their society. We look forward to changes in the Japanese attitude toward Blacks especially in light of the fact that we buy so many of their cars and other products that they manufacture.

Blacks in China

It is believed that Blacks ruled at least in some parts of China from 1100-700 B.C, and that from West Asia to China the land was occupied predominantly by them. The Blacks were forced from East and Southwest Asia by the expansion of the Thai, Annamite, Bak, and Hua Mongoloid people. The Blacks were known in historical literature by many names, including "Negro," "Australoid," and "Oceanean" by the Europeans. The East Indian and Mongoloid groups had other names for these Blacks. Names like: *Dara, Yneh-chin, Yaksha, Suka,* and *K'un-lun, Lushana,* and *Seythians.* The original Black population that lived in China belonged to the Negritos and Australoid groups. It is believed that after 5000 B.C. Africoid people from Kush in Africa began to enter China and Central Asia from Iran, while another group reached China by sea. This double route migration to China by Blacks led to the development of northern and southern branches of Chinese Africoids. In the north they were called *Kui-shuang* or *Yuen-chih* and in the south they were called *Yi* and *li-man Yueh* and *Man.* It is said that Blacks also lived in Mongolia, Turkestan, Transxoiana, the Ili region, and Xingzian province. In northern China, the Africoids founded many civilizations. There were three major empires of China – the Xia Dynasty (1900-1700 B.C.), Shang/Yih Dynasty (1700-1050 B.C.), and the Zou Dynasty. The Black tribes living in China founded the first two dynasties and the other was founded by the Mongoloids.

In Southeast Asia and Southern China, ancient skeletal remains have been found representing the earliest inhabitants to be Australoids and Negrito. The skeletal evidence from the Shantung and Kiangsu in China show the modern Africoid type. Blacks also founded the Yangshao site at Huang Ho basin in North China. In the south-eastern section of China, the people at Hupeh and Guangxi made use of artificial irrigation and by terracing of the mountain slopes. The Blacks of southern China, according to some anthropologists, spoke the Austronesian language like that of the aborigines of Hainan and Taiwan. From southern China, the Oceanic peoples invaded northern China, which was mainly inhabited by Australoids and a smallish Negroid-Mongoloid group. Although the Australoids had been the first inhabitants of China, by 1000 B.C, many of them had been exterminated or absorbed by the taller, heavier Mongoloid Bak tribes that were slowly expanding southward from the north. By 3000 B.C, the Negritos were being forced into isolated areas of China by Proto-Saharan Blacks. About the same time, the Oceanic people were moving northward from the coastal plains area.

Many scholars and laymen have recognized similarities between China and Africa. As an example, the straw hats worn by the people of West Africa are also worn in China. As well, both the ancient Chinese and West Africans had a mound culture that used similar burial customs and common symbols. Many theories have been put forth concerning the origins of these similarities but few of them satisfy scientific proof because they neglect to address the possibility that Blacks lived in China before the advent of the East African slave trade. As noted earlier, the first two dynasties of China are believed to have been founded by Blacks from Africa. These Blacks spoke Dravidian and African languages. The first civilizations were called Xia and Shang. They were ruled by emperors called Xuan Di or Black Emperors. These Blacks introduced farming and writing to China. Trade and travel grew under their leadership. In addition, these Blacks introduced bronze workings to China. They also invented the pounded earth architecture that is associated with early Chinese city-states. The founder of the Xia dynasty was King Yu. Chinese traditions claims that the great Yu was the regulator of the waters and the builder of canals. He also invented wet field agriculture. At the beginning of the Xia dynasty, walls were being built around cities to protect them from invading nomadic tribes. The Xia had writing, inscribed pottery, and bronze vessels and household items.

The most important culture in Chinese history is the Shang or Yin dynasty. The Shang culture was founded by Yi tribes. Both the Yi and Yueh tribes, according to Prof. Shun-sheng Ling, comprised of Blacks. The name Shang refers to the town that was the early capital of the empire. According to a Shang poem, "Heaven bade the dark bird to come down and bear Shang". The earliest Shang capital was located at Zhengzou. There were 30 kings of Shang, and the last 14 Shang kings reigned at An-yang, or Henan in the Yellow River Valley. Today, there are no Black people in China in any meaningful numbers. They were apparently chased out of that country by those who eventually conquered them.

The above serves to provide evidence that Blacks have been part of the Chinese culture and have made great impressions upon the early inhabitants of that country, even though at this time there seems to be no such information being made public to the vast majority of Chinese people. Today, there are stereotypes, which the Chinese themselves - though not prone to be generally hostile in the main sense of the word toward Black people do apply to Blacks. One of these stereotypes is that Blacks are mainly sexual. This the Chinese have blindly borrowed from the Western media. The last time I took stock, however, there were about 1.3 billion Chinese on the mainland, whereas in all of Black Africa, a much larger continent than the country of China, the entire population was just about 700 million. So there is the answer to the Chinese stereotype of the sexual pre-occupation of the Black race as fed to them by the West. Unfortunately, people from other parts of the Orient also wrongfully think the same about Black super sexuality. According to some reports, the Chinese are mostly curious about the modern day Black presence in their country, and most Blacks there are students. The Chinese, in some cases, are apparently worried about Blacks going to China to take away their jobs. This is a cry uttered even by ultra-modern Westerners and should not be used to single out the Chinese as racists. Some of the Chinese men, as with men of any other nation, worry about Black men taking away their women.

One of the advantages that the few Blacks who go to China experience is the curiosity of the Chinese, which serves to make them more willing to be their own judge of character so far as Black people are concerned. This allows them to evaluate on its own merit the character of the Black person they meet. One complaint that foreigners make about China is the willingness to have them pay more than what the Chinese people have to pay for the goods they purchase. They view this as racism, whether they are Black or White. The Chinese also complain about this because they say that the same applies to them if they are from another part of the country, even though they are all Chinese. Outside of China they seem to mix quite a bit in terms of marriages to other races. In Jamaica and other islands of the West Indies, many people are of mixed Black/Chinese ancestry. This is a fairly frequent occurence in Jamaica when I lived there and I have met many mixed marriages of Black and Chinese couples. It is believed that the Hakka Clan from China are mainly the ones who travel to other countries of the world as migrants. While they speak the main languages of China, they also speak their own dialects. They set up businesses and are usually very self sufficient working together. As a result of this the Hakka are considered open minded and cosmopolitan in their outlook towards those they come in contact with and are allegedly less likely to be discriminatory.

Blacks in India

One of the most interesting discoveries I made in my research is that the sub-continent of India at one time had a very large and powerful Black presence. This may not be any surprise to some contemporary scholars of anthropology because, based on recent DNA studies, all modern humanity allegedly originated in Africa. These studies also reveal that African peoples are the world's aboriginal peoples, from whom all modern humans can ultimately trace their ancestral roots. They conclude that if it had not been for the primordial migrations of early African peoples, humanity would have remained essentially and physically Africoid, and the rest of the world outside of the African continent absent of human life. Not only are Black Africans the aboriginal peoples of the planet, however, they claim that there is abundant evidence to show that Blacks created and sustained many of the world's earliest and most enduring civilizations. With this as the backdrop, it should then not surprise anyone that Black Africans at one time or the other would have occupied much of the world — India included.

In Greater India of more than a thousand years before the foundations of Greece and Rome, it is said that proud and industrious Black men and women called Dravidians erected a powerful civilization. This was the Indus Valley civilization, which was India's earliest high culture. There were major cities spread out along the course of the Indus River. This civilization was at its height from about 2200 B. C. - 1700 B. C. This phase of India's history is called the Harappan Civilization, the name coming from Harappa, which was one of the earliest cities in the Indus Valley. In 1922, the large city of Mohenjo-daro was identified about 350 miles northeast of Harappa. Since then, several additional cities have been excavated. These cities all had multi-level houses with sophisticated wells, drainage systems, and bathrooms. A recognized scholar of the Indus Valley civilization, a Dr. Walter A. Fairservis, states that the Harappans cultivated cotton and probably rice, domesticated the chicken, and may have invented the game of chess. Harappa was also one of the two great early sources of the windmill.

The decline of the Indus Valley civilization has been linked to a number of factors. Most importantly, the increasing incursions of the White people known as the Aryans, which were a violent Indo-European tribe initially from central Eurasia and later from Iran. The name Iran itself means the "Land of the Aryan". The Dravidians were pushed into South India as a result of these Aryan incursions into their territory. This fact seems consistent, it is believed, with Dravidian traditions that recall flourishing cities that were either lost or destroyed in antiquity. The term Dravidian is used to describe both an ethnic and a linguistic group. The ethnic group is distinguished by straight to wavy hair combined with Africoid physical features. One Indian academic states that there are two well-defined Black races. One has a Black skin and woolly hair, the other also has exceptionally Black skin with straight hair, aquiline nose, thin lips, and an acute cheekbone angle. The Dravidian of India is of the latter type. Dravidian, in addition to its human component, is also an important family of languages spoken by more than a hundred million people who live primarily in South India. This language is also spoken by the Tamil, Kannada, Malayam, Tegu, and Tulu. The term Dravidian itself is apparently, a corruption of the Aryan term Tamil.

There were three major Dravidian kingdoms in South India: the kingdoms of Pandya, Chera, and Chola. The major city of Pandya was Madurai. To the northwest of Pandya was the kingdom of Chera, now called Kerala, and the kingdom of Chola was where the Apostle Saint Thomas was buried. When Marco Polo visited the Pandyan kingdom in 1288 and 1293, he exclaimed that, "The darkest man is here the most highly esteemed and considered better than the others who are not so dark. Let me add that in very truth these people portray and depict their gods and their idols black and their devils White as snow. For they say that God and all the saints are Black and the devils are all White. That is why they portray them as I have described." The Dravidians were an unusually advanced sea fearing people, with the Cholas in particular distinguishing themselves amongst the dominant maritime powers of the time. It was through its ports that the great kings of Chola traded with Ethiopia, Somalia, Iran, Arabia, Cambodia, China, Sumatra, and Sri Lanka. The Dravidian kingdoms and people were apparently well-known internationally and it is reported that when Augustus became head of the Roman world, the Dravidian kingdoms sent him a note of congratulatory embassy and that the Dravidian kings employed Roman soldiers as bodyguards.

The Aryans, who invaded India and disrupted Black civilization there, were not necessarily superior warriors to the Blacks, but they were much more aggressive. They also developed more efficient weapons and glorified warfare. After centuries of military conflict, the Aryans succeeded in subjugating most of northern India. They then developed a rigid caste system and reduced the conquered Blacks to slaves. It is said that this vicious new order was cold-blooded and racist with the Whites on top, the mixed races in the middle, and the overwhelming number of Blacks at the bottom. The Aryan term "Varna," denoting one's social standing and used interchangeably with "caste," literally means "colour or complexion" and reflects a prevalent racial hierarchy.

India today is truly a racist country, and the caste law, based originally on race, regulates all aspects of life including marriage, education, diet, place of residence, and occupation. As can be inferred from the above, the social caste system of India negatively affects the Blacks there more than the others. But the Aryans claimed that the conquered Black people was Untruth itself; that the Aryans came from the mouth of God, but the Blacks came from the feet of God. This, then, became the reality of life for the Blacks of India. It was written that: "A *Sudra* (Black) who intentionally reviles twice-born men (Whites) by criminal abuse or criminally assaults them with blows shall be deprived of the limb with which he offends. If he has 'criminal' sexual intercourse with an Aryan woman, his organ shall be cut off and all his property confiscated. If the woman has a protector, the *Sudra* shall be executed. If he listens intentionally to a recitation of the *Vedsa* which is traditional Hindu religious texts, his tongue shall be cut out, and if he commits them to memory his body shall be split in half." Servitude to the Aryans became the basis of the lives for the Black people of India, from one generation to the other. With the passage of time, this harsh, colour-oriented, racially based caste system became the foundation of the religion now practiced in India known as Hinduism.

It is interesting to note that when they were in power, the Dravidians the Blacks of India gave their women great freedoms and status, even allowing one of them to become Queen. But with the Aryans, it is was said that a woman was never independent. When she was a child she belonged to her father. When she married she belonged to her husband. If her husband died before she did, she belonged to her sons. Some of those sentiments seem to continue even to this day.

The Blacks of India, and those who were of mixed marriages between Aryans and Sudras, have become the Untouchables. Today they are considered the world's most oppressed people. The largest percentage of all Black peoples to be found in Asia, can be found among the 160 million Untouchables of India. They retreated into the hinterlands of India to escape the advancing Aryans to whom they ultimately succumbed. India's Untouchables number more than the combined populations of England, France, Belgium, and Spain. The existence of Untouchables has been justified within the context of Hindu thought as the ultimate and logical extension of Karma and rebirth. Hindus believe that persons are born Untouchables because of the accumulation of sins in previous lives. Hindu texts describe these people as foul, loathsome, and polluting when any physical contact is made with them. They were and are forced to live on the outskirts of Hindu communities and if they enter Hindu buildings at all, it must be at night. Their very shadows are considered polluting and they were to beat drums and make loud noises to warn of their approach. Cups were tied around their necks to catch any spit so they would not pollute roads and streets. Their meals were eaten from broken dishes, their clothes were taken from dead bodies, and they were forbidden to learn to read or write, and prohibited from listening to any traditional Hindu texts. The primary occupations of the Untouchables included scavenging and street sweeping, cleaning toilets, the public execution of criminals, the disposal of dead bodies and dead animals, and the cleanup of cremation grounds. Their daily lives were filled with degradation, deprivation, and humiliation.

Very little has changed for the Untouchables in the India of today. Recently, it has been observed that they are still not allowed to wear shoes, ride bicycles, use umbrellas, or hold their heads up while they walk in the streets. In the urban areas they are crowded into slums, while in the rural areas they are exploited as landless agricultural labourers and ruled by terror and fear. There are many cases of systemic violence against them. Official figures on violent crimes against them by higher caste Hindus have averaged more than 10,000 cases per year and this figure is rising. In some cases, Indian human rights workers report that a large number of atrocities against the Untouchables including gang-rapes, (why rape the woman you consider yourself so superior to and who's very shadow pollutes you? Is her body fluids that then mixes with yours not be more polluting to you?), arson, and murders, are never reported and when charges are filed, justice is rarely dispensed for the Untouchables. They were referred to sympathetically by nationalist leader, Mohandas K. Gandhi, himself a devout Hindu, as *"Harijans"* meaning children of God. The official name given them in India's constitution of 1951 is "Scheduled Caste" or *"Dali"* meaning crushed and broken. While the status quo is still in vogue, the term reflects a different approach to their oppression.

It is reported that the Dalits are demonstrating an expanding awareness of their African ancestry and their relationship to the struggle of Black people all over the world. They seem quite inspired by African-Americans in particular, whom they almost idolize, and the Black Panther Party was revered. In 1972, they formed the Dalit Panther Party in what was then Bombay. Such a development was noteworthy because Untouchables have historically been so systematically terrorized that many of them even today live in a perpetual state of extreme fear of their upper- caste oppressors. A Dravidian journalist wrote, that African-Americans also must know that their liberation struggle cannot be complete as long as their blood-brothers and sisters living in far off Asia are suffering. It was the contention of this journalist that African-Americans were still suffering but felt that the Blacks of Asia were about two hundred years behind the African-Americans. He indicated that African-American leaders should help their struggle by bringing forth knowledge of the existence of such a huge chunk of Asian Blacks to the notice of both the American Black masses and the Black masses who dwell within the African continent itself.

In the June 2003 issue of *National Geographic*, Hillary Mayall wrote, "Human rights abuses against these people, known as Dalits, are legion". A random sampling of headlines in mainstream Indian newspapers tell their story 'Dalit boy beaten to death for plucking flowers', "Dalit tortured by cops for three days', "Dalit "witch" paraded naked in Bahir", "Dalit killed in lock-up at Kurnool" "Seven Dalits burnt alive in caste clash", "Five Dalits lynched in Haryana", "Dalit woman gang-raped, paraded naked" "Police egged on mob to lynch Dalits".

India's Untouchables are relegated to the lowest jobs, and live in constant fear of being publicly humiliated, paraded naked, beaten, and raped with impunity by upper-caste Hindus seeking to keep them in their place. Merely walking through an upper-caste neighbourhood is a life-threatening offence. Nearly 90 percent of all the poor Indians and 95 percent of all the illiterate Indians are Dalits, according to figures presented at the International Dalit Conference that took place in Vancouver, Canada.

Statistics compiled by India's National Crime Records Bureau for the year 2000 indicates that 25,455 crimes were committed against Dalits. Every hour two Dalits are assaulted, every day three Dalit women are raped, two Dalits are murdered, and two Dalit homes are torched. No one believes these numbers are anywhere close to the reality of the crimes committed against Dalits. Because the police, village councils, and government officials often support the caste system, which as mentioned before is based on the religious teachings of Hinduism, many crimes go unreported due to fear of reprisal, intimidation by police, inability to pay bribes demanded by police, or simply the knowledge that the police will do nothing.

That same year, 68,160 complaints were filed against the police for activities ranging from murder, torture, and collusion in acts of atrocity, to refusal to file a complaint. Sixty-two percent of the cases were dismissed as unsubstantiated, but twenty-six police officers were convicted in court. Despite the fact that untouchability was officially banned when India adopted its constitution in 1950, discrimination against Dalits remain so pervasive that in 1989 the government passed legislation known as The Prevention of Atrocities Act. The act specifically made it illegal to parade people naked through the streets, force them to eat feces, take away their land, foul their water, interfere with their right to vote, and burn down their houses.

Because they are considered impure from birth, Untouchables perform jobs that are traditionally considered unclean or exceedingly menial, for very little pay. Although illegal in India, 40 million people, most of them Dalits, are bonded workers, many working to pay off debts that were incurred generations ago, according to a 1999 report by Human Rights Watch. These people, 15 million of whom are children, work under slave-like conditions hauling rocks or working in fields or factories for less than one USD per day. Dalit women are particularly hard hit. They are frequently raped or beaten as a means of reprisal against male relatives who are thought to have committed some act worthy of upper-caste vengeance. They are subject to arrest if they have male relatives hiding from the authorities. In a case reported in 1999 a 42-year-old Dalit was gang-raped and then burned alive after her husband and two sons had been held in captivity and tortured for eight days. Her crime? Another son had eloped with the daughter of the higher-caste family doing the torturing. The local police knew the Dalit family was being held, but did nothing because of the higher-caste family's local influence. There is very little recourse available to victims.

A 2001 report released by Amnesty International found an extremely high number of sexual assaults on Dalit women, frequently perpetrated by landlords, upper-caste villagers, and police officers. The study estimates that only about five percent of attacks are registered, and that police officers dismiss at least thirty percent of rape complaints as false. The study also found that the police routinely demand bribes, intimidate witnesses, cover up evidence, and beat up the women's husbands. Little or nothing is done to prevent attacks on rape victims by gangs of upper-caste villagers seeking to prevent a case from being pursued. Sometimes the policemen even join in, the study suggests. Rape victims have also been murdered. Such crimes go unpunished. Thousands of pre-teen Dalit girls are forced into prostitution under cover of a religious practice known as "devadasis" which means female servant of God. The girls are dedicated or married to a deity or temple. Once dedicated, they are unable to marry, forced to have sex with upper-caste community members, and eventually sold to an urban brothel.

Within India, grassroots efforts to change are emerging, despite retaliation and intimidation by local officials and upper-caste villagers. In some states, caste conflicts have escalated to caste warfare, and militia-like vigilante groups have conducted raids on villages, burning homes, raping, and massacring the people. These raids are sometimes conducted with the tacit approval of the police. In the province of Bihar, local Dalits are retaliating, committing atrocities also. Non-aligned Dalits are frequently caught in the middle, victims of both groups. There is a growing grassroots movement of activists, trade unions, and other NGOs that are organizing to democratically and peacefully demand their rights, higher wages, and more equitable land distribution. There has been progress in terms of building a human rights movement within India, and in drawing international attention to the issue. In August of 2002, the UN Committee for the Elimination of Racial Discrimination (UN CERD) approved a resolution condemning caste or descent-based discrimination. But at the national level, very little is being done to implement or enforce these laws.

Blacks in England

In England, there is a striking anomaly in how Blacks are treated these days when looked at from the perspective of the British assistance in ending the slave trade in their colonies. It is recorded that the first Black person to reach England was taken to Portsmouth in 1645. He went there as a slave. Portsmouth, England may have seen as many as 700 slaves. This late arrival of may have been in spite of the fact that the first known English slaving voyage to Africa was taken by Captain John Hawkins in 1562 in the reign of Queen Elizabeth 1. It is believed that England had 6 ports for the accommodation of the European slave trade. By the time the British formalised the Slave Trade in 1672 when the Royal African Company was established. However Britain was not a country with a large Black slave presence. Later in this book in the Chapter Should Blacks be compensated for Enslavement, I will detail Britain's involvement in the enslavement of Africans in a more substantial manner. But of all the major countries of the world where there was a Black presence, none has acted more humanely to enslaved Blacks than England. It was the first country to outlaw slavery from its territories and even forbade the transportation of slaves on any ship registered in that country eventually. The greatest and most dedicated Abolitionists of the past came from England. They fought tooth and nail to end the evil practice of slavery. Quite a few African tribal nations and peoples exist today around South Africa because English missionaries and politicians helped them against the hateful and hated Boers who would have brutally enslaved or exterminated them. These include Botswana, Lesotho, and Swaziland as well the Mafeking people in the province of Limpopo, South Africa.

Even outside of England itself, some English people from that country have fought ardently to prevent the ill-treatment of enslaved Black people as well as preventing their enslavement in the first place. The leaders of that country can be credited for opening its doors in the late 1950s and subsequently to the peoples of many of its Commonwealth nations in the effort to rebuild its infrastructure damaged by the Second World War, and providing the immigrants with employment and a chance to improve their lives and those of their families. The country of Zimbabwe, first called Rhodesia because of John Rhodes who with other English people settled and governed it from the European perspective, has in all likelihood the best educated Blacks in all of Africa. Zimbabweans are also known for being the least likely in all of Black Africas to be criminals. This may be changing a bit because of the "criminal" behaviour of its president Robert Mugabee whose policies are causing Zimbabweans so much economic stress. In South Africa, I met many well-educated and very successful Zimbabweans who will credit their success in education to the British system established in their country, even though Rhodesia had a penchant for racist attitudes toward Blacks under Ian Smith.

Despite all this, the English have not always done their very best when they ruled in some African countries and presently England can be a hostile environment for Blacks. While Enoch Powell may have been one of a kind in terms of his outspoken and often elabourate form of bigotry, he was nonetheless voicing the quiet opinion of a lot of Britons who would rather help Blacks and some other non-Whites by stretching their hands across the ocean as opposed to doing so in their own backyards. They consider anything less in distance to be too close up and personal. However, the same can be said of some other White nations as well.

For starters, when one looks at the English Monarchy, it will never be seen that a person of colour has ever been a part of the courtiers of any reigning king or queen. It could be expected that an institution that claimed almost all of Africa and all of India, and some of the Far East as part of its empire that they would have some representation of the various peoples serving in some of its palaces. However, no such thing can be seen. Basically, now, Black Africa is quite neatly snubbed by the English Monarchy and is mainly used as a prop of emotional adrenaline to soothe the ego of a dying and somewhat irrelevant empire which could soon see India, one of its former colonies, becoming much stronger and more relevant than itself from a political and economic standpoint.

One of the first groups to take dead aim at Blacks as they streamed over from the Caribbean was the Police. And this is not really surprising because it happens everywhere else. I have to always wonder why the police in White societies claim the inalienable right to persecute and abuse Black people as soon as they enter their territory. They sometimes cook up stories and file false charges against Blacks at the slightest opportunity and begin the process of harassment for no apparent reason. As with most other White societies, the English think that police generally are men who can do no wrong, and the issues are slanted against the Blacks, and before you know it, some of the people of the nation started to dislike and despise them. I may be wrong but I believe that White societies level their most potent hate against Blacks through the agency of their police services. It would be so much better if they would give Blacks a chance to be good citizens and avoid treating them like criminals even before they commit crimes. Calling people out for things they are not doing is provocation and to continue the mindless and unnecessary accosting and interrogation of innocent people is harrassment.

No one should expect that the Black skin is always a sign of silent and unresisting subservience. I know I have teased even a dumb animal till it became angry and bit me. Yet some people provoke Blacks and expect them to never respond negatively. Sometimes they are even surprised when Blacks give them a logical answer in response to their callous disregard of our humanity. Please be informed that Blacks do have a mind and an IQ. Whites may consider that inferior to theirs, but it exists nonetheless. Were not the best of the British military establishment in Southern Africa at the time soundly thrashed by "uneducated" Zulus in during the tenancy of Prime Minister Benjamin Disraeli in the 1870s? And have they forgotten how they ran in defeat from "uneducated" and "untrained" Maroons in Jamaica's Cockpit Country? The point I am trying to make is: sometimes Black's penchant for resistance/defiance ought to be taken seriously by White societies and addressed in an appropriate manner.

West Indians can tell of racial profiling and harassment by the English police long before the term became a household word in North America. Some can tell stories of being commanded to take off their shoes and walk barefoot in the cold and snow of the English winter, and can also tell of police brass who would go on what they called 'nigger hunts' in their neighbourhoods for Blacks and other non-White immigrants who they seem to always think of as being in their country illegally. The police considered themselves quasi-immigration officers who would use the cover of looking for illegal immigrants to harass Blacks.

There was also what Blacks referred to as the "Hardy Boys." This was a gang of White English hooligans and hoodlums who made it their duty to harass and beat Blacks whenever they found them alone and helpless. I was told by Jamaicans that the saving grace for most of them and their associates was their willingness to throw the ever-plentiful and first known missile - the humble rock. This, they said, saved many of them from the merciless beatings that the Hardy Boys were excellent at inflicting. Many years ago, I was studying martial arts and observed how one of the Black students in the class was fleet of foot. When I asked him how he got to move so fast, he said he learned to run in England because the evening he could not run fast enough the Hardy Boys almost made shish kebobs out of him.

It is believed that the reason for a lot of the tension between them and their hosts, was the unwillingness of the English to make an effort to understand people of other cultures. Also, they were mentally and socially unprepared to accept an influx of people who, being Black, they considered had no right to be in their country. As well, there was the fear of the White men in the society who were jealous and afraid that their women would soon be courted and mated by men of another race and colour.

In recent years, race riots in some of England's cities have shown the plight of Blacks and other ethnic immigrants there, and in the not-so-distant past those who are willing to admit it have seen the willingness of that country to back racist regimes such as the former Rhodesia and South Africa. While the racism of Rhodesia was somewhat benign when comparisons are made to that of South Africa, it is interesting to note that neither England nor the United States hardly ever voted against any of the policies of those two nations, even when those policies were blatantly unfair to Blacks, and that they decided to do something about South African apartheid only when they were embarrassed into doing so. There was a time in the 1970s when racial tension had reached such a fever pitch in England that Edward Heath, the then prime minister, passed a law disallowing Black Britons from leaving and coming back to that country without a passport, but he did not think it was necessary for the Whites to be thus contained. This was brought about by the antics of Enoch Powell, the great racist of modern England. Though that by itself was not so malicious, it showed that there was deference for one group over the other.

Forever and a day, Blacks have to fight against racial problems, and as in many cases some Blacks turned to hate for their oppressors, themselves, and to criminal activities. In England they have infested their own neighbourhoods with crime and drugs. Blacks also have a penchant for revenge that they level against the members of a society that they consider hostile to their presence. Unfortunately when they can't reach the "enemy" they level their frustrations at their own people for a double dose of oppression, one from the White society which is already in vogue and one from these dum dums who turn against their own. At the turn of the twenty-first century, Operation Trident was formed in London's Black communities to see what could be done about Black on Black crimes in these communities. Back in 2002, the Metropolitan Police put resources into the problem, which included radio advertising. Drug-related and drive-by shootings were up, and the problem of solving crimes by Blacks heightened because of silence on the part of those who should be helping. A lot of drug- related crimes were and are being committed by the Jamaican Yardie gangsters, and Operation Trident has concerns about how it is going to tackle the problem of the increasing number of Black British young men who are being sucked into the gun culture imported into these deprived neighbourhoods. The strongest element of concern is that the gun is seen as something that gives these criminals respect and power: two elements so lacking in the lives of young Blacks who have been deprived and despised for too long. Appeals are being made to government ministers to tackle low educational achievement and unemployment, factors which are doing nothing to end the gun culture.

In England, it is believed that the drug industry acts almost like a social service taking care of families, and the government is being asked to tackle the unemployment problem which gives rise to this is in the communities. As it usually happens, some people are frightened and don't know what to do and some crimes are not reported because of poor relations between the police and Blacks. Some Blacks regard the English police force as a "friend" who has lied to them. This makes the work of the police much harder and it will take time to work this kink out. This is pretty standard behaviour where, in a lot of cases, White host countries ignore Blacks in terms of providing education and employment, and then when they turn to bad behaviour and the chicken has flown the coop so to speak, society decides to do something about the problem. Blacks are treated with little relevance until the attitude turns to crime. It is then that everyone realizes that they are dealing with a monster.

Would it not be best if the White societies learn their repeat lessons early and be pre-emptive in their approach to social problems posed by Blacks living among tham, caused by neglect, that then lead to criminal behaviour? The sad truth is that there is almost a whole race of people, the majority of who if there are no changes in their mindset, seem destined to be no more than perpetual dependents on the achievements of Shem and Japheth to exist. If they are given the privilege to come and live among you, you might as well start early to provide them meaningful existences before they by instinct or grudgeful design, start their bad behaviour which eventually will reach you even in your Ivory Tower of Prosperity in numbers large enough to upset the balance of scale relative to socioeconomic peace and quiet.

Whites should not bother hiding behind their walls and think it will not affect them. They should be wise and be pre-emptive since eventually they will have to come face to face with the problem anyway. If Whites are not willing to have Blacks in their countries and neighbourhoods, refrain from accepting them as immigrants to their country. Most Blacks are not seeking to rely on the system of hand outs in a socialist society like that of England, but when opportunities are denied in places of leaarning and of employment, the stark unfairness is easily seen and people have to survive. To do so requires money and if not achieved by honest labout or government handouts, such will come criminal activities. And while the larger number of Blacks are law-abiding and productive, there are those who think they are owed an existence by the rest of the world and points to the past with its record of unfairness and sometimes actual plunder of their forefathers by others, as reasons to expect the White world to yield them is treasures with no meaningful effort on their part. As well Whites sometimes ignore and deny honest efforts by young Blacks who want to make good of their lives, and by this means discourage them and they then turn to crime and unsociable behaviours.

Earlier in this book I mentioned that a lot of Black and White people that I spoke to believe completely that the curse Noah placed upon Canaan is the reason for the plight of the Black race today. For those who hold that belief, there is another aspect of the same prophecy that I want to present here. When Noah cursed Canaan with servant hood, he also stated that Shem would be blessed and that Japheth would be enlarged in his tent, and that Ham would serve them both. This to me would means that Japheth would be a benefactor of Shem at some point and become so enlarged that Ham would serve him. The sons of Japheth are understood to be the European nations of White Caucasians, while at least one of the sons of Shem is the Jewish nation.

It is very obvious that the sons of Ham rely very heavily on both Shem and Japheth for employment. But where has Japheth gotten the wherewithal to be thus enlarged by Shem and be served by Ham/Canaan? Might he be relying on the expertise of the Jewish son of Shem? The Jews are the descendants of Abraham, and God once told Abraham that all the nations of the earth would be blessed through his descendants. I have been told many times even as a small child growing up in Jamaica, that most nations of the earth depend upon the Jews for their financial well-being. And it is my understanding that is it regularly believed even in American financial circles that the Jews drive the engines of prosperity even for that "rich" son of Japheth. I believe that directly and indirectly that is the same for all the nations.

If Ham is the servant of Japheth, it means that Japheth has been granted custodial authority over Ham. In Biblical axiom Japheth has a grave responsibility. He must execute fairly his duty as a custodian and be equitable in dealing with his brother Ham. Japheth should also bear in mind that he is also a beneficiary which means he should not get too huffy puffy realizing that He who gives can also take away. I pen this in the context of the unfairness meted out to Blacks most times in White societies, and is merely catering to the belief stated above. There are many other ways to see this prophecy of Noah's — one aspect is spiritual which I will not go into at this point. There are also many variables relative to this pronouncement but those would take more time than is relevant to get into them. However, I will address the matter once more in this book.

Blacks in Brazil

Blacks in Brazil are presently the most racially oppressed people in the Western Hemisphere. They are much farther down the road of social and economic neglect than Blacks were in the United States some sixty or seventy years ago. Brazil is a country of nearly 80 million Blacks, which is about fifty percent of the population of Brazil, the largest Africoid population in the Western Hemisphere. But Blacks are totally absent from positions of power at all levels of government, the congress, the senate, the judiciary, and the higher ranks of the civil service and the military.

Salvador, a city in Brazil, was for more than 300 years the major slave port and Blacks there make up more than ninety percent of the population. But even there, few of them are to be found in government. Even in the 1970s, Salvador's carnival was for the Whites only. Blacks could only push the floats. They could not even dance around them. Now, they have their own, which understandably is Black-only. They have finally started to teach their own people their history.

About eight million African slaves were taken from all over the African continent and brought to Brazil between 1540 and 1850. This was not surprising because Brazil was a Portuguese colony and contrary to the belief of many, Portugal took more slaves from Africa than any other any other European nation. From a European perspective, Portugal actually started the slave trade. Slavery was abolished in Brazil in 1888. It is said that most of the freed slaves who were then homeless, jobless, and penniless became vagrants. This alarmed the authorities who saw that Brazil's population was mostly Black or mixed-race. The government then decided to encourage European immigration to change the racial demographics of the nation. This move gave the world the impression that Brazil was a racially harmonious country, but in 1946 a study by UNESCO revealed that the practice of racism was widespread and entrenched.

In 1999, fifty years later, a report by the Minority Rights Group International, showed that racial discrimination had not abated and saw that Black and mixed race people from Brazil had higher infant mortality rates, less schooling, more unemployment, and earned much less for doing the same work as the Whites. It also showed that Black Brazilian men are more likely to be shot or arrested as crime suspects, and as in any other racist White nation, when found guilty get longer jail sentences. It is surprising, however, that there is no Black Power Movement in Brazil. There is apparently no strong racial tension and no racial conflict. In a way it means that Blacks in Brazil for the most part are very docile. It is said that Black Americans who live in Salvador report a much happier existence than when they lived in the United States. It is believed that this is because in Brazil if you look White or whitish you are White, while in America as pointed out before, race is defined quite differently. This blurring of racial lines makes it very difficult to fight racism while at the same time it offers Brazil the chance to become a "valid" racial democracy.

This is definitely not the true situation presently. There is a yawning chasm of socio-economic inequity between Blacks and the rest of the population there. Brazil can no longer be viewed by outsiders, nor can it see itself as a bastion of racial harmony. Brazilians now instead see the pervasive force of racism in their society. In a recent poll in Rio de Janeiro, 93 percent of those surveyed said they believe racism exists in Brazil, and 74 percent said there is a lot of racial bias. Brazil's poorest Blacks are targets of racial stereotypes, which often leads to brutal police violence against them. A study by the Institute for Religious Studies found that police in the slums of Rio de Janeiro actually kill nine out of every ten Black suspects they shoot at. This is like using Blacks as target practice for the police and is well more than double the shooting of Whites.

Another recent study in Sao Paolo found that Blacks had the highest unemployment, rarely made it through high school, and were less likely to work at jobs that paid more than $400 per month. Nationwide statistics showed that only about two percent of Black students make it to university compared to 10 ten percent for White students. More that 50 percent of Blacks are illiterate compared to 20 percent for the overall population, and Black infants were twice as likely to die before their first birthday. It used to be concluded by Brazilians that these statistics were simply indicators of economic disparity, but now they are beginning to see that it is racial injustice that is the cause of the problem. It was also believed that racism was not the reason for police brutality against Blacks, a situation made more complex because there are so many Blacks in the police force. Employment by the police is one of the very few avenues by which Blacks can get out of the slums. They themselves do not believe they are racist. However, the police are now trying to change this culture of Black killings, and are training their recruits to be more sensitive to the issues, and more skilled in the use of weapons against Blacks.

Blacks in Brazil are slowly beginning to assert themselves in daily life. Many Black organizations have risen in the past decade. It is said that T-shirts bearing messages are now a common sight in the cities of Sao Paolo and Rio de Janeiro, and that Black hair products and Black-oriented magazines have made their way into the market and onto the newsstands. Blacks are now even appearing in some kinds of television commercials. Black activists say that they are frustrated that Brazilians are still denying that they are racist as individuals, even though large majorities see racism as a problem in their society. They believe they are fighting an invisible enemy though, because in survey after survey Blacks are at the bottom of the totem pole.

Racism in Brazil has always been a complex issue made so because of the wide range of skin colour that is the legacy of generations of miscegenation producing variously coloured off-springs with each shade of colour having a different social significance in the Brazilian context. It is reported that in a survey conducted by the Centre of United Marginalized Populations that respondents chose to identify themselves in ten different shades of skin colour. White Brazilians are quite reticent about making Blacks an integral part of the fabric of that country. However, they are otherwise generally non-violent toward them. This non-violent aspect of the Brazilian society does not include the treatment that the police mete out to the Blacks. But since even the police are willing to make some kind of changes the fight for racial fairness may not take another 300 years for some progress to be seen.

Blacks in Mexico

The history of the Americas was forged by three groups of people—the original inhabitants called the Indians, the Europeans, and the Africans. The

African presence is associated with the slave trade in the U.S., Brazil, Columbia, Peru, the Caribbean, and Central America. The fact that there were slaves in Mexico is practically left out of Mexico's history books. But Mexico was a place where African slaves were taken to for labour, just as other places Mexico at the time which as an up and coming nation needing massive amounts of labour to give birth to their infrastructure. The number of them brought to Mexico was about 200,000, and by 1810 the number of Mexicans who could be considered part-African was about half a million - then more than ten percent of the population. It is believed that some of Mexico's most famous leaders were part-Black. Two of these were Emiliano Zapata, whose village was known to have had many descendants of African ancestry, and Vicente Guerrero, a leading general of the Mexican War of Independence. He was the nation's second president.

It seems intentional that presently the Black presence in Mexico is not as pronounced today as in other countries where they started out as what some refer to as the "third root" of the culture of the Americas. During the colonial era, there were more Africans than Europeans in Mexico. So the Black population did not disappear but was assimilated into the racial mixture which is Mexico today. Because of this mixture, the African presence is discernable in only a few places like Veracruz, the Costa Chica, and the Oaxaca. There is nothing coming out of Mexico on racial disharmony with its Black population.

Blacks in Arab Countries.

According to an article titled "The Forgotten Holocaust: The Eastern Slave Trade," by S.E. Anderson, though Blacks have been mainly used as slaves in Arab and Muslim countries, they have made some positive contributions to these societies. In the beginning, there was some level of mutual respect. Mihdja, it is said, was the first Muslim killed in battle, while another, Bilal, is regarded as the third of the faith. Dhu'l-Nun al-Misri, born in Upper Egypt, is said to be the founder of Sufism. Sufism is the inner, mystical dimension of Islam. Today Sufism's greatest stronghold is in Southern Egypt and Sudan.

It is said that Islamic prosperity was based upon Black as well as Arabic abilities, but that as Islamic prosperity grew, so did an air of hostility towards Blacks, whether they were Muslims or not. After the death of the Prophet Mohammed, even the descendants of Bilal received negative treatment. Arab writings became laced with anti-Black sentiments. One Black writer by the name of Abu 'Ulman" Amr Ibn Bahr Al-Jahiz, who confronted a growing tide of these sentiments, published a very controversial work in a book titled *Kitab Fakhr As-Sudan ' Ala Ak-Bidan*, or "The Book of Glory of the Blacks over the Whites." Al-Jahiz contended that the father of the founder of Islam may have had African ancestry.

The new attitude the Arabs developed toward Blacks marked the beginning of Black African enslavement by them. While the Arab Slave Trade was not entirely based on race, it focused heavily on Africans because Arabs began thinking that sub-Saharan Africans were inferior to them. They started raiding African villages themselves looking for people to buy. Because they were not very successful, they sought the help of sub-Saharan African Muslims who viewed their non-Muslim countrymen as unbelievers and came to the conclusion that because of that they could become slaves. At other times, the Arabs simply demanded humans as tributes from these Africans weary of fighting the incursions of these Islamic Arabs. They took advantage of local wars and bought captives from the winners, and they worked one group against the other and captured or killed those who were the best or strongest so they would not have much resistance relative to their long term purpose. These Arabs would raid African villages at around dinner time, killing the adult men and older women because they were mainly after the younger women and children. The captives would endure long and hard marches through the African country side as the traders gathered more captives. They were bound by hand and neck during these travels and were beaten and raped all along the way. The sick and the dead were simply left behind.

At slave markets, the women and young girls were physically inspected in degrading ways by men who were looking for females to add to their harems. Such inspections would be done both publicly and privately to test their sexual worth. It is said that those who did not survive their time in the slave markets were left out to rot or become eaten by wild animals. Arab enslavement of Africans dealt in the sale of castrated boys who had not only their scrotum but also at times their penises amputated. Because of the unsanitary and unsafe conditions under which these procedures were done, it is estimated that only one out of every ten to thirty boys survived. The others just bled to death or died because of infections.

It is estimated that because of the Arab slave trade, which lasted from 700 to about 1960, when the British and the French used military and economic threats to end the practice in Saudi Arabia, about 14 million Africans were taken into slavery. About 9.6 million of these were women and about 4.4 million were males. In addition, 14 to 20 million men, women and children perished as a result of Arab enslavement. Theses Arabs acted more like ferocious brutish hyenas than human beings, with characteristics more akin to demons than men. Their cruelty more than equalled that which the Europeans exercised toward Black Africans when it came to African slavery. They were unmatched in their thirst for blood and in their desires to rape and take advantage of helpless women and little girls for sexual purposes. Only those in America who, it is reported went as far as cutting unborn Black babies out of their mothers wombs, could compare to the brutality of those satanic Arabs toward Blacks.

It is surprising beyond understanding that details of this aspect of Black African enslavement could be so secreted that very little of this is known today, with very few people speaking about it. On the contrary, we hear so much of European slavery of Black Africans even though their treatment of Black slaves was comparitively benign when looked at from the aspect of Arab enslavement.

CHAPTER THREE
Blacks in Slavery

In this chapter I will be discussing elements of slavery focusing mainly on the Eu-
ropean slave trade. I will look at its cruelties and its lasting negative effects on
Blacks wherever it was practiced. This chapter also looks very briefly at the concept
of compensation for slavery, a matter to be discussed more fully in a separate
chapter. I will look at the culpability of Africans in this trade as they practiced
slavery themselves on their own people and aided and abetted everyone, including
the Arabs.

Studying the history of the West Indies in school, I learned about slavery
in Jamaica, the Caribbean, and in other parts of the world where it existed.
When the Spanish came to these islands, they reportedly killed off most of
the Arawaks and the Caribs, the inhabitants they found there. The islands
were called "Caribbean" because of the Caribs. We were told that sometimes
the Spanish lopped their heads off just for sport. They also enslaved many to
work for them. These native peoples were easy going, peaceful, gentle, and
not used to very hard work, and as a result of this forced labour and harsh
treatment most of them quickly died out. The Spanish decided that the few
remaining ones could not carry on the work assigned to them, and a priest –
out of pity for the plight of these people suggested that those who were in
need of workers should get Africans, a stronger people who were more fitted
for the rigourous work which was required on the Spanish plantations. Thus
began one of the most brutal practices ever perpetrated against any group of
people, and this was a solution the Spanish priest lived to regret that he had
brought forward as a suggestion when he saw the cruelty which accompanied
it. Slave owning as a means of securing agricultural labour was spread all over
the West Indies, the North, South, and Central Americas, and to a lesser extent
parts of Europe, mostly England. In school, I read of the brutality meted out
to these poor Africans from the time they were captured to the time they died.
As mentioned before slavery of Black Africans had been going on for several
centuries before this by the Arab.

It was written in our history books that they were packed together like
sardines in a tin, row upon row, that they defecated on each other on the journeys, that they died of sicknesses they contracted on the way and then were
just thrown overboard. The captives were in a totally helpless state, could offer

no resistance, and were restrained physically from any movements not allowed by their captors. They were referred to as a "group of people nastier than the swine". I was always incensed when I read about these things. How could anyone of average intelligence refer thus to people who they themselves held captive, knowing full well that these people - even if they wanted to - could in no way shape or form help themselves? I grew to passionately hate those who were responsible for treating them this way. I was most appalled to discover that Africans captured their own African brothers and sisters and sold them to the slave traders. Now, though, Black Africans conjure up "righteous indignation" and blame Whites only for these atrocities when they themselves were active participants. The price they were paid for these unfortunate captives never seemed very much. Even useless trinkets given to them by Europeans were enough to incite them to capture their weaker brothers and sisters and then turned them over to these wicked slave traders.

The Gate of No Return in Ouidah, in Benin, and Elmina Castle in Ghana were a couple of the last places in Africa that some of these unfortunate captives saw before they boarded the ships waiting for their journey of doom. Elmina Castle was first established by the Portuguese as a trading post in 1482. It later served as a trading post for the slave trade and served that purpose solely under the Portuguese, Dutch, and British until the practice ended in the 1800s. Now a UNESCO World Heritage Site, time has not erased the smell of human despair in the castle's still dark, mouldy, dank dungeons where millions of people were kept in hodling cells before being shipped off to the distant unknown. The Iron Gate is rusted but it is still there. For more than three hundred years, the chains which bound the African captives together also scraped the stone floors of those dungeons as they made their way to the Door of No Return.

Even though I was aghast at the capture and subsequent ill-treatment of these people, it never dawned on me that hatred from the captors played a role in the process. I thought that the treatment came with the territory and that it was the normal way for things to happen in a situation such as that. I looked more at the misfortune of the slaves being used as a commodity for the purpose of labour. I was much too uninformed at the time to understand that hatred for the slaves themselves was a very large part of the equation. Our history books did not get into details of hate when they talked about the sufferings of the slaves on the plantations and in the homes of their masters.

At times in my studies, the teachers made very negative comments about the slave traders which I thought went deeper than the situation required. I was to conclude later that some of those comments, though unkind, were not without good reason. Further reading as the years went by gave me information of terrible lynchings, hangings, burnings, and merciless beatings of these helpless people for the slightest infractions, and in America I saw actual photographs of White people standing beside and around the bodies of lynching victims gloating as a hunter would do when he shot a deer or some other game. There I saw pictures of Black men dressed in ceremonial white, tied to stakes in a sitting position with White men standing around them waiting gleefully and expectantly for the fires to be lit so they could watch these hapless, helpless souls as they were roasted like pigs being cooked for dinner. I learned later that some of these very wicked men would even cut unborn babies out of the pregnant Black slave women's wombs in their efforts to incite fear into the hearts of other slaves, and to teach permanent lessons of submission to the remaining ones. I was most dismayed to learn that these atrocities took place in America of all places, this "bastion of Christian" virtue. I was more shocked that some White people, with all their talk of superiority, would stoop low enough to be guilty of such demon-inspired behaviour.

I read of the many rebellions led out by brave slaves, and raids on plantations resulting in the deaths of slave owners. Such information I was happy to read about, and saw as nothing other than the reaction of a people provoked to violent action because of the poor treatment they were receiving. I was always very relieved and felt a sense of satisfaction whenever they succeeded in their rebellions. One of Jamaica's national heroes, Paul Bogle, was such a leader even though he was later captured and hanged by the British governor for his daring raids on their plantations. When Queen Victoria called for an investigation of the situation that led to the hanging of Paul Bogle, she had the British governor of Jamaica, John Eyr, whom she held responsible for the ill-treatment of the slaves, recalled to England. Contemplating these things, I later concluded that there must have been strong hatred of one group for the other in this matter of slavery, and subsequently decided that no one would resort to those kinds of misdeeds if they were not indeed full of hatred.

Slavery went on for hundreds of years before anyone decided to end it. There were those who felt that it was very inhuman to enslave another person especially for their entire lives. Some slave owners and even governments did not recognize Black slaves as human beings and justified the wicked treatment meted out to them as deserving. In reality the government of America and other governments of the time designating Blacks as non humans (animals) should have charged their White male citizens who were slave owners who raped and sexually abused Black female slaves with beastiality, and offering an indignity to an (animal), and designate these White males as animals also for cohabiting sexually with (animals). Even Thomas Jefferson, one of America's former presidents should have been charged with infraction. It is strange though, how the offsprings of these rape sessions were born looking like humans, sometimes even taking the lighter complexion of these White human males. These slave owners, etc even used the Bible to validate their wicked treatment of the slaves. Nonetheless, it might ease readers' psyches to know that even White women in North America were not regarded as persons until 1920, a very shocking revelation when one thinks that those who belittled these women so much came through their birth canals, and had them as mothers, sisters and wives.

Interestingly, when I read the story of the emancipation of the slaves, I noticed that nearly all of the people who fought for their freedom were White. This raised a few positives in my mind toward the White race as a whole. Emancipators, as these people were called, seemed to have begun their work for the freedom of the slaves in England. There they were opposed, but the work went on. I read that the Emancipators fought long and hard to obtain freedom for a despised and mistreated people. In America, the fight for the freedom of the slaves by White Emancipators was very difficult and in many instances they lost their citizenship, their property, their families, and even their lives in their efforts to win freedom for the slaves.

It must have been most daunting for the Emancipators to champion this most unpopular cause. They were seen as traitors to their own race. I developed great admiration for their selfless courage and determination to accomplish what they had set out to do, even as I found it hard to comprehend that Whites would actually take up the cause of fighting for Blacks. I read of such greats as William Wilberforce, Sir Thomas "Elephant" Buxton, a British Abolitionist, so named for his size, John Graves Simcoe who later became governor of Upper Canada, and some others who took up the struggle. Starting the struggle in England, they succeeded first in abolishing slavery from the British Empire. Later other countries where slavery existed did the same. Strangely, one of the last places to abolish slavery as it was known then was Africa itself. I learned that the the Civil War fought in America may have been over freedom for the Black slaves.

Much later, I discovered that there were freed Blacks living in America even in the 1600s. These numbered about 60,000 and by the time of the emancipation of slaves there were already about 500,000 freed slaves on its soil.

By the time President Abraham Lincoln signed the Proclamation in 1863, the total number of Blacks in that country was about six million. This by itself, made me wonder about the almost legendary negative reaction of White Americans to Blacks even today, seeing that Blacks have been in that country for so many centuries and in such large numbers. However, even as freed men and women they were denied education, occupation, housing, recognition, and even their humanity.

Finally the Black slaves at the time were "free." This freedom came with many challenges. Not many of them knew "how to be free." Most of them were like kids tossed out of their homes and onto the streets with nowhere to go and nothing to do. Some of their former masters no doubt took delight in their plight and remained their most violent oppressors. The burnings, lynchings, and other atrocities did not stop because slavery had ended. From stories I've read, and stories I've heard from people I spoke to, even governors of States and law enforcement officers participated personally in some of these acts of brutality, at the least by their unwillingness to enforce the law protecting everyone in their jurisdictions as they also believed that Blacks were not humans anyway. The involvement of some of these prominent people was hard to uncover because they hid their crimes when they covered their faces with the hoods of the Ku Klux Klan, a violent-White racist gang to which they belonged, and which had dedicated itself to the total and violent eradication of Blacks in America. They were not exempted from exercising hate and bigotry because of their high office. Even today, hatred for Blacks usually because of skin colour is very much alive in America, and the lynching mentality is still voiced in some circles. A few years ago, I was told by an acquaintance of mine that her friend who worked as the receptionist of a law firm in Texas had a lawyer from a related law firm call her office and during the conversation asked her point blank how many "niggers" her office had "lynched" that day. The caller did not suspect that the receptionist he was speaking to was Black.

Freedom for the slaves did not come with any means of support. They had no previous education and were not given any financial help, land, or housing. Some of them went back to their former masters for employment so they could obtain the necessities on which to subsist. Luckily there was still some work to do as the ex slave owners needed the labour to still carry on with their lives. Some of the freed slaves chose never to go back to their former lives no matter the cost. The ones who worked had to sometimes make purchases from the people who they worked for in which case the cost of the purchases was taken directly from their wages. On Fridays, it was "deduc" day. The employers "deduc" this much and that much from the measly income they paid to these people. At the end of the "deduc'tions," there usually was nothing left over for them to do much with that would start them on the way to becoming self-sustaining. It is reported that they were very often grossly overcharged for their little purchases. And the whole process just went on week after week after week for many years. All this was practiced by people who considered themselves civil and humane just so they could maintain their power over the poor ex-slaves and keep them in the position they designed for them. From such restricted capacity they were supposed to prosper and succeed in America, and were much hated for lack of economic progress.

The situation seems to have been somewhat better for the former slaves of the Caribbean. The Caribbean slave masters were not reported to be as mean or as cruel as their American counterparts, even though it was a Caribbean slave owner by the name of John Lynch who, on a visit to America, gave to them the idea of the lynching (gang slaughter) of Black slaves. Yet according to our history, lynching was not reported to us as being practiced on Caribbean slaves, which made me wonder where John Lynch got the idea. Blacks were more in number in relation to the general population, and they were more willing to fight for themselves. Such were factors favouring the Caribbean slaves. Futhermore, survival was easier in the warm climate with its abundance of edible plants like yams, and fruits such as mangoes. This is not to say that the Caribbean offered no challenges. Slave owners there were no more willing to accept Blacks than the Americans were. In America the slaves were simply far outnumbered, and as well the slaves in the Caribbean, especially in Jamaica came from tribes in Africa which were much more aggressive and rebellious. The Maroons were a case in point.

Not having much to do, and different physical characteristics made Blacks in a mostly White society stood out like a sore thumb. The freed Blacks drew notice to themselves in very negative ways. Most were seen merely as idlers unable to make any contribution to society. They were uneducated, without skill or business acumen. Deprived of any dignity, their plight was great indeed. The Emancipators had done a good work by freeing them, but they had made no plans for the integration of such a large group of unprepared people into the mainstream of society. Few of those who worked to free the slaves wanted anything to do with them in terms of association, and it seemed for a time that slavery with all its evils was better for them than the "freedom" they now had. Most freed slaves spent their days on the corners of streets, neglected by different levels of government and unable to earn their own living. It's not surprising that many turned to crime.

However little or much the material help, the psychological damage of slavery on the Black people would linger for many long years, and affected them more seriously than the perpetrators cared to admit or recognize. These people had even engaged in sexual activities at their masters' wishes and bore children who were raised just to become slaves like themselves. The Black male slave was treated as a mere stud and the women almost as surrogate mothers. The children did not belong to them. These slave masters might just as well have used artificial insemination on Black women to keep the number of future workers growing. That would have accomplished the same thing. After fathering these children, the male slave was then to have nothing to do with the child he brought into the world, and the little he did have to do with these children was only at his master's wish. The Black slaves were also frequently raped by superior White slave masters making colored babies.

It is said that most acquired habits become hereditary tendencies which take about four generations to be eradicated. Is it any wonder, then, that to this day there are so many Black men in the countries where their ancestors were slaves who shoulder so very little or none of the responsibilities of fatherhood for their children? Now the society that enforced such immorality has decided to forget the injustices of the past and to conveniently put aside the reason for much of the Black problem relating to fatherhood, as if it should bear no burden for the cruelty of its history. From time to time, people have arisen and verbally addressed the concept of making right the wrongs of slavery and compensating Blacks for all the indignities they suffered. But nothing has ever been done about it, and I don't believe anything ever will.

In the meantime, the problem of the effects of slavery and the injustices that Blacks suffered linger on, and this is the case not only in American but all over the world where slavery had been practiced. The most protracted and inhumane treatment meted out to, and recorded about any enslaved group of people was and still is being meted out in America, which ironically was called a Christian and a Democratic nation at the time. Black slaves and Black people continue to suffer in many other parts of the world-also-even in their own country at the hands of fellow Blacks and in many places they would never be made welcome for no other reason than what the world thinks the Black skin is indicative of. When all is said and done, maybe one should be more fearful of what the White skin is indicative of.

The Europeans and the Americans were not the first to practice slavery, however. Information is readily attainable that relates that the enslavement of Africans did not begin with the Europeans. Black African slavery existed in Africa itself long before the Europeans went there. And this slavery of Africans by Africans was a way of life hundreds of years before African slavery in the West. The Africa of antiquity was as warlike as the Africa of today, as warlike as Europe, and the captured and subjugated were made slaves by other Africans. Even in peaceable times it seems that slavery of some kind was business as usual for a lot of African countries. If they had not been experienced in the practice of slavery, maybe they would not have been so willing to sell their own people into it on such a large scale.

It is of note that slavery in what used to be Zanzibar was abolished only in 1897, decades after slavery was officially abolished in the British Empire and in North America. It is reported that one of the Sultans of Oman moved his residence to Zanzibar to take advantage of the lucrative slave trade practiced in that African country. There were at least five African countries that had slaves leaving their ports and they were therefore, in collusion with those who started the European version of the slave trade. These are Benin, Cape Verde, Gambia, Ghana, and Senegal.

While there were slaves/servants in every people group, (we see White nannies in America and Canada as an example, and poor Asians serving rich Asians, and so on). Forced slavery was another matter. There are those who apologize for slavery in Africa saying that there it was neither violent nor dehumanizing as it was in the Western world. This they say because Africans enslaved by other Africans became a part of the household and were not forced to live in a new culture thousands of miles from home. But slavery is slavery and wherever it is practiced it is inhuman. Slavery interestingly still exists in parts of Black Africa even today, and as such it is not pleasant by any definition. It is alleged that many thousands of children are sold into slavery in Sudan. Some are sold as child labourers and many others as sex slaves. How sad! The rest of Africa looks on with nary a whimper about the issue, caring nothing about these innocent children on its own continent. However, such is classic African behaviour which prides itself with being too polite to meddle in much of the internal affairs of it's neighbouring African country while at the same time giving the worst passions of human behaviour, and allowing foreigners full control of things for which they should be responsible. I think of these leaders as "meatheads" and I compare them to the woodpeckers whose nests my friends and I raided as children. Every other bird - even the very tiny little grassquits would put up a fight to save its young. But the woodpeckers would fly as swiftly away as they could, leaving their young to be taken by us without any resistance or any protection whatever.

Shame on those African leaders who turn a blind eye on the plight of these poor victims.

There are those Whites who use the Bible to justify slavery because God had given the Children of Israel the right to own slaves as long as they were not Israelites. These people forget that God did not define slavery in the modern sense. They were merely servants in the kindest sense of the word. God gave specific instructions that they were to be treated gently. The life and personhood of those servants were to be strictly guarded, and if the master beat them and made them lose even a tooth, they were to be freed immediately. Those who unjustly murdered servants/slaves were to be punished. Those who advocate slavery under the brutish conditions foisted upon them as we see in this the twenty-first century should go back and reread their Bibles. Interestingly some of the cruellest of slave masters who have been known to beat their slaves to death even for very small infractions were church-going Christians.

CHAPTER FOUR
THE BLACK FAMILY

This chapter makes comparisons between growing up in the Jamaica and growing up in this part of the North American continent. It looks at the value systems, expectations of family members and society, and the negative stereotyping of Black families here as opposed to there. The chapter also delves into the effects of the actions of society on Blacks as individuals as well as on the Black family. I will then look into some studies affecting Black families in the United States and end on the note of challenging Blacks to become active in the matter of self improvement as individuals and families.

The thoughts, feelings, and activities that influenced family life in the part of Jamaica where I grew up were certainly not the same as the stereotypical treatment Blacks receive here on this part of the continent. We were very proud of our heritage in my locale and were not influenced much by any outside influences, probably because as remote country folks we were somewhat insulated from any such stimuli or interference. Taking our cue from families around us, we were as normal as anybody else. I was completely ignorant of the plight of Black families in this part of the world as I now understand it. In the first instance we were all Black, bearing in mind that Blacks come in many different shades. This is not to say that only Black people lived in Jamaica, but the area I grew up in was comprised of 99.9 percent of the American definition of Black people. A few were of East Indian extraction.

The mixture of different races among us was very evident in our physical features. Some had aquiline noses, some had fairly flat ones, some had wavy hair, some looked Caucasian, and some looked Mongoloid. Of course, some were Africoid with many features in between. If I had a thousand life times I would choose to grow up among those same people every time. They were so beautiful, so varied, and cultured, most being very religious and church-going. Our racial mix and upbringing made us feel very proud of whom we were and we had no problems with self-esteem in the general sense of the word. All of us being country folk meant that a few things were the norm. These things included the following: our parents provided a homestead with sufficient land to grow the basic produce that the family would need to survive. Most couples, before they started having children, would ensure that they had a house in which to raise them, even if that was just a hut with

Mother Earth for the floor, straw for the roofing, and mud walls. And truthfully, there were a couple of those among us. Fathers worked the fields. Mothers did the house work and took care of the children. Children chipped in when they were old enough. Girls worked mostly around the house, and boys helped mostly around the fields. The girls kept the house and yard clean and helped to cook meals. The boys prepared the soil for planting, fed the animals, brought in firewood for cooking, picked the fruits, and dug the edible roots for food. If the situation required it, the roles would be reversed meaning that if there were more boys than girls as it was in my family, the boys would do much of the house work, and the girls much of the "bush" work as we called it. I am here writing particularly of life in the rural part of Jamaica where I was reared. I imagine life was quite different in the cities and could have been different in other rural communities.

When city dwellers came among us, or when we went among them, it was easy to detect the disdain they had for us country people, and we in turn were not too fond of them when they showed dislike for us. They liked to call us country bumpkins usually, and when we traveled to the cities in the backs of trucks as opposed to buses or cars they called us "hogs and goats." We hated the connotation but could do very little about it. We prided ourselves on how beautiful and civil we were and felt we could beat most of them in a beauty contest anytime. However, on one occasion when my bigger sister could take being called hogs and goats no longer, she referred to a city male who came around our vehicle mouthing the slogan as a "lowland dog," a very derogatory reference to a Jamaican city dweller. We used that term to denote the fact that we lived in the hills while they lived on the plains. I should let you know that he did not find the reference amusing and set himself in battle array against her, only to be dissuaded by the sheer number of us on her side who would have worked him over quite nicely had he gone beyond just posturing. Not that we really needed to help her. She would have flung him around like a small potato sack all by herself. She used to fight my battles for me in primary school whenever the occasion required it, and was well feared by the boys for her fighting skills. When she closed in on an opponent flinging those fists, even a wild elephant would flee.

School was a must for nearly everyone except for the most hopeless academically who were just too dull of mind to be able to understand the simplest things having to do with learning. Those who were "bright" would be expected to get into further studies and become teachers, nurses, and so on. Those not so bright as boys may look at becoming a policeman, a soldier, or look at a trade such as carpentry, and those who were total dunces were destined to work the fields, or become helping hands at whatever else could be found. The girls who showed no promise in academia were slated to become only housewives if a young man of similar pedigree was available. There were some kids who had no interest in school or church, though both were expected places of attendance in my district. We did not use the term Attention Deficit Disorder or make children who were illiterate think they were rejects of society. We thought that there was still a place for them. Most importantly, we did not associate their inabilities with the colour of their skin. The fact is that children with such "disabilities" were of all stripes and colours, not just the children who had our definition of a Black skin. Even though school was important, children were expected to take time out of class at given times of the year to help their parents with the reaping of crops such as sugar cane, coffee, coco beans, and whatever else they cultivated to make money for the family.

Children were disciplined by parents, older siblings, and adults in the community as a matter of principle. Each child was given clothing, food, and school supplies as parents could afford. The teachers gave us as fair amount of attention as they could even though in my area there could be sometimes more than thirty of us in a class. Sometimes the Ministry of Education sent us school supplies such as exercise books, pens, and pencils as well as some items of food so we could have the basic things they thought we needed both for school and nourishment. We were excited to bring home the various things sent to us by the Ministry. The teachers would tell us a week or so in advance and we would get containers from our parents in which to place these items. Things we got were cheeses, bulgur wheat, cornmeal, and other things. Interestingly most of these things originated in England and America.

Most times we did not have shoes on our feet. They were a luxury for most kids in my area and were especially not given to us when we were very young. Only parents who were a bit well-off could afford to give their children shoes for every day wear. As a result, we mostly walked around with our "ten commandments" on the ground as we called our toes in those days. Long pants came when we were older - about the time we were 12 or 13 years of age. If the parents were a bit well-off or if they had relatives abroad who could send money to their families once in a while this could happen earlier. I can still remember the time when my oldest brother got the fabric from my father to make his first set of long pants. Sleep left him for many nights after taking the measurements for his new digs at the local tailor who just happened to be our much older cousin. Every once in a while, he would say, "Just about now, Mas Ron is making my long trousers." The rest of us boys were more than envious as we impatiently waited for our time to come. This time of waiting was something we could hardly bear. When he finally took delivery of his trousers (long pants), he walked around as if he was on cloud nine, stepping so briskly one would think there were hot burning coals wherever his feet landed, and going around with a perpetual smile on his face. He did not mind that his ten commandments were still showing under the cuffs. But one at a time! The shoes would come later. The first thing he did in the evenings when he got home from the fields and had his dinner was to wash himself and head out in his long pants to be admired and envied by the neighbourhood boys of his age with whom he was hanging out. Normally in my family whenever we got new clothing the first place to see us in them was church. But as he was a non-believer even at that tender age one would not find him even near the entrance door of a church. When he got home he was careful to put his pants on the wooden hangers my Dad made, and hang them in the wardrobe as we called our closets. My father made the wardrobes as well as all the other furniture we needed.

As children we gave unquestioned obedience to our parents. Any disrespect of them or their wishes was punishable with the belt or the whip. A child disrespectful of his or her parents was looked upon as under the curse of God. Our fathers were answered with a "yes Sir, no Sir" and our mothers with a "yes Ma'am, no Ma'am." We could receive the full palm across the side of the face for yawning, scratching, or stretching in the presence of our parents. And getting rid of gas in the hearing or presence of our parents or any other adult came with the "death" penalty. Even burping in the company of our parents after the age of about two or three was discouraged. Disrespect of teachers and adults, even those unrelated to us, was something no sensible child wanted to be guilty of. As a result we mostly grew up very well-behaved. even if that was against our desires.

All our teachers and nurses were much like us in terms of colour and tradition, even if they came from other Parishes or from the cities. This was the case also for most of our politicians and judges when we were lucky enough to get a glimpse of any of them. Our police too were like us as we found out when we saw them in the cities, or when a few of them would come now and again to our area looking for reported *ganja* (marijuana) fields. We would also see them when we went on trips to the cities or on the needed visit to the doctors who were usually in the nearest city, which for me was Old Harbour. We accorded all of them proper respect and honour if not outright fear, and dared not think to do otherwise. Most of us were never comfortable in the presence of the police however, and they were not a part of our daily lives. The average Jamaican did not like the police. We were told that they had to take an oath stating that they would even arrest their mothers if she broke the law. Because mothers then were revered and adored, we considered anyone hurting their own mother as coming under the curse of God. We therefore looked at the police work as a very undesirable profession. This may not have been the case for all Jamaicans but it certainly was for me and those around me.

We did not think we were poor because we were Black. As we all shared the same circumstances basically, the definition and stereotyping did not apply. I did not grow up knowing the word "stereotype." Our teachers and other leaders did not make us feel that it was because we were Black that some of us did not do well in school, for example. Only when I came to this part of North America did I realize that these deficiencies came strictly on a "skin colour" basis, and was made to feel that colour was, and is, the inherent hindrance to our progress and standing in life, and that somehow skin colour was a definite barrier to intelligence and wealth from a genetic standpoint. As far as I could ascertain, we were as legitimate as anyone anywhere and no one brainwashed us to believe otherwise.

I may have wished for a better life, whatever that may have meant back then, but migrating to Canada showed me that in some cases I left the "better life" behind me to seek for what I now sometimes see as base materialism, racial hatred some times toward me, and the perpetual payment of bills. This does not mean that there is no dissatisfaction or need for improvement of life in Jamaica and other Black-dominated economies. Indeed there is. It also does not mean that we as a group of people have done all we can to make the best of our lives. But it is unfair for others to think that the colour of the skin makes us intrinsically inferior and that we have no family values to go with it.

I now conclude that the fact that we had a roof over our heads in the sense that our parents built liveable houses for us providing the most important acquisition in life made us blessed indeed. It did not matter that our houses were not luxurious. The fact is we had mortgage-free homes. And having the basic things to eat comprising of fruits, vegetables, and earth foods, which we had plenty of when I was growing up, placed me in a better position than having to purchase such necessities on a regular basis to survive. As well, having a place to live where I could be kicked out of anytime if I can no longer afford to pay to live there is not really improvement in the general sense of the word. Nonetheless, there are other things for which I am very grateful. I love and admire the nice people I see, I like the four seasons, I love the nice cars and the opportunity to own one, I also love the beautiful accents I hear around me and the beautiful classical music played on the radio. I admire the expertise of the people of this country and how organized and cultured and beautiful they can be.

The discipline, courtesy, and respect our parents taught us for everyone we came in contact with, did not come with skin colour. I was a cab driver in Toronto for some time. One day, an older White woman was riding in the cab and we were having a conversation, which turned to a discussion of politeness and courtesy. I got the distinct impression that she did not believe that there was any where I came from. I said to her that I did not understand why some of the people I was meeting thought that courtesy and politeness was the domain of Whites and that Blacks came from families that taught them nothing about such things. I further stated that all the gracious attitudes that I practiced were taught by my Black parents and other Black people among whom I was brought up. Her response was "Oh really"! I have never forgotten that expression. It was as though it could by no means be possible. What she must have been ignorant of is that the West Indian culture has been heavily influenced by Europeans because they were the colonial masters of those Islands for some time. As I met and spoke with Europeans here, I got the impression that it is mostly the colour of our skins that is the major difference between us. They grew up with some of the same graces that I grew up with. But it must not be forgotten that Africans as well as South West Asians and other non-Europeans were a part of the West Indies also. It cannot then be said that the Europeans were solely responsible for the courtesy that our parents taught their families. The slave owners used Black nannies to raise their children. We were told that the ready switches and the fastidious practices of these nannies were used to keep the children of these White slave owners in line. So, it would seem that Blacks in these cases were responsible for teaching Whites to have good manners.

Where I grew up, the older the person the more respect they got. As a young person I was very anxious to get old so I could get that kind of respect. In Canada, and from what I understand about the U.S. and other industrialized nations, the older you get the more despised you are by quite a large segment of the population, especially the corporate sector and the uppity young heads who think they will never age. This seems to be the case because one's material usefulness is diminished with age, and such a person becomes a drain on the society in terms of medical requirements, the social security system, and the other special needs people develop as they grow older. Getting old in this part of North America is like being Black or like being a member of any other despised group. I have known of situations in Toronto where White children get their parents declared mentally incompetent and send them off to mental institutions and old age homes so they can get their hands on their parents assets ahead of time. I would dare say that growing up in Jamaica with a strong sense of respect for everyone, especially for the old as taught by my parents, has been most beneficial to me. This is not to say that all Jamaicans or all West Indians for that matter have taken full advantage of a better upbringing, or that all members of industrial societies are total reprobates in this regard.

The general consensus of most others in regards to Blacks is that we've all grown up without social graces, without any vision or plans for our lives and our families, no hopes, and no aspirations; that these deficiencies are evident among us because our ancestors being inferior had no knowledge about the importance of these things for their off-springs. They seem to think we are like a ship without a sail, lost at sea with no particular place to go. I have been asked countless times if there are any well-off Black families. Such people need to know that there are some Blacks who have become successful because of good parenting and good family structure and support that have inspired and encouraged their offspring to reach out and do their very best. There are proud fathers and mothers among Black people who have worked very hard to ensure the success of their children and families. We may never become as recognizable because we are not expected to be winners and as such our successes may be kept from public view, sometimes purposely by those who want to present us as unsuccessful. We are so expected to fail that our successes are hardly noticed at all by the mainstream of these societies. How quickly and stealthily the others will operate to hide our positive contributions to society. Only in February, which is called Black History Month is the North American society supposed to reflect on some of the important things Blacks have accomplished. Our reputation as criminals and losers is entrenched though even when it that is false.

This willingness to diminish the few Blacks who succeed comes not only from individuals, but also from institutions and sometimes even governments, which form part of what I call the silent conspiracy against us. These select groups, incidentally, are made up of people who themselves are products of their society, with intentions that are just as self-preserving as those of their peers and who have no training in race relations and are therefore not "de-bigoted" before they are put into positions of public trust. By reason of their positions, these can treat those they dislike with unfairness and discrimination in a sublime and quiet way. Black people can easily become a target for them to disparage and discourage. The more people are pre-occupied with defending themselves, the less energy and time they have for doing the things that can make them productive and successful. It takes more than just the ordinary will power to overcome the many obstacles that are faced by many Blacks both as individuals and families on a daily basis.

Notwithstanding the hindrances, some Blacks do succeed. I recently visited a church group to which I once belonged. I was happily surprised at the successes of some of the young Blacks who were just young children when I used to attend there regularly. Some had become lawyers; others had various bachelors and masters degrees in accounting, business, and other disciplines, and one quite special young woman, now in her early twenties, had obtained her PhD in physical therapy. Of her two older brothers, one had become a dentist practicing in Atlanta, Georgia, and the other obtained his masters degree in engineering from the University of Toronto. I went home feeling not just pride for their successes, but also vindication. It was not too many years before that the school system in the city of Toronto, would have done all it could to ensure their failure and hinder their success.

In order for Blacks to see more success however, there is need for radical changes to our mindset and long term goals. Blacks tend to live only for the day in front of us. Most other races have far-reaching plans not only for their children and grandchildren but for many future generations. This, I believe, is one of the single most important changes we need to make. Maybe we are living with the thought in the back of our minds that slavery could return in this the postmodern era and anything and everything we work for would then be forcibly taken from us. While such a possibility always exists, as long as it is not the reality, we need to take advantage of available opportunities. If we live that kind of mental scenario, our successes will surely be limited.

We need to have our children aim to become lawyers, doctors, judges, dentists and, yes, even politicians right here in North America, on a more regular basis. They need to be in these positions so they can be admired and emulated by their peers, and become worthy role models for other young Blacks. And while we work to become those things, we ought not to become discouraged because the arrows of envy and hate continue to fly in our direction. We will never be able to favourably impress all of those who dislike us where such is the case, because the minds of some will forever remain closed to anything good we would like to do. It is for this reason that our lives ought not to be lived just for the vain reason of showing that we can do well. Our aims for making ourselves better should be deeply ingrained in our subconscious minds as something we are supposed to do for the good of ourselves, the society, and the generations coming after us. We don't want our accomplishments to be superficial. We must aim to build up and benefit whatever society we live in whether Black or White. A lot more of our young men need to be noted for more than just an over abundance of crime and idleness and just hanging out whistling at girls.

That we will never be able to impress all of those who hate us may be understood from this event of a few years ago. Rodney King was captured on video tape being beaten almost to a pulp by White police officers of the LAPD in Los Angeles. In the aftermath of the riot which erupted, a radio station I frequently listen to here in Toronto was interviewing a White woman via the telephone who lived near where the riot had taken place. She stated that White Americans see Blacks "only as criminals". I thought to myself, "You ....." Blacks have become politicians, pastors, business men, lawyers, teachers, judges, and so on right there in your own state and you still see them "only as criminals?"

History and life today indicate that that woman did not speak for all White Americans, but her sentiments indicate that the stereotype is still very much alive. Nonetheless, we still have to go on with our lives and allow small-minded people like her to have their little maggot-brain opinion, and pity them in their little dark tunnels of willing blindness, misinformation, bigotry, and low self-esteem that they have carved out for themselves. It is obvious to me that such people are the by-products of very inferior and closed-minded upbringing. At the same time, I am hoping that since a Black person, Barack Obama, has become the president of the United States of America that more of them and more of us will get the cue and see that success is not based on the colour of one's skin but on attitude.

But, recent studies in the Unites States in regards to Black families have revealed a not-so comforting trend. As America is the leader of the world in almost everything, one would conclude almost every time that what is happening there applies almost everywhere. This study concludes that the Black family in America is failing. If you read the newspapers and the tabloids you see that White families are failing too, and that all kinds of negative stimuli affect every people group in that country, even the highly admired and adored film and entertainment stars of Hollywood. But no negative studies are ever published about them, no matter how low in the gutter some of them sink. Anyway, let me stay on course as far as this affects Blacks, and encourage us to take responsibility for our actions. So what have Blacks in America done this time to deserve the scrutiny and maintain the perpetual negative stereotypes that always seem to dog their every move? First, Blacks continue to have children out of wedlock with many of the fathers being absentees. This no doubt is a sure recipe for continued disaster as we all have seen. It means children are growing up without the presence and influence of one half of the parental support they need for a strong sense of self-esteem, belonging, and emotional security.

In the 1960s, when the late Senator Daniel Patrick Moynihan sounded the alarm about this issue he was not well received, especially when he said that approximately 25 percent of Black children were born out of wedlock. Now, 40 years later the percentage is about 66 percent. When he first reported the phenomenon it was seen as more or less a low income infestation, but now it has gone up the socioeconomic ladder. Social scientists suggest two possible reasons for this: one of them is the disproportionate imprisonment, unemployment, and early death of young Black males making them unavailable for marriage and fatherhood; and at the higher income level we have the fact that Black women are likelier than Black males to complete high school, attend college, and go on to earn academic credentials, which, while making them more eligible for marriage, in the end make it less likely that the greater portion of them will ever find a suitable mate. One possible reason is they would likely want someone as educated as they are to be married to, and given the shortage of eligible Black males, it is obvious that their chances for doing so are quite slim. It is noteworthy also that a lot of the successful Black males marry White women and women of other racial groups. Such is their privilege and is noted here for its material value only because I believe that a person should marry whoever they choose.

Black males, like others, are not born in prisons, or born to become criminal dropouts from schools, and other undesirables of society; so what may be rendering them susceptible to such an eventuality in a lot of cases is the absence of good and properly prepared fathers who should be there with them and act as positive role models for them. The result is that these youths soon become influenced by the evils of television, popular culture, neglect, and so on, and succumb to the very negative influences of criminality when it's pressed upon them by those in their communities who are already involved in undesirable activities. There is also this general disinclination, it seems, among Black males to become responsible fathers in a lot of cases. We just go about dropping fertile sperm into the ever available fallopian tubes of the women who consent to this abuse and move on whether a foetus is the end result or not.

Someone or something needs to trigger the alarm in our heads that this is a very detrimental behaviour, a blight on society, and a curse on our race.

As I have never known a man to have a child without the cooperation of a woman, I must then equally blame those women who provide fifty percent of the opportunity for this to happen. They are just as responsible for the plight of these out of wedlock children as the men are. We just cannot continue to have these irresponsible sexual relationships. We should use some form of birth control so we don't produce all these unwanted children with as dismal a future as we sometimes by default provide for ourselves. The truth is, theirs might even be worse than ours. We continue to perpetuate the problem as fatherless boys become fathers also, even though they have never learned the skills and responsibilities of fatherhood. The children of fatherless homes are more susceptible to the influence of criminals leading them into trouble than are the children of two-parent homes. But there are those who blame Black fathers alone for this problem without ever pointing one finger of responsibility at Black mothers. I am sure the men don't always demand sexual consent via the gun barrel, so how come the women bear no responsibility for this very pervasive yet inappropriate behaviour? And if it becomes a question of not being able to get along with the woman, we must support and do our best to keep in touch with the children if possible. While I know that this neglect of fatherhood by some Black men has some of its roots in the practice of slavery when Black male slaves were made studs by their White owners so a plentiful supply of potential little Black slaves would always be available to work the plantations, as alluded to before, it is time for us to start making the introspective examinations necessary to change this behaviour. We are no longer unwilling studs. We now have a choice.

To compound the problem, we now hear every so often of those who ought to know better behaving like the sexual perverts we are known to be. These "significant" ones are no more concerned about the negative impact that their behaviour will have on the Black population specifically and the society as a whole, than are the uneducated, unknown dwellers of the hated and the civilly neglected Projects.

We have this over-sexualized entertainment craze into which society has fallen and from which so many young people have taken their cue. Even though both Blacks and Whites are guilty of providing this kind of entertainment, Blacks continue to take all or most of the blame, a blame that we probably deserve because many of our entertainment initiatives are so degrading most times. We have become aware of the fact that the more degrading our acts on the screen, the more money they bring in. Nonetheless, I am somewhat tempted to conclude that because of the psychologically traumatic circumstances of rejection, hate, and mistreatment that we have been subjected to, that we are much more likely to descend into the dismal abyss of perversity and moral decay, succombing even more to the stereotype.

In most instances, Blacks have the same positive character traits as any other racial group. Educationally they strive to achieve. Well-researched reports have found that although Black children most times get lower scores than Whites on standardized tests, these same Black children often have higher educational aspirations than the White children in similar economic standing. Some social scientists puzzling over these findings sought for answers to explain it. They conclude that these aspirations of Black children are too lofty and therefore unrealistic. They then conclude that it is necessary to have "educators" lower these aspirations to prevent Black children in American schools from becoming frustrated adults. They become counsellors to them, advising them on the "right" course of action to follow.

The result of these "counselling sessions" is the dampening of the aspirations of these bright Black children, and as they advance through the public school system, and encounter these "counsellors" their aspirations and self-esteem are negatively affected. They become completely discouraged and drop out of school in record numbers. It can be concluded that this is exactly what these counsellors want. They then pile up statistics after statistics of Black student failure in the educational system. Of course, you guessed it, these Black students are then blamed for their inability to stay in school even thought these "Doctor Mengeles" were purposefully and by design, commissioned to maliciously destroy the heretofore untouched brilliant mental "hymens" of these Black youth, making sure that they deposit the seeds of failure into the now shocked minds of these well-intentioned young Blacks. They do it all in the name of "help". Why are the students shocked? For one thing they were expecting that after all the negative publicity about failure and lack of ambition we hear of so much among Blacks, that the White folks who are the first to call these out would be glad to see that these students were trying to head in the other direction. They are much frustrated when they find that envy, jealousy and malice is the standard issue of much of the White race, and that our success as Blacks is the thing they most fear.

Sometimes, I would like to change my "cynical" views on some aspects of life. But then, when I read and hear about things like this, I am tempted to think that I should keep those views. Some White folks reading this might say that it cannot be true. To give them the benefit of the doubt: why should they believe, or how can they believe? It never seems to happen to them. And the fact that these evils are perpetrated by individuals of their own race is reason to bring shame to the honest ones among them. But to me, inherent in all of this, is the concept that Blacks should have been masters of their own destinies and should not have had to be subjected to the designs of others. And this causes me to wonder who is more to be blamed.

It is concluded by these studies that Blacks can be as flexible in family roles as any other group of people. In Black American families, mothers assume some of the traditional roles of fathers, and fathers assume roles traditionally reserved for mothers, and children perform some of the functions of parenting for their younger brothers and sisters. Some people consider Black fathers who do household chores to be dominated by their women. Yet this role adaptation has been a source of help, stability, and advancement of a complete household, meaning a household of two parents. This role flexibility is especially evident in the vast number of Black American families headed by women. Single-parent families are depicted as broken and dysfunctional, while two-parent families are thought of as being intact and healthy. But even though two-parent families can be cohesive and be the best for society, yet a one-parent family need not be detrimental to society either.

The reason single-parent families are so despised in America is because from one perspective such describes a large percentage of the Black population. Taking this one step further, people believe that such children are a drain on the social system where hand-outs have to be made, but also because they think it more likely that such a child, especially if such is a Black, male child, has the greater likelihood of becoming involved in criminal activities. This is not always the case, however, as a lot of Black children from single-parent families have gone on to become educated, successful, and useful members of society. I can cite one example here: Dr. Ben Carson, the head of paediatric neurosurgery at Johns Hopkins Hospital in Maryland, whose mother raised him and his brother on her own. The sad truth about this attitude toward the fatherless Black child is the fact that it makes a mockery of the concept of benevolence the American society is supposedly noted for abroad. While

Americans do give to charity both foreign and domestic, it is almost unforgivable that they despise the unfortunate Black children among them who came to life with no intentions or actions of their own. Too bad that they hate and despise them rather than lend a helping hand. All the while as they neglect what is their responsibility, and wilfully refuse to render acts of kindness to the most helpless among them, their society is crumbling apart from the inside both socially and morally. Will they ever learn that the success of their country is hampered by the way they treat their weakest citizens and that what goes around because of their neglect will come around to haunt and mock them in the future?

Because of family malfunctions of whatever sort, many community-based programs designed to strengthen the functioning of single-parent and two-parent families have been established in some inner city areas. Because two-parent families are more desirable and better overall for Black families, numerous communities have developed programs which serve to enhance the parenting skills of Black fathers. One early program initiated by the National Urban League in the U.S. targets adolescent and young adult Black males with the primary objective of promoting responsibility in matters of sexuality, seeking to prevent them from having children born out of wedlock, and teaches responsible parenting for the benefit of the children of these young Black males, should they have any. I think they should teach the same things to young Black women, some of whom can be as promiscuous and as irresponsible as their male counterparts.

In order for Blacks to take advantage of the many opportunities available for work and school, the studies reveal that there needs to be a structure for mobility. One of the most important sources of mobility in Black families in the United States is a strong kinship network. According to conventional wisdom, the extended family has declined in urban areas. Reports however, continue to show that the proportion of Black extended families increased during the 70s and 80s. During this time, Black extended family households rose from 23 to 26 percent. Reports indicate that, as of the 90s, two out of five Black households were three generational. This trend can be used for the benefit of Black families in many ways. For example, childcare costs less when provided by extended family members. Nine out of every ten babies born to Black unwed teenage mothers live in three-generational households. These mothers have the support of relatives and are less likely to depend on welfare to achieve healthy emotional and social development of their children than teenage mothers who are forced to raise their children without any assistance from relatives.

Then there is the informal adoption of Black children by Black Americans who are relatives, and this has been a traditional base of support for these children for many decades. Such is most often manifested by grandparents, aunts or uncles taking in grandchildren, nieces and nephews to live with them for long or short periods of time. The number of informally adopted children living with relatives has risen sharply among Black American families over the past two decades. Between 1970 and 1990, the number of Black children living in the homes of kin rose from approximately 1.3 to 1.6 million. Many community-based groups provide adoption and family preservation services, which reinforces kinship. One of the oldest groups is Homes for Black Children, which was founded by Sydney Duncan in the 1960s. Alarmed by the large number of Black children available for adoption but who were languishing in foster homes, through Homes for Black Children Duncan was able to find families in the Black community willing and able to provide good environments for children who needed homes. HBC has been able to find homes for more than 700 Black children. HBC now places greater emphasis on family preservation to prevent unnecessary placement of Black children in foster care.

It can be concluded that one of the most important gifts that Black parents have been able to give to their children is the practice of religion. The Black church in America is and has always been the most important independent and self-sufficient institution for most Blacks. The Black church currently provides a wide range of social services directed toward stronger families and enhancing the development of children and youth. In order to increase their assistance to inner-city families, an ever expanding number of Black churches have set up Quality of Life Centres to address the needs of all family members from a holistic perspective. Services include daycare, nurseries, parenting, education, family counselling, remedial educational facilities, family planning, substance abuse prevention, employment training, recreational activities, and services targeted to young people. Black churches have always assisted orphans and homeless children and most Black orphanages were founded by Black religious institutions. Increasing evidence reveals that Blacks with strong religious orientations have a higher socioeconomic status than those with little or no religious commitment. (I will have more on this later.) One study of young males in low-income communities sought to identify reasons these youth were able to attain their goals in spite of deprived backgrounds. The analysis concluded that a deep religious commitment had the strongest correlation with lower rates of school-dropout, delinquency, out-of-wedlock births, and drug abuse. It is clear then that strong religious beliefs can be a major source of family support in Black communities.

Maybe these studies in America reflect the situation for all or most Black societies all over the world. If that is the case, then similar solutions and plans of the organizations able to help could be implemented wherever these problems exist. If the needed help can be given, then the problems can be lessened or eliminated altogether.

Even though we may be having some measure of success, Black parents should become very pro-active, particularly in the early years of their children's lives, preparing them to face the disparities of a society that is most times racially hostile to them. This should happen long before the children are old enough to go to school. By the time the children get to school, they should have some knowledge of these racial pitfalls plaguing society and should be prepared to deal with them. The same holds true for criminal initiation and sexual promiscuity. If a child can be taught to avoid or to be aware of one thing, then we might as well go ahead and make it two or three. This early awareness is even more crucial when the children have to go to a school where they are out-numbered racially. Heaven alone knows how evil the heart of people in charge of the children's education can be, and how early precious and sweet little Black children have been made to feel the racial hatred levied against them from cruel adults who have no regard for their tender age and feelings. These little ones can really be bruised and lacerated mentally and emotionally as little lambs left to be watched by wild and ferocious man eating beasts, setting the stage early for their demise by having seeds of failure and rejection planted in their minds, and causing them mental anguish at so early a stage in their lives. Sometimes they never recover from the initial shock of such a treatment and go on to become the rejects of society, producing nothing and turning to crime to achieve their perverted version of self-esteem. I know of that which I speak. My own children have felt the pain of hate in schools they have attended, and I have heard many stories of teachers and parents who tell their students and children to avoid interacting with a child simply because he or she is Black.

Quite a number of Blacks that I talk with, are afraid and even aloof about the concept of letting their children in on the real world where racial disharmony is concerned, fearing that they will make them aware of something which they may not have to face. They also fear that these children of theirs will then start seeing themselves as inferior to others if they give them this awareness. It is true that racial hatred may not exist in every single place and instance, and that some Blacks may never have had and may never have any firsthand experience with it. If a Black individual living in a multi-racial society can go through life without getting in contact with this virus then good, but I personally can't see how an inferiority complex would develop as a result of making children aware of this probability. Telling children that racism exists should not make them feel inferior especially if along with that bit of information they are also told that they are as important in the scheme of things as anyone else, and that no matter what happens they are expected to make positive contributions to the society in which they live.

While God designed that people should be different racially, and while in all probability He intends that we all get along in spite of our differences, I sometimes wish that Blacks and Whites and people of other races never had to live together, and especially not in such close proximity to each other as is sometimes the case. We all should have been in our own countries, schools, grocery stores, malls, etc., in our own neighbourhoods. We might even have been better off living our lives on separate continents, left alone to determine our own destinies, without the forced social interaction between us. I am tempted to conclude that the only kind of interaction really necessary is that of respectable and profitable business relationships. Social and friendly interaction should be a matter of choice and very optional. If we lived separately, Blacks would not have to be demeaned because of their colour and Whites and other races would not have as many opportunities to practice their love for miss-applied superiority thinking.

A White woman I spoke to about such a thing responded that if such had been the case our future as Blacks would have been most daunting if not completely hopeless. She cited cases of mass starvation in predominantly Black African countries as proof of what she was saying. I unwittingly concurred with her somewhat because she spoke from what, at the time, seemed a caring perspective. But in the back of my mind, I was thinking that it could have been different had Europeans for one not gone and interfered with life on the continent. Back in the early days of European and Arab conquest, Africa had enough to subsist, even if that lacked the technological advancement of the European way of life.

However, because I have disciplined myself to always see both sides of the coin, I could not help but think also at the same time, about the utter incapacity of Africans to make proper use of their vast natural resources, and as usual I was wondering forlornly why it was that Blacks in general are so incapable of making progress by themselves and are always depending on the Whites and others for jobs, and so on? I thought too that some Africans do make use of these natural resources, but only the leaders who are corrupted by foreign entities get any benefit, and they think nothing of the plight of their own people. I should have told her that in the America of her day and mine, a lot of Blacks in a lot of cases were not doing all that well to warrant her making that statement. Some of them live in poverty and squalor reserved for the most repressed economies on earth, and America has done precious little to help those Blacks living right under their noses

All this is not to say that Whites and a few of the others have only done bad for Blacks, or that I am just a mindless racist Black pig, as I am sure that I will be called by some. I don't think I am. I just know that I have no problem speaking my mind about these very important issues. As well, further on in this book you will read where I am clearly in favour of the Whites for the good they have done. So please don't throw this book in the garbage pail just yet. Besides I am sure that I am not the only one who thinks about these things: the difference is that I have decided to put my thoughts in print.

Awareness of the inequities in society should make Black families more determined to do everything possible to instil in their children a sense of value and a winning perspective. Watch less television, especially the type that affords no learning experience except about crime and violence; get your children off video games. There are so many studies by social scientists in which children are blamed for spending too much time in front of the television set and playing video games to the point where their school projects are never completed. Parents also join in to blame their children. But these televisions sets and video games are not usually purchased and made a part of the fixture of the house with funds from the children. It is parents who bring these items into the house, so parents are the ones to blame. Both mothers and fathers should unite together in the monitoring of their children's activities when these activities are time wasting and mentally and academically injurious to their children.

Children should not get everything they ask for. Because the neighbours' children have certain things, it does not mean that your children should have them. It is not always wise to keep up with the Joneses. Many times parents dote on their children, indulging them in slothfulness all the while calling this love. They sometimes do this to be the center of their children's misguided affection. This is poor parenting. One result of indulgence of this kind is low academic performance as the mind becomes sluggish and dull, losing the taste for any challenges not to mention developing a disrelish for discipline and boundaries. These can be further exacerbated resulting in low self-esteem for these children who cannot then keep up with their more disciplined peers in class and other places of competition.

Society mostly blame Black fathers for the breakdown in law and order in their homes and the lack of achievement in their children's lives. But sometimes the blame sits squarely on the shoulders of the mothers who hold the fathers' hands and voices from administering the needed corrections verbally or otherwise, and the setting of sensible limits for the benefit of their children. One can almost conclude that in some cases, it would be better that a lot of our Black men and women (and sometimes those of other races too) be made infertile surgically instead of leaving us to bring children into the world we are not capable of taking care of. We multiply and replenish when we are not able to cherish and nourish. I am not here referring to well-intentioned people with responsibility. I am speaking of those who like to sow and receive wild oats but are incapable of care and responsibility when such take roots and start to encumber the society.

Black families should spend more energy on things that really matter. Countless times I have seen young Blacks just hanging out at shopping malls and plazas doing nothing worthwhile. Why can't the parents get these young men and women away from these places and onto something that can benefit them in the long run? Other people have the same disadvantages as we do, but they have taken measures to help themselves and so should we. As they come out better off than when they began, so can we. We will not see success without a disciplined approach to practicing what will make us successful. To expect otherwise is to expect the unlikely. No one has ever come to anything worthwhile without investing time and putting effort into what they needed to accomplish. Some people are born with a silver spoon in their mouths and things may be better for them starting out. If that is not the case for the rest of us, then hard work is the only answer to our quest for success.

CHAPTER FIVE
BLACKS AND EDUCATION

In this section of the book I look at some of the probable reasons Blacks fail in school as much as they do, by taking into account historical and social factors that might be the cause of this. I offer suggestions on what Black parents and students might be able to do to combat this most unfortunate situation, reverse this trend, and make their lives and those of succeeding generations better through education.

When I migrated to Toronto Canada, I concluded by observation that Blacks had two primary encumbrances in the White society at the grassroots level: these two were the White law enforcement officer and the White school teacher. It seemed as though these two professions were the first lines of defence for the preservation of the status quo in their efforts to dampen any progress Blacks might make. Teachers played their part very well by instilling into the minds of their Black students the thought that they could not accomplish anything worthwhile, and sadly a large number of Blacks have accepted this negative intentional brain washing to their academic and educationally progressive detriment. The foregoing is not a theory as the reader will see from a few of the many examples below.

The law enforcement officers kept Blacks on edge through needless harassment, which kept them from feeling at ease, robbing them of the energy and the concentration which they would otherwise have to improve themselves. Thankfully, much of this is in the past here in Toronto. Before I go any further, let me make it perfectly clear that not every White teacher and not every White law enforcement officer hates and hinders Blacks. But in my experience, and that of many other Blacks that I have spoken to, enough of them do to cause a significant amount of failure of Black students where school is concerned, and much harassment where the police are concerned.

One of the bitterest complaints I heard was from a Black Barbadian young man, detailing how he was denied the privilege of becoming an ophthalmologist. He had gone to a university in the western portion of Ontario to prepare for this profession first by earning his undergraduate degree. He did fabulously all through the program until it was time for him to write his final exam. This was the one that would do it for him. Even though he had always been an honour student at all other times, he failed his final examination. He told me that the professor who gave him the failed mark then used his failed paper to demonstrate to the rest of the class what the answers ought to have been. He had to sit through all of it and endured the humiliation of seeing this done, unable to say or do anything about it. I have often thought how cruel that professor was to do this to this young man.

As it turned out, he could not go on to his chosen profession as he had run out of money and did not have the ability to go back over the program. He took a job as a social worker which he was for the twenty some years that I was acquainted with him. As far as he was concernd, his professor was jealous of the fact that he a Black man wanted to attain to such a prestigious profession and used the only tool he could to willfully deny him of his dream. I know him to have come from a very academically successful family because his younger sibling is a past executive of the Institute of Chartered Accountants of Ontario. At the time this happened there was no hope of this young man complaining to any Human Rights commission or bringing any charges against this professor. The system just did not have the structure in place to resolve that kind of situation.

A former classmate of mine wrote a paper at one of Toronto's universities. Her professor insisted that she was not intelligent enough to write that paper as she was Black, and concluded that she must have bought it somewhere. She challenged him to give her any subject he wished her to write on, and invited him to watch her as she did the work, as that she concluded would dispel any notion of her getting help from another source. He would not oblige her. He preferred to remain bigoted and arrogant, wilfully robbing her of the recognition she deserved. As in the other case cited above there was no point to her trying to do anything legally about it. I studied at one of Toronto's well-known community colleges back in the early Eighties. One lecturer there would not give me one mark above sixty percent, which was the lowest passing grade. I could write an entire chapter as an answer to one question; it was never worth more than sixty percent to him. Others, thankfully, graded me as I deserved, and it made me glad that they were not all of the same mindset.

A few years later, children at my daughter's elementary school were given an opportunity to answer the phones in the late afternoons. I was there on one of these afternoons when it was her turn. The White principal was so incensed that a little Black child should get that privilege; he spent time "checking things out" before he allowed her to pick up the phone. What he had to check out is still a mystery to me. I could not believe that a school principal would stoop low enough to deny a seven-year-old child a simple opportunity like that because her skin color was Black.

Some years later, another daughter of mine was doing very well in school. By then we were living in the Durham Region, east of Toronto. When she made the mistake of telling one of the White teachers that she wanted to become a dentist, she was met with the sternest and most discouraging look and told outright that she did not have the ability to become a dentist, even though she was an A student all round with the ability to become anything she wished. The only reason for this discouraging response by this teacher we concluded was her Black skin. In her business class at the same school, another White teacher became jealous that the students went to her for help with this course, in which she was achieving excellent marks. They had found the teacher mean spirited and were afraid to go to him. He called her a "Czech Terrorist"— whatever that meant. The label was very confusing when looked at from the perspective that she has no ties to Czechs and although of mixed-race, she is Black. This incident was post-9/11 and was considered quite slanderous in that atmosphere. By the time I heard about it, he had been fired from the school due to that and other negative behaviour on his part.

My son, a year younger, wrote a paper given to him at his school, which was also in the Durham Region. Upon reading the paper, his teacher asked him who wrote it for him. His earlier years had been spent in school in Texas, and although Texas is considered by the average Canadian to be very racist compared to Canada, at least three times a week his White teachers, would send us little notes on the excellent progress of this boy. This was at a U.S Exemplary High School. A U.S. Exemplary High School got the title because it is recognized by the U. S. Federal Department of Education as a very high-performance establishment. Yet here in this little pip-squeak school, which as far as I know had no awards for excellence in anything, in little Pickering, which you might miss if you blink as you drive by, he was made to feel that he was not good enough to write a little paper. I mentioned this to a former teacher, himself White and a friend of mine, and his rueful comment was that this was indeed a low blow. My son has not gotten over the inference inherent in that teacher's comment yet. I am led to think that the teachers who practice this negative attitude toward Black students are quite aware of what they are doing. These things are said and done by people who know they that what they do is detrimental and hurtful to the student's self esteem and academic advancement. Because they are professionals, most people will not believe that they would do any such thing. And we Blacks, being in the minority in this and other situations, are not always able to mount an effective opposition to these onslaughts against Black students. In the meantime, those who hurt continue to feel the effects of the degradation. This then leads to despair and a lack of perspective and self-esteem, and eventually to ruined lives especially when these students have no support base to which they can turn for understanding and counsel.

There are many other stories I could tell you my readers about the unfairness of White teachers toward Black students who are made to feel less than humans by those who are bent on keeping them from progressing and then blaming them when they drop out of school, turn to crime and drugs, and become a menace to society. These people then love to cite statistics on the failure of Black students as if they themselves made not a single contribution to such failure.

The above, I'm thankful to say, does not mean that all Black students suffer the same fate; and at the same time some of them, when treated unfairly, become even more determined to let nothing stand in their way to get an education. If people would just think about it they will find that God has not destined anyone to fail. It is the conditioning that they get from parents and society that makes the difference in their lives. Those who are negatively affected should think of that. Some Black students do overcome the encumbrances and go on to make good of their lives. But a different story is written for the ones who have become too discouraged to revive.

It is important that Black students who are experiencing racism at school speak to those of their parents who are interested in their children's success. Some parents I know have had to go to the schools and confront teachers who are standing in the way of their children's education. At times, the oppressive hands of these teachers are lifted because they are terribly afraid and even ashamed when they are discovered and branded as racist and unfair, which indeed those teachers are. Sometimes they have to be reminded that there is a Human Rights Commission now that listens and to which complains can be lodged about their attitudes towards these students before they will release their "death grip" on them. Some Black parents show no care for their children's education, and so some Black children never get the support they need from the most important people in their lives. But that is both wrong and very unfortunate. We can't just become so pre-occupied with eking out a living that the plight our children face on a daily basis gets overlooked. When they have the system against them and parents who don't really understand or care, it becomes overwhelming, depression sets in, and disappointment and failure are the inevitable results.

Children are naturally afraid and terrified of authority. Most Black children are more so when they live in societies where they are in the minority. When they are placed in mostly White schools, and are sometimes the only Black in a class, how frightening the situation becomes when negative comments are made about them by the teachers and other students who make them the butt of their jokes. Every mistake they make is attributed to their Black skin, and they are made to feel so low that instead of concentrating on their school work, they concentrate instead on the problems they face even just being in school. Should some Black students even have to apologize for breathing? What a wretched existence they have to start their young lives with! No wonder they become traumatized and do poorly or drop out of school altogether when they face such challenges. No one, it seems, likes them. They may even be walking the streets in the conscious thought that almost every person they meet, even other Black people, dislike them. These otherwise normal and healthy children then start being disruptive in schools and wherever else they go, or become completely withdrawn and uncooperative.

The system gladly points to their lack of progress as just cause to keep them back or even have them expelled from schools. Society accepts the bunk that these students are non-achievers. Black parents themselves may, and often do, become disappointed and angry at the poor level of their children's performance and further discourage them without having any meaningful dialogue with them about probable reasons for their failure. Some of these children, because of bad relationships may not trust their parents enough to tell them their problems. Many children would rather tell someone other than an immediate family member what their problems really are. One friend suggested that children need adults other than their parents to confide in, saying we should be there for each other's kids.are. This is a very unfortunate situation and a very unwise course of action for these young people to follow because silence can lead to further complications of a situation and may delay solving a very pressing problem until it is too late.

Social scientists will usually look kindly on the White child who has been emotionally traumatized by unfavourable circumstances and displays a less than normal behaviour, but they are very strong in their condemnation of the Black child who has been brought up under similar circumstances or even those much worse. Those in charge need to realize that children will fight back one way or another. The course of action they will take may not necessarily be criminal, but they will find a way to avenge themselves. I can recall the day August 6th, 1962 when my family was getting ready for Jamaica's Independence

Celebration. My father had upset me, and it was not for the first time. I decided that I would have my revenge. So, even though he was very authoritarian, I decided that I would defy him by not going to the celebrations to be held on the primary school grounds. I hid around the house till they all left. They must have thought that I had gone ahead of them. As soon as they left I simply went inside and slept, angry that I wasn't going, but holding my father responsible for that. I was so happy when they all came back very frustrated, telling me how much they had searched for me there at the end of the festivities but could not find me. I was so very glad inside to have upset my father, even though it cost me a night of celebration. The point I am trying to make is that the psyches of children have not changed and things will only get worse if adults don't handle them the right way.

But why are White educators so willing to assume the role of keeping their societies free from educated Blacks? In truth, I believe that the answer lies in the basic nature of every human being. We are all insecure and afraid that what we have can be taken from us and our children, and that what we have grown to think belongs solely to us, ought not to be shared with anyone else. We believe that the established order of things should remain as is, and when those unlike us come among us, we become very defensive and protective of the status quo. Thiss is not just a "White people" problem. The bug affects us all. When I was teaching in Jamaica, I used to meet foreign teachers working in some of our schools. As local teachers we did not like the fact that they paid no taxes and were given free housing as an inducement to work in our country, while we had to pay these taxes and find our own housing. We saw it as something the government should not be doing for foreigners. At the time, I was unable to see that these teachers might have taken a pay cut to work in Jamaica, and might have left better facilities in their home countries, and maybe even their families, to work there. Whether their service was of benefit to the Jamaican students they taught was another matter and not a conclusion I could come to.

I was having a conversation quite a few years ago with a White Torontonian and asked her why people there were as unfriendly toward Blacks, as indeed they were. The answer was that they did not care so much about who came to live in their country as such as long as the newcomers did not take their jobs away from them. I then began to wonder if this was the same mindset of most of the teachers. Some of them have children too and may be imagining that future jobs and opportunities might be lost to them if too many people, especially Black people, are competing for those job opportunities. While she was not a teacher, she had used the words "we," and to my mind it was likely that she was speaking for most Canadians. It is a fact that people in some professionals have more opportunities to practice their brand of discrimination and exclusiveness much more freely than others. This allows these practitioners to enforce their way of thinking on those in their charge. The teaching profession, I believe, is one of those. I will hasten to say again that this does not include all White teachers because I know there are those among them who do not practice these evils. I have studied under some of them who were fair and even-handed in their approach to their profession, and I have met some of these even in 'ultra-racist' America, as noted before.

When I began to understand these things, I concluded that I was previously misinformed about Canada not being a racist country. I had read of about the Underground Railroad and was pleasantly surprised to learn that a country of White people would be so willing to help a group of escaping Black slaves. It impressed me favourably, but later on I learned that Canada had a skeletons in its national closet, in reference not only to Blacks but also to the Native Indians. Still later on, I learned that even though Canada was the destination for the Underground Railroad escapees, there had been institutionalized racism in this country and quite a bit of disfavour for Blacks in the early days of Upper Canada. There were even segregated schools in Ontario, Manitoba, and Nova Scotia from the early nineteenth to much of the twentieth century. However, Canada's racial history was not even one hundredth of a percent as violent as that of its great racist neighbour to the south. And truly, while there are uncomfortable and sometimes quietly pernicious inequities for us in Canada, Blacks in general do not suffer the overt and shameless racial biases inherent in the American experience. In Canada, Blacks now may legally and without much fear of personal danger, eat in any restaurant, go to any place of entertainment, go to any school, and buy a house in any community, etc., even though a report on racial discrimination in the Toronto *Sun* in March of 2008 shows that Blacks are still the most likely people to be shown racial intolerance. I cannot deny that this might not be due in part to the recent bad behaviour of young Blacks, mostly males who do nothing but kill each other, sell drugs, and are the ones using guns to terrorise the GTA.

But, as bad as things may be in Canada, they were and still are much worse south of the border. From the pages of history, Blacks in the legalized slavery days of America did not even have the right to be educated privately or publicly. In fact, it was downright illegal even to teach them to read. When, after many years, Blacks could finally go to school, there were few schools willing to accept them. Later on, they got their own schools and unsurprisingly, the schools for the Whites were and still are well-funded, well-staffed, and well-cared for in terms of the maintenance of the physical structure of the buildings. The schools for the Blacks were and still are under-funded, understaffed, and the buildings decrepit and run-down. There is no mystery here. It was and may still be government policy in the United States to give Blacks much less than Whites receive. It was, and is institutionalized racism at its worst because it denies one of the most basic and fundamental rights to the citizens of a country: the right to a good education. Countries like China, and Cuba have the right to laugh loudly at Uncle Sam when he preaches to them about improving their human rights record. At least in Cuba, of all places, all citizens have equal rights to an education even though some of them are Black. But here we have the so-called most advanced country on the planet still practises institutionalized racism in the post-modern era against the people to whom it owes so much of its present wealth.

It takes money to provide a good education. Money usually comes from the government or from very rich institutions and wealthy individuals. If the Black people in America are too poor to give donations to their schools for the support of staff, for needed supplies, and for the upkeep of the school buildings, their schools will not be able to operate as efficiently as schools should. The government is responsible for providing proper learning facilities for its students regardless of colour. Where this is not the case, the quality of education that the Blacks receive will naturally be much inferior to what the Whites receive; , and this under circumstances and conditions certainly not conducive to learning.

Children of poor parents generally live in poor neighbourhoods, are poorly fed, and poorly clothed. They eat less of the foods essential to the proper nourishment of their bodies and to support mental and physical health. They have little or no money to buy the things they need for schools and other necessities, and live in far less healthy conditions than the rich. I will always believe that Blacks ought to do all they can to help themselves, but they started out with a handicap. It was the handicap of being Black in a White society, which really, after slavery was abolished, had no use for them and denied them even their humanity. Because of this, many opportunities were never given to them. The result of this denial of entitlement to the Blacks where education is concerned is discouragement, failure, and a lack of motivation. They look across the racial divide and see that for no other reason than skin colour, their White counterparts are given everything they want, and they are not always in a position to level the grossly uneven playing field. As a result we see idleness, crime, drugs, and the super jails that America builds to house those who "become" criminals. Maybe it would be better to redirect the money for penal construction and use it instead for the renovation of Black schools. I am aware that this would mean that there would not be so many job opportunities for the prison sector, but the American economy is versatile enough to accommodate them in other areas.

Poorly educated people are a blithe to their society. America is not better off for having denied such a large segment of its population the right to a good and equitable education, which is one of the preambles to living a decent life, and it will be much worse off in the end if it allows this unfair practice to continue. Yasuhiro Nakasone, when he was prime minister of Japan, alluded to this when he insisted that the reason for America's low performance in (some areas of academia) on an international level was because of the Black people among them. I stand to be corrected here if I am wrong, but I believe the reason for his conclusion is that when some tests are administered, the overall numerical population index of the country participating is considered. If such is the case, the higher the number of illiterates in the populace of the participating country, the lower the mean average would be. Nakasone himself hated Blacks, but he made a good point about the illiteracy of Black Americans, although this is not all their fault. He illustrated, albeit unwillingly, the point that keeping a group of people in your society as an underclass by denying them the right to an education will not benefit the nation overall. One of the ideas I always cherished was the thought that leaders should operate free from any racial bias. I used to believe that they were a special breed who had accepted their positions without taint toward anyone. But in some parts of America, as well as other White-ruled countries, even leaders actively engaged in the act of keeping Blacks out of schools. Even presidents of that country took jabs at Black people, and by their actions fostered sentiments of racism against them. One wonders what they could have gained from such a practice? Men of such high offices stooped so low to bring grief and mental anguish to their own citizens.

It is true that some things have changed and are continuing to change for the better in terms of education and in terms of Black achievement and wealth. More and more Blacks are earning some respect from some of these societies by reason of the dollar bills flowing to their bank accounts. As they earn money in sports and entertainment, their financial health increases, and maybe with this increased wealth, successful and wealthy Blacks can now become philanthropists giving money to Black schools and other Black institutions, which are always in need of financial help. America's local, state, and federal governments do not yet empower themselves to stop Black wealth from flowing to these Black institutions. So, while there is time and opportunity to do so, wealthy Blacks should make as large contributions as they can to help the poorer Blacks get an education. In some places, California for example, they are still unwilling to give Blacks a fair shake so they come up with Black-focused schools and Ebonics to make it seem that their failure is progress, not admitting that their "progress" is still set up to make Blacks fail. It would seem that if an employer were hunting for prospects he would not readily hire someone from such a school because the curriculum would not be seen to be general enough to include all the benefits of a traditional education.

(You might say to me "What about Africa and the other countries of poverty where Blacks live?" I am coming to that. As well it's a different economy with a different set of rules. Let us finish with things here first).

Sometimes though, we Blacks refuse to see the forest because of the trees. My children, as I said before, used to go to a U. S. Exemplary school. The average grade for students in that school was ninety ninety-five percent. There were some other Black students admitted to the school who did nothing but blame the teachers for their lack of progress. They criticised other Black students, my daughter included, for "acting White" because they were working hard and making good grades while the uncooperative students just fooled around, disrespected their teachers, and wanted things to just fall into their laps. I know for certain that at least some of the teachers at that school, even though they were White, were doing a very good job of helping students. I know firsthand of the personal attention they paid to my children, even taking time to hand write personal notes to us, the parents, keeping us informed on the academic progress the children were making. They would send these notes two or three times per week as said before. So, in this situation, I know for sure that it was not their fault that those Black students were not up to par with their grades. It was the students who needed to change their attitudes and their reasons for being in school. These students were not taking advantage of the opportunity to help themselves, and this leads me to confirm that there is a subculture of indolence in the lives of some Blacks on this side of the continent. As Blacks, we need to keep hunting for the nuggets of gold that hard work and persevering efforts deliver. The world will always give its treasures to those looking for them. Think about this seriously and remind yourself of how hopeless and helpless Blacks were when they set foot on American soil and see how well some of them are doing today.

I mentioned earlier that governmental bodies in the U.S refused Blacks educational opportunities as well as other resources where they could have made progress if allowed. Such a practice was mostly historical, but it still exists today. When Mr. Bill Clinton was president of the United States, the administration stopped Mr. Muammar Gaddafi, the president of Libya, from donating a billion dollars to America's Blacks. Such a donation was to be given to the Black Muslims, or otherwise called the Nation of Islam, and was to be used, as far as I can remember, for the improvement of Black schools and other Black institutions in America. I was in the United States then and remember the offer very well. The administration's reasoning was that Libya was a terrorist state and because of that the gift was swiftly and initially declined. The New York Times reported that Louis Farrakan, the Black Muslim leader at the time made plans to spend the money more generously, but had appeal the administration's decision. I thought it was too bad that the administration did not accept the gift or offer to substitute the refused gift with federal funds, at least the part it determined would go to the schools. When Clinton was president, America saw prosperity on a scale unprecedented in the modern history of the country, and he left office with America enjoying what was probably the largest budgetary surplus in its history. A billion dollars or a fraction thereof, would have been nothing for his government to give for the improvement of Black schools. I wondered then if Mr. Gaddafi had specified that the money go to America's White schools instead, if the administration would have put any stumbling block in the way. I tried to keep my ears open for further news on the matter because as mentioned earlier, the Black Muslims had decided to challenge the refusal of the gift in court, but I have never heard if the money was ever allowed to be donated. (I have not included this incident because I agree or disagree with everything or anything the Black Muslims and the Nation of Islam do; I included it to illustrate a point of inconsistency to my way of thinking.)[20]

Black achievement in American schools was always held back by most Whites, in one way or another. From the very early days, Blacks were not supposed to be taught how to read or write and any White person caught teaching them was subject to very heavy punishments. A Black slave who was fortunate to learn from his or her White slave owner and caught teaching other Black slaves could be killed by anyone White who discovered what was happening.

Over the years, Blacks came to be viewed as inferior in aspirations and intellect. But it was not because of any inherent inferiority that Black people were not literate. It was because of a system which controlled their lives and placed restrictions upon them, hindering them in every possible way. There were even times when slaves were beaten for daring to pray and had to do so very secretly and very late at night when their "Christian" slave masers were fast asleep.

As time went by, the restrictions were eased in some corners and Black students could sometimes attend a few institutions of learning aided and supported by some of the Whites who were sympathetic to them. Now, there are Blacks in almost every profession, though the representation in numbers are much smaller than it they should be. There are even some noted Black institutions of learning. Still, there are many hills to climb and a long road to travel before progress is more than just a drop in the bucket. It may take many more generations before progress is more visible and pervasive enough for the negative stereotypes to go away. Sure we have Oprah Winfrey, Tiger Woods, and Michael Jordan to name a few hugely successful Black Americans. But the bulk of Black progress does not seem to come so much from academia as it does from other sources. It is in sports and entertainment that Blacks make the bulk of their presence known in the America of today. This may be a good way out of poverty, but it should not be the only way.

And yet, even when Blacks make progress educationally, the Whites pretend that it is because they have to lower the standards so Blacks can pass exams. The interesting thing is that in the vast majority of cases they are still using the same text books and other educational materials in the schools where Blacks and Whites study together. Unless they tell the Blacks in advance what the test questions are, Blacks will have to cover the entire material in preparation for these tests and examinations like everyone else. If educators water down the text books or the test material and have the Blacks study from those instead, they should then be blamed if they put unqualified people in professions where the citizens will experience less of the quality of life due to this "lack of qualification" for some of the graduates from their schools. Do they allow Blacks to get by with wrong answers to the same questions, or do they allow lower passing grades for Blacks? If that is what is done, then shame on these educators and their system of deference that they have put in place. Why do these "educators" not see that it is the social conditioning and the mental trauma that they have brought upon Blacks that have caused them to be low performers most times when such is the case? Blacks have had to bear the mental pain of White inconsistencies for centuries. Blacks do everything pre-occupied with the thought that they are despised by these people. There is a lot of energy spent in emotional and mental preoccupation of overly stressful situations purposefully brought on to people who have had more than enough, and such energy could have been used to do something much more worthwhile. Stop the unnecessary hate of Blacks yourself and stop training your children to hate them also. It is becasue your offsprings see you hating them that they continue the same course. If you were made to feel the same hate you give them all your life, how would it make you feel, and how productive would you be?

The better solution for Blacks is to empower them in their own surroundings, stop yelling the poison of self-deprecation at them, allow them their rightful amount of self esteem of which they have been robbed, and in a short time there will be progress that was never expected. Or is this what people are afraid of? Put birds of a feather together, but give them the same flight range and opportunities. Putting unwilling Blacks or Whites in a place where they are uncomfortable because of government-enforced social norms, causes tension and simply puts both groups under undue pressure which lessens their ability to concentrate on what they should be doing. Since success and achievement is learned over time and is passed on from one generation to another, the Whites must then be almost entirely blamed for stifling the ability of American Blacks initially and not bringing them into the fold of higher learning much sooner than they did.

How can an education system lower the qualifications to be a doctor or a lawyer, for example, and put those people less qualified to serve in such capacities? Wouldn't sick patients be placed in danger, and defendants stand less of a chance for justice in the courts? Were the qualifications lowered for Dr. Ben Carson to make him the internationally known neurosurgeon that he is today? And were they lowered for the Black astronauts who went up into space? Were standards lowered for Colin Powell, past Chairman of the Joint Chiefs of Staff for the American military, Justice Clarence Thomas of the U. S. Supreme Court, or Condoleezza Rice, the past American Secretary of State? Were they lowered for President Barack Obama who has now become leader of that country, elected by mostly Whites? And has it been lowered for other Black people who have reached the high pinnacles of educational and career achievements that they have? The truth, I believe, on some of these issues is that many White people are still jealous and are full of envy over every little bit of progress that Black people make. They are obsessed about keeping their "superior" positions and feel threatened that Blacks so recently slaves will catch up to them so soon. They seem to also believe that it is genetically impossible for Blacks to be intelligent. Why so? Did not God say that He saw that whenever any two men set their minds to accomplish something they will achieve it? God did not say any two White men or any two Oriental men. He said "any two men". That includes any race or color of men and it is God who speaks. Some of the White folks should stop believeing and stop spreading their own mindless lies. If you can lower your standards and still maintain functionality, it means then that your system may have been purposefully over bloated in the first place.

Almost everything that Blacks set out to accomplish in White-dominated societies leaves them with at least one very enervating preoccupation—they have to fight against the stereotypes placed in their minds about their limitations, and they have to seek to do their best to concentrate on the task at hand. This begins at a very early age, happens in all countries and places where Blacks are in the minority, and stays with most from birth to death. Let me illustrate: my family and I spent some time in the Philippines where my wife is from. The children were very young then. My daughter was eight years old, and my son was seven. Because of our racially mixed marriage, our children are different in their physical appearance. Davina, the girl does not look Oriental while Gregory looks Oriental like his mother. She was told by one of her Filipino teachers that they did not care about her because she was Black. He never had that problem. She was and still is a very sensitive and sweet child, and suffered a lot of mental anguish over this. It was very difficult for her to concentrate on her lessons after that. It was a preoccupation she had to go to classes and live with for as long as we were in that country. Such a preoccupation would make it hard for any child of any race or age to study with. It was hard for me to conceive of an adult putting such stress on a child so young. I pray that I will never do such a thing to any child even if the parents of that child were my worst enemies. And even if I were a racist, I would seek to ensure that I never practiced racist behaviour against an innocent child. Yet this is what technologically "sophisticated" and "advanced" White societies and the societies of other races have been practicing against Black children for hundreds if not thousands of years.

Though the history of their rights to education in White societies has been less than fair, Blacks need to take seriously their quest for an education. No nation, race, or people will accomplish much without proper training and a good education of some kind. Those ahead of us know this and it is precisely why they deny education to Blacks. In places like Texas, it is mandatory that children go to school, no matter what the circumstances are. With such a law in place, educators cannot legally hinder children from going to school. If Blacks want to dispel the stereotypes in a place like that, then now is the time. It may be difficult for children who have seen their parents living on welfare all their lives to suddenly rise to the challenge of school work and make good, but it is not impossible. Parents don't always have to be educated to have educated children, although such is a more likely scenario. Children with minds of their own and a determined will can achieve, even when their parents have led very humble lives. One of the most successful law practices I heard of in the United States is owned by a Black lawyer who won either the second largest or third largest financial settlement in American history at the time I read the story. He owns several luxury motor cars, his own airplane, and lives in a huge house with a home theatre that seats 25 people. His two sons are probably lawyers by now {they were studying law when I read about this}, and he even had White lawyers working at his practice. His father had been a humble sharecropper, but he was determined to do well, and hence his success. Unfortunately, not too many of us have that kind of drive.

CHAPTER SIX
BLACKS AND THE
SOCIAL STEREOTYPE

Why do Blacks and most other non-White groups depend so much on the expertise of the White race? What is it about Whites that makes them the masters of the planet in so many instances? Why is it that Blacks in general are mostly at the bottom of the pile when it comes to material and financial progress, and why is it that it is mostly when the non-White people join with Whites, especially those in the West, that they see progress in their economies, etc? Why are Blacks so dependent on others economically? There are nations of White people living progressively without the help of Blacks, but in Black-dominated countries where there is some progress and a growing economy, somebody White is almost always behind the wheel. Why is this so? I will attempt to answer these and other puzzling questions in this chapter. The role of religion and spirituality in the lives of those who succeed, and the lack of the same in the lives of those who do not, will also be looked at.

I was listening one day to a talk show on one of Canada's most popular radio stations, broadcasting from Toronto. The topic of discussion was: Should the Black man be allowed to live in Toronto? I was a frequent listener to this radio station as well as to this man's program. I developed a liking for him because I thought he was fair-minded and very balanced. A lot of other Blacks were known to listen to that station as well. But I was very surprised at the question he asked on the air that day: a question on which he expected to receive opinions from his listeners. To me, the question smacked of racial bias, and came across as quite offensive. In retrospect, I should probably not have been surprised, because of an incident on a previous program some years before during Caribana. Caribana is a West Indian Festival celebrated every summer in the city. It draws a lot of people from all over North America and even as far away as Europe to watch and enjoy the festivities. It is, quite naturally, attended by a large number of Blacks. The broadcaster was asked if he was going to go into the downtown area of the city. Thinking he was off the air he replied that he did not want to be downtown at that time because he did not wish to be in contact with so many "niggers". Calls poured in from disappointed Blacks who had previously thought of him as their "friend" and were shocked to hear him use the "N" word, as such is now referred to these days.

The discussion about Blacks living in Toronto chilled me. This was the early Nineties, and history says that Canada was a place that opened up its arms to Black people fleeing slavery south of the border way back in the 1700s and probably even before. They had even been a part of the early fabric of the country in quite prominent ways, so one would have thought that such a question had no place on the air in Toronto, of all places. The subject was being discussed by him and his callers as if every Black person in Toronto had plugs in their ears, or as if we did not have the intelligence to understand what they were saying on the radio, if we were bright enough to be listening in the first place. I was suddenly led to recall the total vulnerability I felt living in a White-dominated society. And being naturally concerned about potential racial violence, I immediately wished I was back in my little corner of the world where I was treated in my teenage years more like a prince as opposed to the almost total irrelevance which I felt living in this new society.

His listeners had various answers to this question. I just had to call in! The answer I gave, though it seemed unrelated to the question, was compatible with the twist the callers had given to the question as it seemed to address the worth of Blacks and their "entitlement" to live in a city like Toronto. Part of my answer was to remind listeners that Blacks were a helpless lot when they were set free from slavery. They were not given land, housing, or education, but they had to survive like other living creatures did. I told him that if he had a number of animals but refused to feed some, the unfed ones would either starve to death or turn to violence to get a morsel of food so they could survive. I told him also that when I came to Toronto, my expectation of White people was that of nobility, generosity, and natural goodness because they had so much to offer in terms of knowledge, talent and expertise, and because they presented themselves to be the superior people; but how disappointed I was to find so many of them jealous, socially insecure, hateful, and ready to pounce on every little Black person they came across. I ended my answer by letting him know that as a person the behaviour of the Black man in Toronto at the time did not warrant such a topic on his show. He never responded to any of my comments, and instead he quickly switched to another topic without even explaining why.

I was riding the subway one day in Toronto when my eyes glanced at quite an attractive young White woman reading a book. She looked very kindly back at me and smiled sheepishly then kept reading. Without her knowledge, I was able to read a few lines from the page she was on. The American writer of the book was, in the few lines I read, expressing his disgust at the fact that every Black person he knew there was working for the White man. His inference was their lack of originality or initiative where creating their own economy and subsequently jobs, was concerned. The pleasantness left my face, and I looked away in dismay and shame from the young woman and the book she was reading. How this writer could have been so uninformed, I thought to myself. Had he closed his mind to the fact that almost everything the Black man did there in America in the early days to help himself business wise was destroyed by some of his people? There is history of other places where Blacks had a measure of prosperity also, but it too was destroyed by those stronger than they. It is interesting to me that people can hide so well behind their practice of keeping others from progressing, and then blame the same people they oppress for their lack of progress.

In the Seventies, I was speaking to my barber in Toronto. I asked him about his job and the process he had to go through to make it as a licensed barber. He told me that the people who gave him the license said that they gave it only because in their opinion, he would likely be cutting only the hair of Black people. I took this to mean that they would do the same thing in other areas also when they felt like it, limiting the opportunities they would give to Blacks.

What is it about Blacks that has led others to make us of so little consequence in their society? Is it because of our physical appearance or is it because of how we behave? Why do they have no respect for us? Maybe it is because generally we are so weak economically, politically, and militarily.

Many years ago, I was in conversation with this "superior" White fellow that I met in Toronto's East End. We were both employed as security guards for an apartment building. Although he said he was French Canadian, he had lived in New York for a number of years. His comments were quite derogatory in regards to Black people. Whenever I did my job of opening the door and greeting the people, he asked if I was unconscious of the fact that I was Black. I could not see what that had to do with anything. From his perspective, maybe I was too self-confident.

He told me that in New York a number of them simulated a conversation a Black man had with God. The man asked God why he was so Black and was told that the colour of his skin protected him from the heat of the jungle. He asked God why his hair was so kinky. The answer; it was so because whenever he climbed trees, in which he was supposed to live, his hair would not get entangled in the branches. He asked God why his nose and mouth were so big and broad. God answered that such was necessary because the environment in which he lived was hot and steamy and heat diminished the amount of oxygen in the air, so whenever he took his breath, the size of his nose and mouth would ensure he picked up enough oxygen for his body in every breath. Then the final question: What was he doing in New York? There was no answer for that question. Interestingly there was no question about why Tarzan did not have such characteristics.

I was not amused in any way. I wanted to tell him that the Black man was not in New York, or probably any other city in the Western world, by choice. He was taken there forcibly and enslaved by people who thought they were superior to him. But now these people had not the intestinal fortitude to live up to the attributes of superiority and instead "degraded" themselves to profit from the forced efforts of their inferiors, and further degraded themselves to disenfranchise and even mock these same people who had helped to make them fat and wealthy. This fellow and his cronies placed a much greater value on physical appearance than on the inner person, and while I cannot deny that I myself have questioned why we have to look so different from others, I have wondered also if just looking different had to make others hate us so completely.

Incidentally, this superior young man through all this, was flatulating so terribly and letting out such a pungent odour, that getting out of the room became my only pre-occupation just to catch my breath. I wanted to open the door full-fledged and let clean air flow in, but I had not been brought up to do things to humiliate others, even when they were humiliating me, and I did not want to crush his superior ego. Nonetheless, this kind of public release of flatulence was a behaviour my "inferior" Black parents taught me not to practice because they considered such behaviour to be disgraceful.

I was sitting in a Bible study class in Texas one Saturday morning. The group was mostly White and included a man who had a last name I knew was not English, and as he said his name "came out of Portugal." He had never taken a liking to me. That morning, he kept interrupting me every time I tried to speak in the class, and when he could no longer contain himself, he blurted out unashamedly about how in times past the colour of my skin was a sin. I looked at my beautiful copper coloured skin and could see no "sin" written anywhere on it. I can recall how many times White-skinned people had come up to me and told me how much trouble they have trying to get a skin colour like mine. He kept up his ranting and I wanted to ask him how "righteous" his White skin had been when it was cutting Black babies unborn out of their mothers' wombs; how "righteous" his White penis had been when it was raping little Black girls in their single digit years and when it was bursting up the rectums of little Black boys; how "righteous" his colour was when it was lynching Blacks for no other crime than being Black, and treating others worse than the brute beasts would have treated them. But I did ask all those things. I held my discreet 'Black' tongue. The reason? There were some White people, including his wife, in the class, all of whom I knew and had a great deal of respect for and I did not want to embarrass or offend them.

Later on, to his credit, he offered help to me and my family when we needed a car to get around as he was in the car selling business. And, quite by accident, a few years later when he was leaving his house to surrender himself to jail for a crime he allegedly committed, his wife told mine that I was the only person from the church or anywhere else who called that morning to give him a word of encouragement. Seemed like my skin colour was not so sinful after all, and for his favour to me, neither was his, really!

In America, many Hispanic men are married to White American women, and there seem to be no problems with that arrangement. One evening, I was conversing with my White female supervisor about the fact that White America was so accepting of this arrangement, even though some of the Hispanics themselves had very dark skins, while at the same time these same people were so much against mixed marriages when it involved a Black man. Her answer was that the features of the Hispanics were more pleasing. I wanted to ask her if Americans would then accept those Black men who were very pleasing in appearance, but I didn't bother because I was afraid the answer would still indicate a dislike for such an arrangement.

I think of the advertising I see around me as one of the barometers that I use to gauge the multicultural orientation of businesses that use such a medium to get their products and ideas out into the market place. Whenever such advertising includes pictures of people, I always look to see the racial mosaic of such endeavours. The reason this is important to me is because it accomplishes two things in my mind. One I have already spoken to. The other is the overall impression it leaves on the people who look at such advertising. You may recall that earlier I wrote on the influence of picture images of people, which influenced me somehow to develop dislike for myself and others of the Black race because we were never presented in a positive light in those books, etc. back then. If we are only placed visually where we are being disparraged or where we degrade ourselves such as in criminal acts, society and the rest of us will never have reason to endow us with anything else but disgust.

It is for this reason that when I first came to Toronto I wondered why there were no Black news reporters on any television stations in the city. There were also no Black journalists in any of Toronto's daily newspapers. I suppose, back then we did not matter in the eyes of those who owned the media. It could also be concluded that our numbers then did not warrant our representation in those areas, or maybe we had no one among Blacks educated in the field of journalism, so, consequently, we need not be there. I did meet one Black gentleman who said he worked for the traffic department of CFTO Television. I did not know at the time that such a term could be used for anything connected with a television station and inquired what that meant in the context of his job. After he explained, I asked him why I never saw him on TV. He said that his job was not the type of work where he needed to be on camera.

Subconsciously, I was thinking that since our social profile was so low, maybe publicly featuring an individual such as he would indicate that Blacks could be useful in such areas. I asked him why Blacks were never represented in that kind of positive publicity. He said, as Black people we have to learn to live with that kind of anonymity. He seemed completely contented with himself as he said this, and I wished I were not haunted with this kind of preoccupation all the days of my life.

That kind of anonymity was to continue in the city of Toronto for a few more years until finally, in the late Seventies, one of the city's more popular television stations hired a Black man as a reporter. Looking at American stations I would see Blacks there from time to time. When I went to live in Texas, there were Black reporters aplenty. I was taken aback by this. I wondered about that fact in relation to the situation in Toronto where it was believed that the society had evolved much more in its multicultural outlook than Texas of all places with its history steeped in racial discrimination. Nonetheless, by the time I came back to Toronto in 2001, the cultural mosaic and racial demographics had changed considerably and almost beyond recognition, and now Toronto itself is full of Black and other non-White news reporters. This, I believe, is a good thing as it will show Blacks in a little better light than we have been placed all these years. I especially like when they have a Black person reporting on Black crime because it sends a subliminal message that we are not all "criminals" and that we are not all in "support" of Black crime.

When I was in South Africa, I felt completely represented with all the Blacks I saw there on television. They are plentiful as actors and actresses in soap eras and movies of every kind. They were also political commentators, news reporters, the financial analysts, the opera singers, the talk show hosts and hostesses, and all that it took for functional television exposure. Most surprising, their professionalism was beyond belief for how good it was. I was most delighted to see that. Not that I liked it because there were no Whites because there were many Whites also. But I liked the fact that Blacks had been given the opportunity to come of age so to speak, in a place such as that. And as well I learned that Nigeria is the third largest movie producer in the world. Their contrubution to the movie industry has earned them the name of Nollywood after Hollywood in America and Bollywood in Bombay India. Using mainly digital camerals, the Nigerian producers are able to bring a movie to market in about ten days.

One of the concerns I have, is how we are seen internationally. In matters of economics we lag far behind. I am told that there are many successful Black businessmen in Africa. And really I've read and heard of a few. But maybe success can be seen as relative. The point though - how often have we seen or heard of a large Black-African owned corporation of much meaningful worth with an international presence? And has anyone noticed that not even one country from the continent of Africa has risen to the status of a developed nation, apart from South Africa, which incidentally has to credit the European for that achievement. Zimbabwe used to be called the Bread Basket of Africa under White rule but we now see that under the Black rule of Robert Mugabe that disaster has now befallen that nation.

It is said that some nations of Africa are forging reasonably successful economies, and I was looking to Nigeria with its oil producing capacity to become that prominent Black African nation of international economic presence and prestige. Presently, it is among the "Next Eleven," which is good, but a few bad apples from that country are making the rounds as con men, sometimes "morally" supported by some of their politicians. Presently, I get emails almost on a daily basis from that country, telling me I have won or inherited millions of dollars. The senders never seem to read my replies indicating my lack of interest and my ridicule of their attempts to get me to send them money so they can send cheques to me.

We also have Ghana and a few other places trying to come alive economically. But most African countries are still mired in poverty and corruption and remain beggar states, always looking to the West for handouts. I am well aware that the former European colonialists are partly to blame for the economic plight of most of those nations because they plundered them when they ruled. And when they were "forced" to give them autonomy, they maliciously ensured that they left almost nothing in the public purse with which the new leaders could start. Sometimes they purposely left the most uneducated and despotic men they could find to be leaders, probably knowing full well that with those, failure was assured. They were and are unfit and unable to administer, having no training in governance and in the areas of wealth and job creation. Still, I wonder how many more decades or centuries it will take for Africa to initiate what the Europeans and some other nations count as second nature in terms of economic progress.

Despite their meanness to Blacks and other people sometimes, I am forever admiring the ingenuity of the White race. They are able to initiate progressive economies and create jobs almost anywhere. Given time and opportunity they could turn the Shahara Desert into a fertile oasis. All that most Black-run countries, even in Black Africa, can originate on any large scale is quite a lot of chaos. Even in most of Black Africa, the "cradle of mankind" and a continent where there are so many natural resources along with gold, diamonds and platinum galore, we see so much that is not progressive. Yes, I have gone to Africa and seen arts and crafts which are the works of genius, but it seems like no Black person (including myself) has even been able to complete the invention of a bicycle relying solely on Black resources though we have over a billion of us worldwide. When Black History month comes around we hear that Blacks invented this and Blacks invented that. Some is true, but we always allow the Whites to get the credit. And besides, it's not from Africa.

It is about time that some Black leader, somewhere, address these issues and is seen to be doing something about them. The economic future does not lie in allowing animals to destroy the flora and allowing con men to run rampant in some of Africa's countries. The rest of the world seems little interested presently in addressing the ever-present economic problems of Africa, even though G7 nations and the World Bank are always lending/giving Africa a little pittance here and a little pittance there. To me these nations are merely trying to give Africa a little of the interest which has accrued on all that they have stolen from the continent. Maybe Africa is not yet ready for anything bigger. They ought to have grabbed the bulls by the horns and take control of their own resources.

Many might say that Africans have no need for any way of life other than the primitive one they have been used to for centuries, or that there is progress in places where one or two countries have car assembly factories, and where some of them are attempting to develop stock exchanges and really trying to make a difference. To this I say, Keep it up! And while one cannot deny that there is a bit of advancement in some cases, it needs to be a lot more plentiful and obvious, and Africa needs a lot more of the expertise that the West takes for granted. African leaders and people need to be educated to the benefits of economic progress and should develop social attitudes which see beyond just blind tribalism and cronyism for the overall good of everyone. Africa needs a lot more stable political environments, less hostility to its own, and should rid itself of its propensity to be bought and sold by foreigners who are ever so gleeful about paying off its leaders so they can rape and pilfer the people and resources. Until Africa makes radical and meaningful changes, a lot of good foreign businessmen will continue to avoid the continent and only those who seek to benefit themselves unscrupulously will do any business there.

Two of Asia's giants, India and China, are vying for investment opportunities which they claim they see on the continent of Africa. There are indeed potential opportunities for the future, especially in the area of Information Technology, and in the development of the remainder of Africa's resources. I did not like either of them because China, it seems, was only putting in infrastructure to the benefit of itself to move goods it needs to trade in. It goes in and puts in a little roadway from the loading dock on the port to a warehouse nearby and then do photo ops and ribbon cutting to the delight of the glady glady African leaders of that particular country who are too dense to see that there will be miniscule if any benefit to their people. China brings its own people to do most or all of the work. India I would not touch with a ten-foot pole because its peoples are usually aloof to Blacks, (remember the Dalits), and as self-serving as the Chinese, and think of themselves better than everyone and anyone else. Neither, I think, would care anything for the average African citizen. If Africans at the grass roots level would benefit, I would be all for such investment. But they won't. Hopefully this wont be the second round of rape and pillage for the rest of Africa's resources by foreigners before some African visionary arises to negotiate a better deal for Africa's peoples.

But going back to Black ineptitude: even back in my very early years I used to wonder why we did not have anything sold in Jamaica that was manufactured in Africa. Always, I would see things that were made in the USA, made in Great Britain (yes, Britain was called great some time ago), and once in a while in other countries. Just about everyone I knew who left Jamaica to go to a foreign country to make a better life for themselves and their families ended up going to England, or to America. No one I knew ever went to Africa, which to me was a natural fit because so many people around me had part or all of their ancestral roots from there. Only the Rastafarians, who were plentiful around us, talked about going back to Africa because of Haile Selassie. They promised that they would take me with them from the time I was just about six or seven. I don't know if my parents would have allowed them to take me at such a tender age, but as late as December of 2007, when my Canadian-born son went to visit my Jamaican homestead, none of those who planned to go had left. They had either died or were on the verge of dying and still had not gone to Africa.

One day, however, I was looking through a book my mother had just bought from a traveling book salesman, and there I saw a picture of Ethiopian airline pilots mapping out a flight path. I knew enough to know that Ethiopia was part of Africa even though I was only about seven or eight years old at the time because I was already able to read. My eyes almost popped out of my head, and my blood almost stopped flowing. I could not in my wildest imagination at the time come up with Black African airline pilots, but I instantly wished there were many more of them.

African leaders in very many cases still allow foreigners to plunder their natural resources mercilessly for the benefit of their foreign corporations, but as Africa goes only the good of the blind, greedy, gullible leaders themselves, whose functional intelligence it seems sometimes does not go beyond junior kindergarten, is of interest to them. They seem to have no care for their own people, and if and when they appear to show some care such is always only along tribal lines. I was watching a documentary on television where some foreigners went to a certain African country and had the government agree with them to set up a situation where they could "pretend" that they were acting for the benefit of the elephant population. They got the government to pass laws against the poaching of these animals, as when an indigenous African would kill an elephant for its tusks. The group then started "caring," they imagined themselves, for a certain herd of elephants. When the herd reached a certain number, the foreigners gathered up their weapons and surrounded it and massacred as many of them as they could. I saw some majestic and healthy animals cut down in that documentary that evening. They had convinced the government that this "cull" of these members of the group of elephants' was for the benefit of the elephant population in general. Why did they have to kill the strong, healty ones? Why not the old and the infirm?

Do I need to tell you that they then robbed these dead animals of their tusks so they could sell the ivory for profit? I could hardly contain myself in my seat that evening. "How absolutely insane", I thought. The government went against its own penniless people, who might take an few elephants a year just to get by and put a morsel of food in their children's mouths, but then allowed the foreigners to deceive them and through that process took out a lot more elephants than the few that would have been taken by its own people. I sat there in wonderment, thinking about when Black Africa might learn anything sensible. When will they mature and stop being the laughing stock of foreigners who, it would seem, rightly view some of them as stupid for doing things like this? I have heard it said that it is because they are a peaceful people in general, and I may have decided to believe that some time ago. But present-day situations have changed my mind. Please allow me to exchange the word "peaceful" for "gullible" when the situation demands that.

Much of Africa is really a continent at war with itself, killing off its neighbours and people of other tribes, having some of its military and other groups of renegades, raping and mutilating untold numbers of women and young girls. Some governments of the nations of the continent of Africa are not always peace-loving at all. Maybe it is part of the coming of age that they are experiencing as it was in Europe of some decades ago. But to equate inefficiency, cowardice and gullibility with peace is quite a bit stupid. Some of these leaders have not a tinge of economic savvy.

A case in point for gullibility is the Truth and Reconciliation initiatives of the Black leaders when they took over South Africa a few years ago. While I am not looking for vengeance, I certainly believe that for all the crimes and the brutality that the former White rulers committed against the Black South Africans, every single one of those responsible, including their past presidents who ordered these crimes, should have been tried and upon conviction been publicly executed. This is what would have happened to them if they had been Black. Instead, we see these spineless Black leaders coming up with some rubbish called Truth and Reconciliation as a fair means of addressing a course of action that maliciously and violently took the lives of so many innocent people, and which have kept millions of others in extreme poverty and wretchedness for so many long years.

Some might conclude that Africans need a formal education to make the difference, and in many cases this may just be quite true. But a formal education alone is not the only prerequisite for a worthy, and a visionary leader. In the early days of America, some of its presidents did not have a formal education, but they had the good of their country and their people at heart, and as such made a big difference. On the contrary, the education of an African leader such as Robert Mugabe of Zimbabwe, with his multiple university degrees earned when he was jailed for anti-government activities, has produced no beneficial results for the people of his country. His education has not helped him with any vision and economic foresight, a character trait inherent in most leaders of Western nations. He presides over a country that was quite prosperous when he took it over, but which he has now led into the very iron jaws of abject poverty and misery. Like most of his contemporaries, he cares for no one but himself and those immediately around him. He has placed his country in such dire straits it is hard to comprehend that such could have been the case when one looks carefully at the one turned over to him. I hope he'll be gone soon and Zimbabwe can again become the breadbasket of Africa.

It is said that a lot of African leaders rape the treasuries of their own countries, then pile up millions, even billions, in foreign bank accounts while their people starve to death right in front of their eyes. How many times have we in the West heard that even the basic necessities of food and medicine being sent to some of these African countries for the desolate and miserably poor living in refugee camps, have been forcibly taken from aid workers by the soldiers of some of these leaders and used solely for their benefit instead, even though it would appear that they already have enough for themselves. When it is found that African leaders have all that money in foreign Western banks, why don't these banks give all this money back for the peoples of those nations? We have the United Nations that pretends that it cares for the people of the world. Why not do it through them?

When I was coming of age, one of the characteristics that I most admired in Western nations run by White leaders, especially America, was their interest for their people. The leaders acted mostly for the good of the entire country. No matter what political party won an election, the out-going leader would encourage support for the new leader. I knew by then that the Black citizens might not have been of primary concern, but these are White nations and that's another story.

It would be so good to see that kind of objectivity exercised by Black leaders everywhere, as opposed to the short-sighted behaviour of malice toward those of the opposing political parties. There seems to be this inherent disposition of Black leaders to be dictatorial, thinking that they should be rulers for life, or that opposition to their self seeking attitudes is always a personal vendetta against them. No leader should be allowed to continue in a position where he is not acting in the best interests of the people. We may indeed have a point when we want to hold to the fire the feet of those White leaders who formulate policies or act in ways that hurt Blacks, but we should also be able to do it when Black leaders do the same for albeit different reasons, whether tribal, regional, or political. The fact is, it is still a form of discrimination.

The Black leaders in the Caribbean do not usually tend toward the same undemocratic ideals as their African counter-parts. Most of the time, they govern under stable political and economical situations, even if the economies are very small and based almost entirely on tourism and the export of some food products—such as the famous yellow fruit that everyone loves, but for which the Caribbean is demeaningly referred to as the Banana Republic, and sometimes bauxite. Having almost no natural resource they depend largely on tourism for most of their foreign exchange earnings. While the leaders and people are more educated because leaders have worked on stamping out illiteracy, their economies still lag far behind those of developed countries. Most of the Caribbean islands are seen as debtor nations and again, even though I hate to admit it, Blacks all over the world seem to always be the people least likely to have corporations and industries producing jobs and money to sustain ourselves. It is almost like there is this universal curse that we are faced with in this regard. As well, the darker the skin, and the more Africoid the people of a nation, the less likely are they to get help from those who have gone on up the road of prosperity.

A lot of Oriental nations have had measurably progressive economies over the past few decades, and others of them have gained the status of developed nations. They were helped by Western countries and are allowed to sell their goods and manufactured products to the ever increasing consumer-driven economies of these prosperous Western Nations, mainly America. When the Bush administration came to power in the 2001, I kept my ears and eyes open to what the newly elected president and his cabinet would do for the Black and Hispanic nations just on its outer flanks. I was very disappointed when the administration decided that it would not allow the flow of goods, free or otherwise, from the Caribbean nations and those of Black Africa to be sold in its markets. It did, however open its doors to goods coming from Hispanic America. Quite a load of bigotry, I thought, from the "greatest" nation on earth whose leaders go about trumpeting democracy and human rights all over the world. It seems to me that the Black nations, even the few which are friendly toward America, must first change the skin colour of their people to participate even a little in the prosperity of those nations which "have arrived".

I had a conversation with a Welshman when I visited South Africa. He had lived in 18 countries of the continent he told me. He and his friends held countless discussions on the aspect of the lack of economic progress in Black Africa. This lack of economic progress, they felt, was symptomatic of all other forms of progress as such related to Africans. They concluded that one reason for the progress of the European was the creativity they had to exercise because of the environment they had to contend with in Europe. They had to be creative in winter, for example, and had to find a way to make artificial heat to keep them warm. Africans, on the other hand, had no such need. I mentioned to him that the Indians of North America faced the same challenges of winter as Europeans did, but they simply cut enough firewood to burn to get the warmth they needed for the winter. As well Africans had all that heat to endure almost all year round but never invented the air conditioner. Then he and I wondered out loud about other reasons, such as whether the problem had to do with the heat of the sun, as indeed the closer people live to the equator the less innovative they were. When we look at South and North, whether the people are Black, Asian, or Austroloid, less progress seems the order of the day. That too was inconclusive because White ingenuity did not end for the Dutch in South Africa nor the Whites of Australia and New Zealand. So the answer is yet a mystery.

It cannot be made any more obvious that Blacks lack international presence and achievement economically, which is so badly needed to raise our profile in the world in which we live. We do have some achievement in sports and entertainment, but in those disciplines we are no longer unique. The others are taking over in those areas quite rapidly. We need to make an effort to enter the professions. Besides, sports careers only last for so long and are only for the super gifted in most cases.

The Japanese have made their mark. The Chinese are becoming an economic force to contend with. The Arab nations have their oil and their leaders were able to negotiate good arrangements for the benefit of their peoples. The Indians are making their presence known in technology. Nigeria has some oil, and I was hoping that with money coming from that natural resource they would have ventured out into other areas economically and gain that presence. But I have yet to see that. Africa has probably the richest deposits of gold, diamonds, and platinum, not to mention the vast amount of timber which some of the countries of Europe harvest with very little if any benefit going to the average African. I am left wondering when we might start doing something bold and daring like demanding more for our natural resources there, spread a bit of the wealth to our people so we can move up a bit faster in the world. Can some of you parents who have smart kids encourage them to enroll in schools of technology and acquire the skills needed to become mathematicians, physicists, architects, engineers, and all the other skills needed to invent things so Blacks can start doing the things that the Whites have been doing for years to accomplish what they have? With these skills they can then go to Africa and develop the continent for the uplifting of the people. Its time we start seeing automobiles, computers, appliances, and so on being designed and built in Africa by Africans. My life is passing before me, and I would like to see us make some real progress before I expire.

The world community admires and respects economic achievements when you can do it on your own, and is astonished at the almost total failure of the Black world when it comes to such a thing. Some of the White folks strain their necks to see if we will someday come up with something positive for them to take seriously. I had a White Briton as a passenger in my cab once who told me that he had lived in Africa for some years. He told me that he could not understand how he, a foreigner, was on their continent in their country and they were his servants. He was completely dumbfounded that it was not the other way around. He was even more astonished that he found no desire on the part of the people he met to accomplish anything worthwhile. At least in his mind he did not doom us to be the eternal servants of Shem and Japheth, so you see it is a conditional thing and when the mind believes otherwise and there is a change in perspective things will be different. When I hear things like that from other people, it reinforces my thinking that the mental limitations that we have placed on ourselves have become the mother of all encumbrances to Black achievement. We must do something to end this. We must start originating our own success. That was the way the other people started. We must begin, even if it is by making bricks out of African mud (there is plenty there) and start selling them somewhere. One of these nations can make the bricks and another can start making water skins out of the hides of wildebeests. (They roam the African Savannah in large numbers). Mud bricks and animal water skins must have a market somewhere.

Sometimes, I ask people who I meet from other parts of the world questions about economic progress where they come from. They probably have no idea why I ask, but I have my reasons. If the person comes from a predominantly Black country, I always ask who has the money there and who make up the larger percentage of business-owners. The answers are rarely what I would like to hear, and this brings me consternation. I always want to know what the progress of the Black man is in different parts of the world. It is almost an obsession to me. In all areas representing financial progress, we are lagging behind.

My Black acquaintances and I always discuss hard and fast the social issues of the Black race. I always find someone who tells me the Black race is what it is because we are just coming up in the world or because the others have always had the upper hand or some such answer. I like to go back way beyond "just coming up into the world," especially when anthropologists say that we were the original peoples. I want to know why the others have always had the upper hand. I want to know who or what set things up the way it is, and I want to know why it was that the Black race fell so far down the totem pole of recognition and economic achievement. I am convinced that the three sons of Noah all started out on an equal footing. Was there some social or religious set of norms that we violated which brought us down to the level of poverty and loss that we have descended to? This matter has bothered me for almost as long as I've been able to contemplate the issues of social ostracism and the financial deprivation of the Black race, and I have been searching for answers ever since.

One theory I would like to explore that might help to alleviate all or most of the confusion posed by the speculations heretofore discussed is the possibility of a relationship with the true and living God making the difference in progress or the lack thereof. God created us all as equals with the same potential for achievement and success. I will repeat something here. In the early days of man's history on this earth, He said that He saw that if any two men set their minds on accomplishing something, they would succeed at it. He did not say two White, Black, Yellow or Brown men. He said any two men. This means to me that we started out with equal potential for success. I further understand from reading the Bible that what we do and think has a definite bearing on the outcome of our lives. I read from the same Bible that the people who know their God will be strong and do exploits. The converse of that would be that the people who do not know their God will not be strong and will not do very well in terms of exploits. This, according to the Bible, does not refer to just any god. It meant the God who is the Creator. God at the same time has given a measure of success to all because He is a good and generous God, and as David, the Sweet Singer of Israel past said – "He sends His rain on the just and on the unjust". But I conclude that the people who believe in the true God, and act accordingly, have the greater chance to succeed with their plans for their lives. Religious history can teach us a few things about this probability, and I would like to consider a Biblical reference to one group of individuals. According to that great book, when the people of the Bible obeyed their God and did what He requested from them, they were successful in all that they did socially and economically. When they did not do God's will, they experienced many difficulties. They lost wars, they lost their crops to drought or to the locusts, they had famines, and their country was over-run by their enemies. This I found interesting. By that example obedience to God brought peace and prosperity, disobedience to Him brought about the opposite.

While exploring this theory, I will admit that I do not think that that single factor is the only component responsible for the success and prosperity of people, as I believe that they must also be diligent and hard-working, even though dilligence and hard work is also a directive of God. I don't necessarily believe that a short time of disregard for God will bring poverty upon anyone immediately, and below you will read the reason for my opinion. But it was amazing how even the enemies of these people recognized the benefit of their being true to their God. Some of their conquerors, Nebuchadnezzar the king of Babylon for one, told them that it was because of their disobedience to their God that he was able to conquer them.

In my search for answers to the challenges and impediments facing the Black race, I have had to take a good, hard look at the continent of Africa where most Blacks reside. I see a place steeped in voodoo, black magic, and demon, and spirit worship. I see a place where cannibalism has gone on for centuries. It is a place where human beings have fallen so far from God's ideal for mankind that there has literally been no progress among the tribes and nations that practice such crafts, even to this very day. Was this the sort of thing my grandmother meant when she told us of Dark Africa? I don't know because she never went into details about it, and at the time I did not think to ask her. I just thought and thought about what she said. Actually, some of the same could be said of the people living in the jungles of South America and a lot of the nations of south-east and south-west Asia, and about the First Nations of America and Canada.

Conversely, a lot of the European nations that have become followers of the true God especially since the apostle Paul was called over into Macedonia have had relative success and prosperity. Then, for quite some centuries, even these nations ceased to progress even though they had developed a rich and favourable culture economically in their early years. Though they did not really lose all that they had gained during those years, they did not seem to add much to it for some time. But since the 1500s, they have again rebounded. Since the time of the Protestant Reformation when people again reconnected with the true knowledge of God, something which had been kept from them for hundreds of years, Europe has again experienced a revival of economic and social progress in a massive way. You will notice I said the *true knowledge of God* this time. I wrote that for a reason. The true knowledge of God had been purposefully kept from them for a long time.

Let us look at the American nation which started to come onto the world stage in the 1600s. That country was set up on Protestant and Republican principles, with its constitution allowing its people the freedom to worship God according to the dictates of their consciences. They had actually set out for that land from Europe because they wanted to be free to worship the God of heaven in the first place, and though they had problems even before they disembarked from the ship that took them to America, by and large they were determined to accomplish their purpose. The budding nation did not promote any religion directly, but it could be seen that Protestantism was the hallmark of its intent. So far, its success has been unparalleled in the history of any nation to ever grace the face of the earth. No other nation grew up as fast, as prosperous, and as powerful as did America, and none has had prosperity for so long a period of time. There is no denying that. Despite America now operating as a debtor nation, it is still the envy of the world—even of much older European nations.

Yes America committed a great crime against humanity in the forced enslavement and gross ill-treatment of the Black people on its soil. This is a sin for which that country continues to be guilty because none of its leaders has ever apologized for such inhumanity, and many of its people would still have Blacks in slavery and the cruellest of bondage if they were allowed to do so. I believe that a just God, who blessed King Nebuchadnezzar yet punished him when he became too cruel and unreasonable, will most certainly bring about justice for all wrong doing in His own time. But as we have seen in times past, God works with the human race despite its sins and evil ways, and so God continues to work with America. Its continues to deny the Blacks a level playing field in the marketplace of opportunities, but a lot of its people are most generous in the act of giving even to those who hate them, and especially do they give in times of calamity.

Could it be because of America's early trust in God, despite its sin of enslaving Blacks, that it has been such a prosperous nation? Is there a lesson here for the rest of the nations of the world including progress-starved Africa to learn? I have observed that even the Oriental and other nations now experiencing prosperity, saw no such thing until they became friendly and formed alliances with America and other Western, Protestant, Christian nations. Though this last statement may offend some people, I issue a challenge to them to prove otherwise. The same statements can be made about the pagan nations of South West and South East Asia and about the other nations steeped in their Communist ideals. Try comparing the prosperity of the two Koreas today.

I would also like to proffer the opinion that the most successful Blacks in the world are American Blacks. They are the descendants of former slaves. Most of their ancestors were, in all probability, devil worshippers before they were forced to go to America. These their off-springs, who have since accepted the worship of God, have now seen success they would probably only dream about if they were on the other side of the ocean. It is a known fact that most of the more successful Black singers in America started off and learned their singing skills in Christian churches. You will notice that I did not say all of them, and you will remember that earlier on I hinted ever so faintly that not everyone in a nation needs to be servants of God to have personal successes or for that nation to have national greatness. God would have willingly saved Sodom and Gomorrah if only ten righteous persons had been found there, even though it was obvious that thousands resided within the walls of those cities.

I believe that I will get a lot of flack from the above opinion but I am not worried about that. I have run into a lot of hotwater even from one or two of my own children who strongly oppose the concept. However, in my mind it has validity. They wonder why God has not yet punished America for slavery but allowed the curse on the descendants of Ham. I remind them that even though God allowed the curse, it took Him quit a few hundred years to do so and that it was because the children of Ham continued in their own ways. America, through its legislature did put an end to slavery and a just God has to take that into consideration much like He has blessed many of the sons of Ham becasue they have turned to Him.

Another hypothesis I would like to explore is the concept of desire, determination, and relevance in light of the general thrust of this book. I have heard it said that if the White man had not come to the continent of North America things would still have continued to be the way they had been for untold generations prior. There would still be tepees, massive herds of buffalos, hunting and fishing for food in their primitive forms, no vehicles and no railways, and so on. The people who hold this view believe that the original North Americans had no reason to live otherwise than they did, and that such would have continued to be the case even till today. They believe that the modern way of life, as dictated by the White race, was not relevant to the Indians' way of life.

If such is the case, then we must assume that progress as we define it was and is relative to our past way of life and experiences, our present situation, and our aspirations. This, then, means therefore that no group of people should be criticized for choosing to live their existence in the same way their ancestors lived for centuries before them.

I don't believe that anyone should disagree that what has been working for others for a very long time might not continue to work for them in the future, given the same set of circumstances. But, interestingly, the people who hold that view may say that the White man was himself once a cave-dweller and lived much the same existence for many generations, which he saw when he came to North America. This, then, gives rise to another thought: is there something or someone driving the human race relentlessly toward what can be called modernization or civilization as we say; that it just got to the White man first, and then we should simply sit back and wait for it to arrive at our doors, just like it got to the door of the White man? Now if the preceeding were true, it would then be only a matter of time before native peoples, as we like to refer to people of undeveloped countries, get the bug of progress biting at their heels and would all be well on their way to the grand place of "civilization" as determined by destiny, whether they wanted to be or not.

This thought for me then becomes enigmatic when I consider a story I heard some time ago about one of the Chiefs of the First Nations who visited Washington. It was quite a few decades ago by our reckoning, but fairly recently for him in terms of the transition from his North America to that of the European. When he saw the progress that the White man had made in so short a period of time, he exclaimed that "the Great Spirit loves His White children best." Since I heard that story I have wondered what made him come to that conclusion. Did he see something that he believed his people should have had if they were as loved by the Great Spirit which was better than what they then possessed? Can we then conclude that he believed that his people did not possess the endowments that would give them what he saw these others had achieved in such a short space of time? Please bear in mind that the Native North Americans did not know, worship, or have the same God that these "White children" had.

Now that I have explored the theory as it relates to the situation above, allow me to turn it over to the situation of the Africans. Are they themselves living their lives happily without the need of the things the West takes for granted? And, if such is the case, would they then be entitled to the same rationalization as other native peoples? Should we agree they are all living happily the way things are? Let me say here very quickly that I don't cater to the thought that there is contentment for the "uncivilized life" that is lived by the primitive peoples of the world, and let me say also that I have good reasons for coming to this conclusion. Every time these people come in contact with what the developed world referred to as "civilization," they suddenly seem to "want" everything they see. Incidentally, the need is always there for medicine, better clothing, better food, better skills, better housing and so on. Allow me to refer to these things as the "benefits of civilization." I was told by one person who visited the Holy Land how desperate the nomadic shepherds were for the American dollar. They would try almost any trick to rid you of any that you might have. I still get a bit of haziness in the head whenever I recall this bit of revelation wondering what in the world do they "need" it for?

One might argue that the White man's way of life is extremely materialistic, and therefore that perhaps those other people who have not experienced that way of life might not be as materialistic, or such should be modified to contextually fit the situation where that arises. One could counter that argument by saying that the other side of the coin, extreme asceticism, lived just to make a point, is also then extreme and of the kind which is quite detrimental to the well-being of those people who are by design or circumstance forced to live with it. I really can't see how anyone would agree that the primitive way of life is the better way to live. I mean primitive not in the sense of values where such can mean respect for morals and respect for contemporaries, I mean primitive in the sense of social, economic, technological, and educational advancement benefiting quality of life. I don't believe that God intended that people He created in His image should live a life that could reasonably be compared to that of wild animals where such is the case.

Then there are those who argue that the reason the White race is so successful is because its members are aggressive and very manipulative of others. I believe that in some cases this is true and will not argue against it. But I believe also that they are just responding to a drive within themselves to make their lives better. I will say, too, that what they have achieved has also been of much benefit to those they have chosen to share with, and that they should therefore be congratulated for so doing on both fronts. Are we to concede that this 'aggressiveness and manipulation' of others is evidence that they are inherently gifted with a power that others of us do not possess, since we are left to cower in front of this "awesome" gift of theirs, and be thus manipulated and taken advantage of, and just be left to whine and whimper unsolaced like a coyote robbed of her prey and is bereft of any power to mount an effective counter offensive to regain what she thought was rightfully hers and her cubs'?

If we agree that the civilized way is the best way to live, we must then conclude that there are reasons uncivilized peoples have been living the way they do and that such reasons might well include the limitation of their ability to make changes themselves to their lifestyle. The challenge then is to find out what has kept them from making these changes after so many centuries of their existence in what seems like an endless cycle of poverty and loss.

There is plenty of undeniable proof that the underprivileged peoples of the planet need and do hunger for something much better. Just take a look at your television screen the next time there is an appeal from an international child adoption agency or some such thing, and you will see the expectant faces of those who need help. There is this visible yearning for a better life.

This convinces me beyond any shadow of a doubt that there is not really any reason to think that civilization as referenced in this volume is irrelevant to the lives of anyone, or that given the choice anyone would elect to live without the comforts and prosperity known to be derived from the efforts of the White race. If everyone were given the opportunity to live with the comforts that civilization has to offer, I think most of those not presently doing so would hasten to trade the places they now occupy for the better place, and hence we can conclude that most people have the desire to change their situation from what it is to what it can become. If we conclude that the White man once lived the caveman state of life, we must then also conclude that there is something very special about him that caused him to be the first to rise up out of that state of being; something superior to what the others possess. I will assume that the reader will agree that there is then something that gave the European the advantage over the others, and it would be quite interesting for us all to discover just what that might be if you disagree that the God he served had nothing to do with it.

Maybe another reason we have been socially rejected by so many is because of our colour and appearance. I had a girlfriend of East Indian extraction who was quite disgusted with the fact that along with being Black, we also had to have kinky hair. It seems that in some cases people treat us as if we are completely responsible for the body in which we came to the planet.

I am very sensitive if I am caught in a situation where I have to be among people who I don't know with straight hair because of my kinky hair. I will say that if I were blue black that it would be more of a trauma for me than the color I now possess in the context of my mindset because society has caused myself and others like me to be so cognisant of that one factor. So many people think that we are less than human because of this when in reality it is just pigmentation.

It is such a sad reality that a lot of people on both sides of the divide are so conscious about that. One side of me tells me that people have a right to their feelings and inclinations as long as they don't perpetrate physical harm on anyone. The other side of me says that I have seen those same people treat the beast of the earth with much more care and tenderness than they do a live, talking, human being just because the appearance is not in keeping with their sentiments. Maybe they are afraid of what those humans (if they consider us humans yet) will need - jobs, housing, education, co-mingling, socializing, equality, and so on. Animals can be cute and nostalgic, adult humans, especially when their skin colour is Black and they lack "physical beauty", are a different lot.

We also have the natural barrier to social interaction by any two persons or groups of persons who do not know each other bringing other complications to social interaction. A team of janitors of whatever colour would probably not necessarily be comfortable with another team of janitors of a different colour, at least not until they have grown to know each other. If a group of Whites were riding an elevator when it stopped on my floor I would probably not get into it unless there were at least one person in it whom I knew. The same would probably be the case if I was among a group of Blacks with whom I was not familiar, although my comfort level would be a bit higher. So, part of the reason for our rejection in certain situations may not always have to do with how we look physically but because people are more comfortable being with others who are more like them. And this is just an innocent, subconscious reality for most humans.

But why you ask has God chosen to bless the Whites so abundantly instead of the others? Why not the Orientals and the Brown people? Why could it not be the Black people? My answer is that God blesses everyone, but in the context of the above paragraphs, we cant expect Him to always step down from Heaven and pick the fruit and put it in our mouths for us. We need to get the will and move the limbs to do things for ourselves. I may have also said previously that I believe that in most cases, the Whites are much more likely than the others to share what they have acquired and be much more generous with what they have achieved.

CHAPTER SEVEN
BLACKS AND THE WORKPLACE

This section of the book looks at probable reasons for high unemployment among Blacks. It discusses the reasons from the employer's perspectives as well as the reasons we as Blacks may not be employable at times. The chapter also encourages Blacks to be more pro-active and look to become employers themselves.

It seems that not long ago and still in some cases when employment was or is offered by people of other races, that Blacks face more discrimination than all other people groups combined. Some reasons may well be of our own making and some are definitely not. I will discuss what I think are the marks against us which are of our own making later. Right now I will concentrate on reasons I think are not of our making.

There seems to be what I will refer to as a "hierarchy of entitlement" to employment in these cases. Not surprisingly, this describes nearly all employers in the prosperous Western countries, and I believe, is usually based on the colour of the skin. From what I know in regards to this matter, the consensus is that Whites are first, and naturally so because they are the primary job creators anyway, and in a sense should not really be held to account for not always readily employing us as we should have developed economies and create jobs like they have done.

Next for jobs are the Orientals, followed by the Brown people, and after they have had their fill at the trough, if anything is left over we the Blacks might then be lucky enough to get employment. There may be cases when the White employer, because of compassion, or because of government regulation do employ Blacks ignoring the criteria above, as we sometimes see by the process called Affirmative Action Programs instituted in some countries such as America where there has been historical denial of jobs where Blacks are concerned. Some quota system seems to be set in place in Canada also, even though it is not called Affirmative Action here. In quite a few of cases, the government, at least here in Canada employs a lot of Blacks even though in the not-too-distant past this was not the case. I suppose the government cannot break its own laws of being an equal opportunity employer having to set the right example for private companies to follow.

It is to be expected that ethnic immigrant business establishments will not be quick to employ Black people here in North America if they employ them at all. They use language most times as a barrier against employing anyone but their own people. Sometimes one might see token representations of White people, for example, at an other than White restaurants and they typically act as hosts or hostesses.

We inherently feel closer to those who are most like us culturally and physically, and employers are often left to conclude that it is their right to employ whom they please. As said before, they are the ones who created their businesses and subsequent jobs and really in fairness to that kind of mindset one could conclude that they do have the right to determine whom they will employ. However, the foregoing should not be taken to mean that I necessarily agree with the concept. I believe that the way things are structured in the world presently, employers should not completely ignore the responsibility that providence has placed upon the privileged to employ those who are not able to develop and run businesses of their own. Employing people from all sectors of society should be looked upon as the proper thing to do for the overall good of everyone.

One of the encumbrances to employment opportunities for everyone in general in a White society as an example may be that as a group, they have no need to associate with or employ those of any other race to get things done because they have mastered all the knowledge and skill that is required to maintain their economies from all angles whether their need is local or international. Such an achievement can make them quite unwilling indeed to employ those they see as irrelevant to their enterprises. The White race has evolved to the point that they can exist alone if they really want to with no need for the help or support of any other.

People in general simply wish to remain as homogenous as possible. Because of people's disposition to be by ourselves, we sometimes have the problem of employment discrimination, or put another way - employment selection based on the employer's wishes. As can be deduced from the first paragraph of this chapter, Whites are not the only ones capable of thinking this way, and are certainly not the only ones who put it into practice.

In a level world, no one should be forced to employ or befriend those they really feel no responsibility for, but I guess that things have not been set up that way. From the time we started to live on planet Earth, care and forethought for others have existed as a role given to some to fulfil. As a result, we will sometimes find ourselves having to do the things we are really unwilling to do. Things like employing those we don't really like or want to have around us.

To justify Black exclusion from employment opportunities where such exists, there are some stereotypes that prevail in conjunction with skin colour. For one, it has been said numerous times that Blacks are lazy and that is the reason that most of us are not successful. It is further thought that if we are not diligent as a matter of principle we will not be diligent at our jobs either. If evidence points in that direction, then that is something to think about. But those who come to such a conclusion on this side of the globe, prove that they are not aware of the history of their nations. They are not aware at all of the fact that in many cases Blacks have been among the hardest workers in the North American society. They worked for more than two centuries, sometimes seven days per week, to satisfy their slave masters' wishes. They picked the cotton and reaped the crops and performed other tasks which were integral to the American economy as well as that of other countries.

The colour of the skin is not a true indicator of laziness, though I will admit that attitudes might indeed be. And people diligently looking for work should not have the label of laziness attached to them. If they were lazy why would they be seeking for work? Given the same opportunities, the minds and abilities of all races can be as inventive and productive as the most equipped In the past, Blacks have proven that we are capable contextually speaking, and with the right training and education, of doing anything that the others can do. It would be nice if Blacks could be judged in terms of their individual capacities as opposed to being lumped together as just the product of a singular thought, and that singular thought, that of indolence and everything uncomplimentary.

Blacks were efficient cattle herders in America in the early days and were just as efficiently as the Whites. They were some of the most productive cowboys when they were given the chance. They were also some of the best soldiers in the Unites States Army. Information on the Tuskegee Airmen will lead readers to discover the ability and expertise of Blacks when given the opportunity. They distinguished themselves very well and fulfilled all the requirements it would take to support all the functions of a flying air crew. Standards were not lowered for them. So why are we not good anymore, or why are we just selectively good?

Whites in North America should not forget who picked their cotton, reaped their fields, cooked their meals, and took care of their children. Much of North America is what it is today because of Black labour. While the Whites may have been in charge of everything, the Blacks had to provide the manpower needed both to start and to keep the engines moving. It is infair to label a whole race of people as lazy and that becomes a statement so credible that generations have been denied the right to make a living, educate themselves, and feel that they are respectable and productive members of the societies in which they live.

Another of the stereotypes is that Blacks are dumb and our IQs are not up to standard, making it difficult for us to function as efficient members of society. This is malicious and derogatory as well as untrue. While that may truly be said of some people who do not have exposure to some things and therefore are truly illiterate, yet no part of creation is so dull that it cannot function. If the animal world is so intelligent, why would human beings created by God not have the same inherent capacity to be intelligent? Any group of people, no matter how primitive, is able to function for its survival. While not everyone may be wise in everything, given the opportunity, skills and knowledge can become the domain of the vast majority. It is true that I just wrote a whole chapter on Black ineptitude outlining the lack of initiative by a great many. However, it does not apply to everyone.

I once watched a television program about a Pigmy father teaching his son how to survive in the forest which was their home. He was teaching his boy how to use his bow and arrow to hunt for food. His instructions seemed very primitive, and absurd to me, and I started to be amused at the simplicity of what was being taught. But then reality struck me. This was the boy's PhD in survival technology as far as his environment was concerned, and such was most vital to his life and circumstance. So who was I to be critical of it? Such skills were all he needed to live.

In the more advanced Western Societies in which some Blacks live, we know that much more is required and Blacks in many cases have shown themselves more than capable of the acquisition of whatever skill is required to make their contribution.

I have heard it said many times that in order for a Black person to compete in the marketplace of opportunities, he or she has to be at least twice as good as his or her White counterpart. Would that not then mean that the few successful Blacks in society are smarter than the White person of comparable success? The same smartness shown by Blacks to do what the White people do in the past is still with them today and may even be getting better as time goes by. Blacks have been good builders, business men and women, and professionals here in North America, relatively speaking. Even in Canada where present-day success is only just now being seen, Blacks were very successful in the days when Canada was just becoming a country. Some of them, who had just escaped through the Underground Railroad, in just a few short years became doctors, lawyers, and business men and women of note.

Even during the times when Blacks were most oppressed and were denied the most basic privileges in North America and other places, there were the few who rose up from the ashes to lead relatively successful lives. Some have received credit for their genius and some have been denied. When people had been reduced to slavery, doing manual labour for many generations, it is not easy for others to think that they can be made capable to work in jobs fulfilling the needed functions of a business. Even if they have gained the education and training necessary, society promotes the idea that the education and training they received is inferior to that of the status quo. But this too is unfair and only the tarnished minds of mean spirited individuals will contrive these conclusions to the detriment of Blacks. Education and training is rarely if ever initiated by Blacks, so the status quo is doing society a disservice if they give inferior education and training to others to prepare them for service to the same society.

I believe that another reason we are considered unsuited for some jobs that the employment marketplace offers is just because of strong dislike and jealousy. Try looking back on the face of a recruiter as you walked out of an interview. You might see a brow so knitted and a face so contorted by hate just because, it seems you being Black had the audacity to be looking for a job in their company. You might just be scared out of your pants.

In the early seventies, a lot of employers in Canada were fooled into thinking that Black people who applied for jobs were White Britons because they had English last names, and because the accents sounded British. In these situations they were shocked when they saw us but would still do the interview. We knew by their attitudes that they were just going through the motions and as we were there already we just went along with them. As Blacks, all we could do was to laugh at the antics of these people even though in our hearts we were disappointed. Needless to say, we knew we would never get the jobs.

In the not-too-distant past, employers in Toronto would hire one fair-skinned Black person as a token and to avoid being called racist. I had an interview at a general insurance company here in the early Eighties when insurance companies did not really think a Black person was good enough to work in their offices. On my way in, I saw a White receptionist at the desk, but on my way out they had replaced her with a very fair-skinned Black woman, probably the only Black person they had in that organization. I noted that the interviewer went out of the room a few minutes ahead of me after the session ended even though there was really no reason to leave me there by myself. I read through it soundly, because in the interview I knew by the questions that they would never have employed me. I believe that they placed the Black woman at the reception desk just before I went out to fool me into thinking that they were an equal opportunity employer race-wise. Most Blacks became aware that racism in Canada, though a place not really known to be racist, was very covert and very subtle in the work place and everywhere else. I had no bitterness toward those people as I always thought that people have the right to do what they wish with what belonged to them. Most of us Blacks would laugh at the cowardly way they chose to do it. Why not just say plainly that they did not want us in their companies? In America, the approach to work place discrimination, as in most other cases there is open, and though sometimes abrasive, as Blacks we would rather face it head-on because at least we know it is there. It is best to know we are not welcome so we don't show up at all.

Envy and fear that they will succeed and acquire the same material possessions as those employing them, I believe, are other reasons that Blacks are denied employment. In Canada of the 1970s and 1980s, some White people were very upset that Black and Brown immigrants were coming here and purchasing 'expensive' homes so soon after their arrival in the country. They would express their anger by writing to the newspapers and voicing their opinion on Talk Radio. I used to wonder about that. I used to think that if they could do that so soon after coming to Canada, then the people complaining must not be taking advantage of the opportunities the immigrants saw. It led me to believe that those complaining were very much full of insecurity and envy about the success of the newcomers. Why else would they have complained?

On the other hand there are things Blacks may be responsible for. One of them is our sometimes casual and easy-going attitude which could be interpreted as carelessness. I know for sure that this offends a lot of people. They think this makes us less likely to conform to workplace rules and restrictions. I know for example, that a lot of Blacks from the West Indies do not appear to take life seriously and do not appear businesslike enough for most other North American people. They laugh and fool around a lot, shooting the bull, so to speak. It is not necessarily because of lack of seriousness about life's responsibilities that that this is the case. It is just their inclination to be carefree, outgoing, and to engage freely in conversation with everyone and anyone who will chat to them. This may sometimes raise eyebrows with employers or prospective ones who believe that in the workplace there is room only one thing only. That one thing is work. Any other preoccupation is disallowed. Does a carefree attitude hinder the progress of work? Well, I think it could. I think that it could interrupt the diligent and prompt performance of work. I have gone to places of employment and found Blacks and others there who will still be chatting with their co-workers about their own business while people, including me, are standing in line waiting for the service. I get the impression that if I dare to ask them to serve me instead of wasting their employers' time, I would be sure to get a cussing. This does not describe all Blacks because some are honest enough to do an honest day's work. One might say that a lot of people goof off at work and shoot the bull. Maybe, but I am sort of thinking that we need to be more eager to prove ourselves than the others all because of how things are looked at and what is expected of us. "Children" can get away with things that strangers can't.

Needless to say, sometimes the attitude toward service to clients can be a real hindrance to finding or keeping jobs in the workplace. I have gone to business establishments owned by non- White immigrants to Canada where immediate attention to customers did not seem like a high priority though they are in the service business. I think some of these people come from places where even though they depend on their businesses to make their living, they think themselves superior to their customers who who must wait on them till they feel good and ready to serve them. Take that attitude to a work environment where customer service is a very important criteria, and one can readily see the outcome. This attitude pervades much of Third World and describes the behaviour of some Blacks also. Should a prospective employer be concerned about the attitude and the quality of work that will be done by a prospective employee? I think so. It is up to the prospective employee to make an effort to fit the mold. When people spend most of or a good part of the work day carelessly, what eventually gets done ends up being substandard and may have to be subsequently corrected. This takes another day which could have been spent doing something else. This can be costly and can also be looked upon as a form of stealing.

Appearance and the manner of dressing can also be detrimental to employment possibilities. Sometimes, it is such a fine line to walk, however, that one may not know for sure what to do in a given situation, but there are places and organizations which are able to help with advice in the area of "Dressing for Success." There are also books available that one can read to become informed on the issue. There are employers who, for example, require Black women to straighten their hair for their workplace feeling that doing so will raise or keep up the image of their company. I see nothing wrong with that unless religious reasons dictate otherwise and the employer is willing to accommodate that. If there is unwillingness on the part of the employer, then employment should be sought elsewhere. There is really no point being on a job if requirements that cannot be met are an issue. I can see where braids or dreadlocks in some places of employment might definitely be a distraction. It is wise to conform to the standards of an employer even if this "violates" our own inclinations. Among our males, being clean shaven with a relatively low cut hair might help our cause quite a bit. How often do we see those of us who look so scraggy with hair uncut for what seem like years without any thought that we come under the scrutiny of those who are in positions to judge us by our appearance? Some of us with very dark skins sometimes dress ourselves in very dark clothing instead of light coloured garments. Light colored garments can enhance our appearance to our benefit. We have been born Black already and, like it or not, the Black skin has its many disadvantages. It is up to us to make the changes necessary to help ourselves. After all, we are the ones needing help and employment, much of which we cannot create on our own. So if we have a standard to conform to we should do our best to fall in line.

At other times we have to avoid over-dressing. I once went on an interview where I was dressed in a navy blue suit, black shoes, a light blue shirt, and a purple-brownish tie. I thought that because the employer was an insurance company, I needed to look as conservative as possible, and in Canada in the Seventies and Eighties much conservatism was required, but I must have appeared much over-dressed because the first words out of the mouth of the person interviewing me were, "Let us see if you plan to come here and become president of this Company". I knew instinctively that I might as well have just gotten up and walked out of that room then and there instead of enduring the futility of an interview. In the Toronto of the early Eighties, a Black man would not stand a snowball's chance in hell of ever landing such a position, no matter how qualified he was. Clearly in his mind the job I was being interviewed for required a bit of dressing down.

Then there is the question of being antiseptic at work. This may be a word you have not used in the context I am placing it here, but I will exlain. Some people go around with unwashed mouths, too much fragrance, inappropriate clothing, and other aspects of uncomeliness. They may brush their teeth very regularly but only every Saturday. Showers may only be once or twice per week.

The clothes hang loosely and one might feel like pulling up theirs every time they look at them just to make sure that theirs is not falling down. The perfume they use is fairley cheap and the scent sends nostrils sensitive to allergens scurrying for cover. Their socks or stockings smell and nobody really wants to be around them. When they open their mouths to speak you see food particles between their teeth and their breath is so foul it takes yours away. Armpits: phew!!!. If any of this describes you then you must not even think to go to your place of employment unless you rectify the offending practice.

Many times Blacks have been told that they are over-qualified for the jobs they are seeking. While this could be remotely true, it is more likely that this is the employers' way of saying they don't really want us in their places of business. I went on another interview once, was given the job with a start date, then got a call a few hours later saying that the existing staff considered me too qualified for the job. I sought basically the same position with the same qualifications at other places and was denied because I was not qualified enough. While Whites may sometimes be given the same excuses, Blacks always see job opportunities in these countries as something for them to refuse and we cannot appreciate the fact that they get the same answers as we do for the same reasons. It can be a very disappointing process at times, leaving a Black person feeling unwanted.

Seeing also that most humans prefer to be with those most like themselves, it is up to those who wish to live in the society in which they find themselves "to do as the Romans do when in Rome". Sometimes as Blacks we need to change what makes us look more for manual labour than for the refinement of an office or a position in business. It may be that the lack of sophistication of our mannerisms and personalities hinder us at times. And for those of us who lack them, it is noteworthy that a lot of these qualities can be acquired. What can also be acquired and ought to be acquired very quickly, is respect for others and the willingness to put aside what we have grown up with in our cultures, which may be unacceptable in the culture of others.

Unsociable behaviour in the workplace can be very embarrassing and if people see that in us before they give us work, it will certainly work against us. I had an occasion to visit a government office on Bay Street in Toronto a few years ago. I had to go to a floor which required the riding of the elevator. I punched the button and when the elevator opened for me there was a Black fellow in it whistling like a bird. He had taken the elevator on the lower level. There were other people on the same elevator, and except for him and me, they were all White. I hoped hard that this man would immediately stop his embarrassing whistling out of shame for this uncouth behaviour. This was sophisticated Canada on Bay Street, Canada's Business District. But would he stop? He continued whistling all the way till I got out of the elevator. I don't know where he found breath in his lungs to continue whistling for so long. Thankfully, my floor came up and I could finally get out. I was so ashamed! Even the other people in the elevator seemed embarrassed. At one point, I had felt like sticking my finger in his mouth to interrupt the whistle, but I was too shy to do so. I think if I were a prospective employer riding in that elevator, I would deny him a job if he came to me. I think if I were his supervisor and heard him whistling in the elevator like that I would call him into my office and let him know how uncivilized his behaviour was, if not downright fire him. Poor social behaviour puts any prospective employer in an awkward position if a job is available to be offered. We should be ever careful to observe what is not acceptable around us and make an effort to change whatever it is.

I have heard of Black employees who feel entitled to carry a small television to their work stations so they can watch their favourite programs while at work. I have also heard of those who insist on having a small radio or CD player strapped to their ears so they can listen to their favourite music as they work at their jobs. No matter how you cut it, I can't see that as a proper thing to do. I have always felt that if someone is kind enough to employ me, enabling me to make money to pay my bills and provide myself a place to live, food to eat, and clothes to wear, the least I can do is give that person or entity my honest and undivided attention when I am on their premises to do the job they have hired me to do. Anything else is quite foolish and should be considered outright robbery of an employer's time.

It seems nowadays that more and more White employers are becoming increasingly susceptible to criticism and the label of racism, and are willing to let Black employees get away with things they wouldn't allow just a few short years ago. Part of the reason for this new development may be the network of government organizations where people who feel they have been wronged can lodge complaints. No employer wants to be called in for violation of government regulations, which could result in fines of loss of licenses in some cases. And sometimes some of us are likely to call down fire and brimstone on those who in our opinion have historically denied us now that we have the right to do so. I must say that I blame governments for their rush to equalize opportunities by penalizing companies not hiring enough Blacks, especially when we may not be qualified to do the work required. In many cases, the governments are to blame for not ensuring the opportunities for Blacks to have gotten the proper educational tools required for employment. What those companies may inturn do, however, is deny employment altogether to Blacks looking for work. So if we are seeking our own pleasure at work and complaining when we should not, we might just be "denying" ourselves employment.

Sometimes we may be going from a welfare situation into a school and from school into the workplace. We then may need some kind of orientation toward this new way of life. The need may be there to be coached about dress, appearance, expectations, and how to fit into the workplace. This may be the responsibility of some support groups or government agencies established to orient people going from one way of existence to another.

In recent studies by various groups all over America, conclusions have been arrived at which still show a growing disparity between employment prospects for Blacks versus Whites. The national average unemployment rate for Blacks is more than twice that of Whites. The Blacks have an average rate over 10% while the Whites have an average rate of just 4.7%. The overall wages for Whites are still higher than that of Blacks, and promotions are usually given to Whites even where the Blacks have the same qualifications. Many sources can be cited which concur with the findings being discussed here. Work for young Black males in America is hard to come by at best, especially where they do not have much of an education above high school or sometimes no high school education at all.

This part of the finding should not be surprising, however, because work is hard to come by for anyone Black or White who does not have at least a high school diploma. In this case it is wise to further one's qualification to get employment. This is never too late to do especially if you are still young. I know you want that flashy car yesterday and you think the time spent in school may be better spent looking for work. But dont worry. Chances are the world will still be here when you have finished making yourself more qualified.

Some Blacks and some Black organizations appeal to governmental agencies to address employment inequities. It is true that these government organizations have done a bit recently to address the disparity, but a lot more still needs to be done. At the same time, they live under a capitalist system in the United States which glorifies personal efforts for the acquisition of material things, so the need for individual effort is a fact that Blacks need to wake up to. Once this is fully realized, we will hopefully develop the mindset which will qualify and enable Blacks to achieve this. I am fully conscious of the stumbling blocks that have been set up at times, but as indicated before, we can use these as stepping-stones instead. Other non-White peoples who are quite recent immigrants to North America seem quite able to create opportunities for themselves and subsist on the support of their own communities in terms of employment. What are we waiting for?

It is an historical fact that America has been denying opportunities to Blacks from the day that they set foot on American soil. A lot has been done to make life very difficult for them in every situation, but gains have also been made. We could even call the gains strides in some respects. In a single generation, America has given birth to many Black millionaires and multimillionaires. This has come about because of our proficiency in sports and entertainment mainly. But some have come about through education, entrepreneurship, and business acumen developed since emancipation. The earnings of Black Americans are now counted in the billions of dollars. One of the things rich Blacks need to do is employ their wealth and earnings to make it beneficial to Blacks as a whole. When this is done, Blacks may no longer need to cry to governments to right the wrongs done so far as employment is concerned. We need to get it into our minds that such will work over the long run. How long did it take Bill Gates to amass billions, and what did he do? Blacks should stop depending on Whites for everything. We now have some of the resources needed to benefit our own people. And we can certainly benefit from each other in the true spirit of reciprocity when we support each other in our business ventures. Blacks number about 39.2 million in America alone; almost 90% of those who are able to work are working. They are also the second largest consumer group. Black-owned businesses, where they exist, can tap into such a number and financial resource and market products and services.

According to the latest available report on Black earnings in America, the figure is about $771 billion per year. The yearly GDP of South Africa, to name one country, was about $483 billion the last time I checked with roughly the same amount of people. What I am saying is; this is quite a large sum of money with a lot of the spending from this going to mostly White-owned businesses. We cannot refuse to support the businesses of Whites because the vast majority of the jobs we have from which these incomes are earned, come from them in the first place. I personally cannot express enough gratitude to companies like General Motors, The Ford Motor Company, and Chrysler Motors for all the jobs they gave to West Indian Blacks when we just came to Canada. If is was not for them, many of us would have starved. Anyway we must make an effort to develop worthwhile enterprises as Blacks also, and bring ourselves into positions of some degree of self-reliance so we can offer jobs to our own people.

If this model is put in place and perfected by Blacks in America, it can become the example for Blacks all over the world. This will be so because American Blacks are not the only ones to consider. Blacks in every nation where they are, face the problems of unemployment and a shortage of Black businesses, and as the rest of the world looks to America as a model of prosperity and economic leadership, the rest of the Black world can also look to Black Americans for the same kind of economic leadership and prosperity that they can achieve as well. We can learn from the productive tenacity and creativity of the White race. As I said before, when they came to North America the countries were mostly wildernesses. In a short time, relatively speaking, the new-comers have revolutionized the continent till now skyscrapers are everywhere they want them to be, and grand enterprises, businesses, and jobs and employment opportunities are aplenty. As the White people started out of almost nothing but a desire and a plan, so can we. Maybe so should we. It will do us good in the long run.

CHAPTER EIGHT
BLACKS AND THE LAW

There are two aspects of human nature. One is revealed by fear and deprivation, the other by security and love. It is for us to encourage the latter and discourage the former if we are to make progress. Progress in society cannot be measured by the accomplishment of only those that we feel we should empower. Interpreted — People should not feel that only when members of their color and race succeed that their obligation ceases. As you read this chapter, keep in mind that it is sometimes because some are left to feel disenchanted, disenfranchised, and disallowed that they become unsociable, vengeful, unproductive, and criminal. Resolve to be tender with the young, sympathetic to the poor, tolerant of the weak and the wronged, and remember that at some time in your life you yourself may have been one of these. This chapter will speak at length about crime and Blacks both in Canada and the United States of America. I will be looking as well on the historical presence of Blacks in Canad up to the present time. Also I will take a look at Blacks and their reaction to law enforcement in White societies.

If there is only one segment of White society where there is a group to be feared by Blacks, it is the group dispensing "justice". The judicial system in White-run countries seems to overwhelm and mystify them. The system seems like the natural-born enemy of Blacks in these countries. Never in the history of the fight for justice, has a group of people met such a formidable opponent. It is alleged that members of the justice system in America have even disguised themselves in the coverings of White supremacists to commit some of the worst atrocities against Black people. Most of these crimes have taken place in the Southern States of the United States of America. But the unfair treatment of Blacks by Whites, so far as "justice" is concerned, exists all over America and all over the world; sometimes even in their own countries by their own people. Stories full of bigotry from places including the United States, England, Brazil, and the former South Africa, just to name a few, abound where law enforcement agencies have practiced and are still practicing these acts of bigotry against Blacks. Sometimes this is so pervasive and open that it is spoken of as a thing that "Blacks just have to accept". This conclusion itself is a travesty of justice. And those responsible are themselves so very capable of ignoring the law that they are not even aware of the irony of their conclusions that Blacks just have to get used to their gross injustices.

There probably are not too many Blacks, especially Black males, who would think of most White police officers as having their best interests on their minds, or as being someone they can trust. Quite the opposite: because the White police officer is held out to be credible, and a person who can do no wrong in the eyes of almost all the White citizens in their jurisdictions, he can do almost anything he wants to Blacks, even to the killing of innocent Black women as has, happened more than once. Fairly recently in St Petersburg, Florida, two White police men shot and killed a young Black woman who was just sitting in her car. They alleged she was a threat of some kind to them. While situations may be changing in some areas, and for that credit is due, the long-standing distrust of law enforcement officers by Blacks will take more than just a bit of whitewash to eradicate. The truth is that police, White or otherwise can, and sometimes lie, rob and cheat like anybody else. They have also falsified statements to get criminal convictions of people they know to be completely innocent of any wrong doing

At the same time, some Blacks do not do themselves any favours by being criminally minded and by being a problem to society, taking vengeance on mostly innocent people because of wrongs they feel society has done to them. They kill, steal, and destroy to get even it seems or just to be wicked. In such cases, the law enforcers cannot and should not be blamed if and when they apply the law, which is usually full-force when it comes to Blacks. It is not unusual for those who pass sentence to wait till there is a poor, insignificant Black man before them to "teach society a lesson" on how to behave, but immediately turn around and give the lightest sentence possible to those who are White and guilty of even a greater although not totally unrelated offence. I have often wondered why they would do that to us insignificant Blacks as if in our sphere we are so influential that the rest of society will learn from our mistakes.

Taking a Look on the Situation of Blacks in Canada.

The Situation for Blacks in Canada

Although the contents of this sub-heading might have been more logically dealt with in an earlier part of this book, I will here take a look at the situation for Blacks here in Canada from an historic perspective, employing the view that Canada is not known as a racist nation by any acts of federal parliament. However, the social conscience of its citizenry will be briefly looked at in the past as well as in the present.

Canada was considered a safe haven for Blacks in its early years when it was just becoming a nation. It may still be looked upon as the same today by those who think they know, and really it is still a very good country relatively speaking because Canada has never acted out the same deep-seated, institutionalized, violent, racist behaviour toward Blacks as some other "civilized" nations have done. This however, does not mean that Canadians did not or have never had any racial biases. They did and still have some of it. As with any other society where there is a variety of peoples there will be pockets of discomfort as well as individual hate. This is 2009, but Blacks have told me that they've been called "Black ugly monkey" on the job, have been told that slavery should not have ended when it did, and should be continuing even now and involved them, and so on. Young Black people trying to sell books in some White neighbourhoods to earn a little money to get an education have also been called "niggers" and have been chased off White people's lawns and porches as a reward for their efforts. So the concept of Canada being free from racism is just a myth.

Yet, it is not as bad as it could be because I see, hear, and work with White people here who make a conscious effort to avoid the pitfalls of racism in their behaviour and who will go overboard to accommodate Black and other non-White people. When my wife and I ran a small business most of our clients were White. Had it not been for their purchases we would not have been able to survive. True, it is that when I go to see some of them they are flabbergasted to see a Black man showing up at their door who "apparently" knows how to design, sell, and install kitchen cabinets. Sometimes their eyes begin an upward climb toward their foreheads because of their complete astonishment. Those people have never bought a kitchen from me, but we could not have had much of a business if I was depending on the purchases of Black people only. Interestingly, even some Blacks have a negative reaction to me when I show up at their door, and even go so far as telling me they did not know that a Black person in Canada could have such a business. I usually look at these poor mentally diminished souls with great pity, or depending on my mood; with angry impatience. While I can appreciate the reticence of the Whites, I see in the attitudes of Blacks the reason this book should be written.

We even have some municipal Black politicians elected to office in Canada when the majority of the constituents in their ridings are White, and there are other visible signs of Blacks in places and jobs were they would not have been just a few years ago.

Lincoln Alexander, Canada's first Black MP and the former Lieutenant

Governor of Ontario and former federal Cabinet Minister Jean Augustine are both prominent political figures, and a notable MPP - Alvin Curling was speaker of the Ontario Legislature for a couple of years, and later ambassador to the Dominican Republic. Although it was never publicly stated, rumour has it that he was recalled by the recently elected Progressive Conservative government which is a party rightly or wrongly known for its conservative attitude much like the Republic Party of the United States of America. His appointment as an ambassador had been made by the Liberal Prime Minister just before he was defeated at the polls. Anyway, it is up to newly elected governments to overturn appointments that have been made by the outgoing governments in this country and racism may not have been a factor with Alvin Curling. In recent elections I have not seen any Black candidates fielded federally or provincially, although there were some in municipal elections. This I think is a mistake—a sign that Blacks are not taking advantage of an open opportunity in Canada to elevate themselves through politics. In the meantime, the other ethnic groups are getting into politics at a steady rate.

As the Lieutenant Governor of the province of Ontario for a while, Mr. Lincoln Alexander conducted himself with the utmost dignity and class. Recently, the former prime minister, the Right Honourable Mr. Paul Martin, recommended the appointment of Her Excellency the Right Honourable Madame Michaelle Jean, of Haitian descent, as Governor General of the country. She is the third female and the first Black to hold this post. Actually, it is visible to me that though she is legally Black, she is of mixed ancestry, and married to a White caucasion even though I do not believe that that influenced the appointment in any way. While this appointment may have angered some White people who do not like to see Blacks progress in their society, I believe this to be a good thing for the Blacks in Canada when seen from the perspective that we are better than just being good-for-nothings. Madame Michaelle Jean's appointed could not be terminated by the new Conservative government though it might have wanted to because Canada's laws do not allow for the termination of a governor general without reason.

The national personality of Canada toward Blacks can in no way be compared to that of the brutal former South Africa, the class-conscious England, or the once-and still somewhat violent United States relative to their treatment of Blacks. In the present case of America's "physical non-violent" attitude towards Blacks, I am holding my breath becasue its history of hating Blacks is long, it is a big country with lots of guns; with a temper as volatile as a recently active volcano, and has many Whites who still hate Blacks.

Canada as a country had African slaves in the early days of its history. The first slave transported directly from Africa to Canada was a child brought to Quebec in 1628 by the English privateer David Kirke, and sold to a local resident on Kirke's departure in 1629. Canada's first free Black visitor was Mathieu D'Acosta who came to what later became Canada as a translator traveling with Samuel de Champlain. Between 1628 and the British Conquest in 1759, 1132 slaves of African descent were brought to New France. Governor Denonville sought permission to establish an African slave trade in 1688, but such was denied. Most of the slaves who came to Canada came from the British colonies of North America and the French West Indian Islands. Roughly 60% of the slaves brought in were males, and they were mostly brought into the urban centres as domestic servants. They were mostly owned singly or in small groups and would serve the same person or family all their lives. They were not traded as in other countries.

Black slaves lived in the British regions of Canada in the seventeenth and eighteenth centuries. One hundred and four of them were listed in the 1767 census of Nova Scotia, and overall their numbers were small until the Loyalists influx after 1783. As White Loyalists fled the New American Republic, they took about two thousand Black slaves with them.

Approximately 1200 were taken to the Maritime Provinces of Nova Scotia, New Brunswick, and Prince Edward Island, 300 to Lower Canada (Quebec), and about 500 to Upper Canada (Ontario). As in New France, Black slaves were employed as domestic servants, farm hands, and skilled artisans. The system of gang labour and its institutions of control and brutality did not develop here, and in Canada slaves were taught and allowed to read and write as they were not considered a threat to their slave masters if they were able to do so. Christian conversions were encouraged, and the slaves' right to marry in Canada was recognized by law. There was early segregation in Nova Scotia, Manitoba, and Upper Canada. But, in 1793 Upper Canada became the first territory in the British Empire to legislate the gradual abolition of slavery. By 1800, the other provinces of British North America effectively limited slavery through the courts, and strict rules of ownership were required. Slavery did, however, remain legal till the British Parliament emancipated the slaves throughout the empire, effective in 1834.

It can rightly be concluded, as a number of Canadians have told me, that this country's treatment of Blacks was certainly not as cruel as the treatment of its native peoples. Until it was mentioned to me in the late seventies, I had no idea that Canada was tainted with any racial bias. Actually, Canada was one country I knew nothing about till I was about nine or ten years old. It was about that time that I heard that one of my uncles was married to a Canadian. Also, when Jamaica's second Prime Minister, Sir Donald Sangster, had a brain haemorrhage in 1967, I as well as most other Jamaicans heard on the news that he was sent to Canada for treatment.

The treatment of Blacks in the province of Nova Scotia, Canada has historically been very poor indeed, if even only from the perspective of civil neglect. One of the oldest Black communities in Canada, Africville in Nova Scotia has come to represent one of Canada's worst incidents of discrimination against Black people, both from an individual and governmental perspective. Africville was a community settled in Nova Scotia by slaves who were promised freedom and land if they supported the British in the American war for independence. It became home to about 400 Black settlers who built homes, businesses, and churches there. The surrounding city of Halifax began building offensive structures such as factories and sewage drains around Africville. It finally became home to a prison, Halifax's night soil disposal pit, an infectious disease hospital, an open city dump, an incinerator, and a slaughter house during the time that African Canadians lived on the site. These activities resulted in highly unsanitary and undesirable conditions creating an almost squalid environment. As late as 1970, Africville did not have clean water, or electricity.

Eventually, even the Halifax City Council realized that the area around Africville had conditions which were quite unsuitable for human living. But when requested, they refused to install running water and other utilities. This was prime water front real estate and eventually, the city decided to expropriate the land in the area. They offered the residents far less than fair market value for their homes and property and when the people refused, they sent bulldozers in to raze the homes and businesses these people had built up to sustain themselves. Some residents were given less than five hundred dollars for their property, and some were given nothing at all.

Nova Scotia continues to be one of the worst places for Blacks to live in Canada, and, not surprisingly, it continues to be one of the poorest provinces also, much like the Southern States of the U.S. where the poorest, most backward states are the ones that were the meanest to Black slaves, and are still most hateful of Blacks in general today.

In many places across Canada, there is much unwelcome to members of the Black race. It is believed by some that specific places in Alberta, Manitoba, and Saskatchewan are areas for Blacks to stay away from for their own social well-being and peace of mind. In Quebec, there is allegedly a strong dislike for anyone who is not French and who does not speak the language. Most Haitians who live in Canada live in Quebec because they speak French, but being Black they are not beloved by many in that province. And given the history of the province towards Blacks, one should expect, there are places in Nova Scotia where Blacks would not be welcome at all.

The government of Canada has enacted human rights laws to protect all its citizens. However, its police forces in some of its major cities single out Blacks for harsh and unreasonable treatment in comparison to others. It is alleged that this is the case in cities like Halifax, Montreal, Calgary, and Edmonton; and Toronto has had its own proven history of police intolerance toward Blacks. I can speak to the attitudes of the police towards Blacks in the Toronto of the Seventies and Eighties, and will have more to say about it below. I will also attest to the fact that the treatment of Blacks by the police in the Toronto of today has much improved. However, Black criminals are presently giving the Toronto Police Service their biggest challenge.

The Toronto Perspective.

This part of the chapter deals with the racial tension in Toronto in the mid-Seventies when Black immigration was heating up. It describes the reaction of the citizenry and its police force in the face of an unwelcome rising Black population. It will detail a number of incidents that made the atmosphere very tense for the general populace of Toronto in the Seventies.

One of the most chilling experiences I had in my life was in Toronto, Canada in the early Seventies. I had been here for only about three weeks. I had been told that the policemen here in Toronto did not like Black people driving certain cars. This was information though I believed, I was appalled to receive. It made no sense to me that the police should be that concerned about the cars Black people drove. I began wondering if Blacks were asking the Toronto police to subsidize their monthly car expenses. One such car was the Cougar made by the Ford Motor Company. I lived on a street where a Black Jamaican who owned a Cougar had relatives, whom he would visit from time to time. One day, a parking enforcement officer who just happened by decided to give him a ticket for parking on that street. He protested, saying that by no means and especially at that time of the day was he parked illegally. He got the ticket anyway, and he and the parking enforcement officer who was White, got into a very heated, very loud argument. The "N" word came up, and he was told by the parking enforcement officer that if he had been in some other place he would have been shot. I took that to mean in America. This Jamaican was a very high-strung fellow and completely lost his composure because of what came out of the enforcement officer's mouth. He got into his car and drove at the parking officer as with the strongest intention to stike him down with it. His brakes screeched loudly as he came to a frightfully close stop, of what seemed less than a foot away from the officer. It was a miracle that he stopped at all. The parking enforcement officer maintained his composure even though his eyes bulged in massive fright, and the three or four of us who were watching the whole thing were frozen in fear and unspoken apprehension.

The episode ended up with the officer saying that the motorist would be further charged with excessive noise, and the motorist said he would go to City Hall, whatever that was, and file a complaint against the officer for discrimination. I thought to myself that if excessive noise was the only additional charge, he would be very lucky indeed. It seemed like something much worse to me, but I did not have the power to charge anyone with anything. At the time, I did not know what City Hall was, and I did not hear anything more about the incident so I can't tell what happened. But I knew that I immediately wished to go right back where I had come from. I had just experienced something that I thought only happened in America, and it was the first time I had actually experienced such a direct White/Black confrontation. It made me most uncomfortable.

When I first came to Canada, there were very few Blacks living in Toronto, but as the years went by, an increasing number began to flood some of the neighbourhoods of the city and the police rose to the challenge of dealing with this new influx of people with a different skin colour, a more casual way of looking at life, and maybe representing a possible perceived threat, though this was yet unproven. Most Black West Indians love to laugh and have a good time, and they find humour in the simplest little things even though the world may be falling apart around them. Most people in Toronto at the time seemed to think that being grumpy and walking around with grim faces was a sign that you were serious about life, and maybe everyone thought that they needed to bring our sunny dispositions under control. I remember walking down St. Clair Ave. at Vaughan Rd. one day, talking and laughing with my friend, when a White fellow came up to us and asked us what we were so happy about. I felt as though being happy as a Black individual was an anti-social behaviour in Toronto. Superficial though it might seem, in my mind back then I could not come up with any other reason than colour for the police targeting Blacks for harassment in the city. Even though I had read and heard of those who persecuted Blacks, I was too daft to believe that they did that to people who were doing no wrong at all.

Not long after I came to Toronto, an associate of mine and I were riding the bus home from work. We stood close to a White man seated on the bus who showed signs of irritation, so we started moving away from him. He stated that he did not like Black guys, which meant us. It was the first time I had hatred verbalized against me from someone I had never met before, and I was shocked to believe such a thing was possible.

A few years into life in Canada, crime was starting to become a problem. I might not have the exact reason for that, but people who are mistreated without just cause usually fight back in the way no one really wants. Really, in those days crime, even among Black people in Toronto, was something unheard of and therefore I believe it was nothing to worry about. It was not that Toronto had a sudden surge in crime which the people had to deal with immediately following a rise in Black immigration. Yet there were many incidents of unfair treatment being meted out to Blacks by the police. They were unfairly targeted for traffic violations and readily stopped when they drove half-decent cars. There were cases when they were allegedly even physically hurt. In one particular case, it was alleged that a Black motorist had his arm twisted and broken at a police station because he protested loudly against some unfair treatment he thought he was receiving and was dumb enough to protest. The few cases of crime were being reported as if it was an epidemic, and as some of the incidences of crime were relatively unknown by the Toronto public it made it all sound quite dramatic.

The chief of the Toronto police at the time started to talk about crimes that the immigrants were committing. This to me was nothing more than fabrications to justify the ill-treatment of Black immigrants by members of his police force. When he was taken to task for his comment, he changed his wording to say that he meant the illegal immigrants. This answer was even more baffling because I could not see why an "illegal" immigrant would put himself in such a predicament. While a criminal at large will remain a criminal, being an immigrant, legal or illegal, does not of itself increase the likelihood that one will commit a crime. Nonetheless it appeared that White people in general became alarmed at the increasing number of Blacks and other minorities coming into Toronto, and the police seemed to have picked up on that and decided to do something about it. Some in the Black community concluded that there was intimidation and a reign of fear by the Toronto police.

It is alleged that some police officers even became "immigration officers" on the streets in an effort to find those who had no permanent residence papers so they could have them deported in an effort to contain a potential "problem." (In those days it was customary for the Canadian government to allow people to come in as visitors and then apply for permanent residence status from within the country). But the Blacks saw everything the police did as harassment. Black immigrants started to speak out, and those who were here legally figured they had the right to be here and as such they expected to be treated fairly.

Reading the newspapers, one got the impression that the general consensus of the Toronto populace was that Black immigrants did not have the right or the relevance to speak out. We were, after all, just newcomers and in most cases unwanted newcomers. But Blacks from the West Indies, especially from Jamaica, are cut to the quick when they are treated poorly and will rarely remain silent. We were not all brought up with the same self-depreciating mentality as are Blacks who have grown up on this part of the continent. Jamaicans as a group will take a very callous attitude when pushed to the limit and usually entertain no feelings of inferiority to anyone. They act with reckless abandon and an almost total disregard for the rule of law when provoked or poorly treated without just cause. A professor at York University did a study a few years after these incidents started occurring and reported that of all the West Indians, Jamaicans were the most likely to rebel against injustices. This is an attitude that people from developed countries do not accept from such an "insignificant" group of people and are usually too proud to accommodate it. Jamaicans do not like to be accused of something of which they are not guilty.

It was not too very long before the Blacks began to be placed in the traditional roles that the White societies carve out for them. Not every employer would employ them, not all schools welcomed their presence, and not all landlords would rent to them. There was a time when real estate agents were told by White homeowners not to bring potential Black and other non-White buyers to view their houses, and so on, and soon enough they congregated in certain areas which accepted them. One of the neighbourhoods—the Jane/Finch corridor became legendary for its "criminal" activities. Of course, whether real or imagined, any place in the White world where there is a disproportionate number of Black residents suddenly becomes a place of criminal activity if they wish to so classify it.

Civic Toronto seemed very eager to "grow up" and be "crowned" with its very own darling "ghetto of crime." Those who could were very quick to place labels. The news reporters seemed ecstatic that they could finally say that Toronto was becoming like the major crime cities of their great neighbour to the south. I guess it made them feel that the city had finally come of age, but there were those who were saddened by it, myself included. And I especially could not compare Toronto with places like Detroit for example which was recording upwards of 900 murders annually. Toronto would have been "lucky" to see 90 such murders. But it was not very long after when a White guard who worked at Toronto's Don Jail told me that there was a whole floor there in perpetual reservation for Black criminals, especially Jamaicans. I did not like the sound of that. Quite frankly I was very disappointed at that revelation.

But the truth was that 51 Division, in the Dundas and Beverley Streets area in the heart of downtown Toronto where no Blacks lived at the time, had more crimes than the Jane/Finch corridor. Crime statistics back then allegedly proved that this was true. But the reason it did not make the news was because the area was White and White people don't commit crimes, only Black people do. Even White passengers would tell me sometimes while driving in my cab that they thought the label was unfair. For my part, I just wondered why Toronto was so quick to label its Black neighbourhood a haven for crime and why newscasters were so quick to second the notion. Back then, there was not the epidemic of criminals selling drugs, committing rapes, and brutalizing residents as there probably is now. At least, that was not what I was hearing and I have always been quite a sponge for things happening around me. At the time, driving a cab gave me much opportunity to read the newspapers, the Toronto *Sun* being the paper of choice because its size, compared to the Toronto *Star* or the *Globe and Mail*, meant it was more easily read in a cab.

Reading the newspapers gave me a clear perspective of what the people of the city were thinking and the Toronto *Sun*, a paper then known for its dislike for Blacks, was editorially condescending and critical of us in their written opinions, and would publish, it seems with relish, all the bad things their readers had to say about Black people. The Toronto *Star* was somewhat objective. I can't speak for the *Globe and Mail* because I did not read it much.

Later on, in the mid-Seventies to the Eighties, there were some very high-profile criminal cases arising. One of them was the killing of a White taxi driver by some young Black males. I remember his last name was Stoddard. I had just begun driving a cab after finishing an accounting program at George Brown College, but finding nothing to do in that field. My greatest fear at the time was Whites taking revenge. This killing alarmed everyone including me. On a Saturday night shortly after, I picked up a fare who wanted to go to Scarborough where Mr. Stoddard had been killed. He was a very muscular and rough looking White dude. I was as frightened as a cat and would have gladly relinquished this fare but could not because City Ordinances did not allow a cab driver to refuse a passenger for no good reason. I was so worried of him that he might hurt me I had to find a way to get on his good side, so I flattered him about his looks and about how many girls he must be able to pick up. I just did not want him avenging Mr. Stoddard's death on me. He smiled, and I felt a bit easier having broken the ice, but I remained uncomfortable all the way to Scarborough from downtown Toronto.

The killing of Mr. Stoddard was followed by some young White fellow in Scarborough who came out brandishing a weapon at the Cedarbrae Mall, threatening to kill as many Blacks as he could. The police rushed in great haste to take care of that situation realizing its potential for great trouble.

These events might seem very insignificant to readers, but keep in mind that the Toronto of the Seventies was a place of such peace and quiet that any of these incidents caused alarm. Even now, in the twenty-first century, this city of more than two million and with a surrounding population of more than five million sees less than100 murders per year.

There were other criminal activities by members of the Black community, which began to alarm most if not everyone, and some members of the community began "deserving" the label being placed on us. It was getting emotionally uncomfortable for me to go places because as someone Black I was very visible. There was never a time when I agreed, or ever will agree to any kind of criminal activity by Blacks as I believe that though they might be provoked to action, they ought to act within the confines of the law.

However there were also many incidents, large and small, where police bigotry was evident. I experienced a few of them personally. I was driving around Dundas and Bay Sts. in my cab. At the time the spot was being worked by two police officers. One was White, and the other was Black- a rarity at the time. Just in front of me was a White driver who made the same error I made. The White police officer turned him back with a warning. When he came to me, he wrote me a traffic citation. I was very angry at the obvious inconsistency. I could also see the obvious frustration on the face of the Black officer who could do nothing about it, but I understood the problem he was facing, because the few Black policemen on the Toronto police force at that time were apparently not given an easy ride by their White counterparts. Even on the same police force they were treating the few token Blacks, which they grudgingly employed, in the same profession as if they were nobodies. The owner of the cab was with me that morning and decided that he would go to court on my behalf and contest the ticket. When he pointed out the stark inconsistency to the presiding judge, the fine was doubled. I had no choice but to pay it. That was only one of them. If I were to write about all the incidents of ill-treatment that Blacks allegedly suffered at the hands of the Metropolitan Toronto Police back then, I would probably never finish writing this book.

But, there were incidents that deserves particular attention because they were very troubling for those times. It was the killing of Albert Johnson by White police officers, in his own house, and in front of his family, one of them his very young daughter who said repeatedly that her father was kneeling down and begging for his life when the police broke into his house and murdered him. To those who may not like the word "murder" in regards to this, I will emphasize that cold-blooded murder was exactly what it was. The autopsy report stated that the bullet entered his body at an angle. And indeed the police claimed that he was coming down the stairs at them with a knife when they shot him. The autopsy report did not indicate the position the angle. I believe this was a deliberate omission. I believe if it was an upward angle, the people who conducted the autopsy would have been more than happy to point that out to vindicate the police. And why would Albert Johnson be coming from upstairs with a knife when he ran inside his house from the outside to hide himself when the police showed up at his house that morning? How would he be able to get a knife so quickly when they came in right after him? I believe that the angle at which the bullet entered his body was downward, corroborating the little girl's story of her father being shot while on his knees begging for his life. I remember watching the news on television and seeing a reporter asking a police sergeant about his version of events, which was contrary to that given by the little girl. The reporter asked him if he was willing to "doubt" the little girl. At that point, the sergeant switched the conversation to the investigation that would be taking place, saying that such would reveal what really happened.

Such an investigation would always take place whenever a person was shot by a Toronto police officer. But this incident in the minds and hearts of Toronto's Blacks would prove their charge of judicial racism against them.

Albert Johnson apparently first came to the attention of the police because of some domestic problems with his wife and he was ever hounded by them after that. It was as if he provided an opportunity for them to harass a Black man. Back then the police had precious little to do and his house was just a few blocks from a police station. It is alleged that he had been very badly beaten by the police on more than one occasion. The doctor who attended him allegedly stated that he had never seen a case of police brutality as bad as his, and it was further alleged that Albert was taking the matter before the courts in a law suit against the Metropolitan Toronto Police Force and the individual officer/s accused of beating him. It was a law suit most believed was too clear cut to go any other way but in his favour and would convict the police officers responsible. Some of the members of the Black community including myself believe to this very day that it was for this reason that on that fateful Sunday morning the police "received a call" about a neighbourhood disturbance coming from his house. It is my understanding that the emergency services have never been able to find any record of this call in their database.

A reporter who I believe was as bigoted as the policemen who murdered Albert Johnson called him a "loser", pandering to majority sentiment against Blacks at the time. This man, who had been in Canada for a very short time, had already been able to purchase his own house, something some people living here all their lives were not able to do. This alone proved to me and others who were mentally balanced, that he was no loser. Maybe the reporter himself still lived in a rental apartment. Because some things were not going well for Albert Johnson at that particular time, that reporter who was obviously on the side of hate and injustice, wanted people to believe that he was a loser.

A few weeks after Albert Johnson was murdered by the police, I was driving my taxi in roughly the same neighbourhood where he had lived. My actual location was in front of 730 Dovercourt, an apartment building where I had just dropped off a passenger. Another cabbie, not more than a about a hundred yards away, was having an altercation with a fare and someone called the police. As good cabbies do, I delayed my leaving to see what would happen, and to assist if I could. But this was a volatile area at the time. I did not want to get too close to the other cab driver. Not many minutes went by before the police arrived. One of them came by and asked me if I was the driver having the problem. Other officers went on to the other driver. I stretched out my hand and pointed toward the location of the other cab driver stating verbally at the same time that he was the one having the problem.

The police man straight punched at my out-stretched hand for reasons unknown to me but did not hit me because from his position his reach was short of the mark. He probably wanted me to retaliate so he could kill me. I looked at him for a few seconds in surprise and confusion. I thought to myself, "Toronto is in complete turmoil over the Albert Johnson affair and here was this White policeman trying to provoke a confrontation with another Black man." I immediately walked to my cab and with much relief drove away as quickly as I could, thanking God that this policeman did not use the few seconds I used to stare at him as a pretext for killing me as some of his contemporaries had done to Albert Johnson. I was glad also that he did not ask my name. It being so close to that of Albert Johnson's, only heaven knows what kind of demons it may have stirred up in him.

The city of Toronto was in a huge social and emotional upheaval because of the Albert Johnson situation for quite some time. There were no showdowns between Blacks and Whites, but for a lot of Blacks I knew then it was a time of great fear and apprehension. I dreaded walking the streets and going into public places. And being a cab driver at the time, the fear was much heightened especially when I had to drive at night. I had never had to live through something like that before, and all the stories I had read about the racial hatred between Whites and Blacks caused me to fear being physically harmed by Whites when I was going about my daily affairs. There was much anger and tension among the Black people, but they were as helpless as anyone could be to do anything about the situation. As we spoke about the matter, a lot of us thought that but for the mercy of God any White Toronto police officer could mow down any number of Blacks for no apparent reason even in our homes without any serious repercussions against him. The Albert Johnson killing was a case in point. Such thoughts may have been just the result of fear, but at the time they were uppermost in our minds. Maybe the Whites felt the very same fear and apprehension as the Blacks felt and were just as afraid about being killed by avenging Blacks. In reality though, Blacks had been the first to show the tendency toward that kind of violence when they killed Mr. Stoddard.

The inquest that followed in the Albert Johnson case not surprisingly went in favour of the police. But I believe it was a huge embarrassment to the powers that be. The "Justice System" in Toronto was seen for what it was—bigoted and stacked against Blacks, at least in that situation. It might as well just have been referred to by some other name. No one who mattered seemed to care, and we were too weak and powerless to do much about it except to whine as loudly as we could. As a result of Johnson's killing, however, a lot of changes were made to police procedures, which not only benefited the Black community, at least on paper, but benefited all other racial groups including the Whites. It was because of that situation that even short little White menand the vertically challenged members of other races can now be police officers. Before that, the height of applicants had to be no less than five feet nine inches, to the best of my recollection with appropriate weight requirement. Police relationships with Toronto's Blacks, which were always hostile anyway, suffered a lot more in the ensuing months as the police brass grudgingly put some of those changes into effect. Radio talk shows and newspaper comments sent in by readers were very critical of Blacks, labelling us as criminals. The Editorial staff of the Toronto *Sun* was especially critical of Blacks and its readers showed how very unbalanced they were. Their letters to the editor awash with bigotry and hate. One female reporter, no longer at that paper but still in the news business, may remember a phone call made to her even though she may never meet the caller. I told her that we were not all criminals and that most of us like most White Torontonians were were just trying to exist and make something useful of our lives. To her credit, she is no longer the firebrand of racial hatred that she once was, and I have even grown to love hearing her voice on CFRB when she makes her comments.

I carefully read the newspapers to gauge the pulse of the people of the city. In all my reading, I came across only one person, writing in the commentary section who was trying to put things in perspective. I remember him saying that he was Canadian to the core, and had a lot of friends who he spoke to about the situation, none of whom he said felt like the ones writing in, and he was baffled at the reaction of those who wrote as they were one hundred percent against Blacks. Then, later, the Toronto *Star* commissioned two of its staff writers to explore the feelings of Toronto's Whites. One of those reporters was White and the other was Black. He was the only Black person writing for any of Toronto's daily newspapers. This however may not have been indicative of racism at the time. There probably was no other trained Black journalist in the city. The White journalist described how depressed he was at the responses he was getting from people who were glad that Blacks were getting what they "deserved" and that they should "know their place". Such sentiments just made me feel entirely unwelcome in the city. One young White fellow, a passenger in my cab, was rejoicing enthusiastically at the fact that Black people in this country "are going down, man! They are going down". I wanted to ask him when were they ever "up." But as he was saying this, he was getting ready to pay me for the fare and I did not want to be antagonistic and lose the money I had rightfully earned. He left the cab telling me, "I'm with you, man! I'm with you!" My feet felt as heavy as concrete blocks when I tried to drive away. I felt like heading right back to Bellas Gate, St. Catherine, Jamaica. I had no such challenges there.

If only Michael Manley's Jamaica were the same as the country I had left it!

I could not understand the label they placed on us here in Toronto at that time. Some of us came from places where words like "cocaine," "drugs," and "break and enter, etc." were words unheard of in the context they were being used here. I can recall the embarrassment of being stopped by a White policeman who wanted to see my driving particulars and then proceeded to look at my left forearm. I asked him why he was doing that and he never gave me an answer, but an acquaintance of mine told me later that he was looking for needle marks. Prior to coming to Toronto, there were many aspects of criminality I had no knowledge about. Not that we did not have crime in Jamaica, it just never impacted me because I was a "country boy," and had no personal experience with crime. There were others like me as well, so why we were all looked upon as criminals I will never know. Some of the sentiments and references made against us opened my mind on to things that before I never thought of.

A few Blacks became leaders in trying to tackle issues of police harrassment, the bad publicity, and other matters of Black disenchantment. They used such media as the radio and television when they were invited by different program directors. There were members of the establishment who wanted to hear what the Black leaders had to say. We were already a part of the racial demographics of the city, and since most Blacks were here legally, I suppose they could not just wish the "problem" of the Black presence away. Therefore, they had to work with it the best way they could, which I believe in their way of thinking meant that they had to at least establish a dialogue with Blacks. Notable Blacks included Charles Roach, a prominent Black lawyer at the time, and Dudley Lawes, who became a "Black Activist.". There were others whose names I cannot recall, but these two men who seemed to be front and centre of the fight for the fair treatment of Blacks, were never given enough credit for the work they did. Even Blacks, because they were scared and afraid of a White backlash would attack their work of bringing the Black plight to the forefront. But Providence must have allowed them the space and time to complete a needed work. They have subsequently become very tame: maybe their work is done or maybe they no longer think the fight is relevant. I know that much later on Dudley Lawes had been charged for allegedly smuggling human cargo across the border into the United States. I have never heard about the outcome of the charge relative to his guilt or innocence. I do know that he had said he was not guilty of such a charge.

Then there was a Black professor whose name was Wilson Head working at York University who used to speak up for Blacks detaileding evidences of the dislikes and ill-treatment of the police towards them. He received a lot of complains of unfair traffic stops of Blacks by the police especially when they were driving nice cars. They allegedly had a lot of racail slurs hurled at them by the police, many being called "nigger" by the Toronto police. He claimed at the time he was never stopped by the police for vehicular reasons because he drove a Volkswagon Bug. One evening, he was having a meeting in the Bloor/Spadina area of Toronto. It was reported that he was attacked and as-saulted by someone White and someone who was never caught. When they called the police on his behalf, it is alleged that one lone police officer showed up after a longer time than usual. It was reported that the officer had taken public transit to go and deal with the 'emergency' call. Since then, I had never heard Professor Head's voice speaking publicly in favour of Black justice in the Toronto area, or of speaking against the Toronto police. Even as I write this so many years later I chuckle about it just like I did back then. I know that this can be construed as me making fun of a bad situation. The fact is the professor was not badly hurt and I just smiled at the innovative way the police came up with to silence his criticism of them.

There were other incidents after the Albert Johnson affair, which were discrediting both to the police and the Black community. One was the killing of a Black patron by White policemen at a night club on King St W. in down-town Toronto. Police had gone there after receiving complains of some dis-turbance. When they arrived, they accosted the culprit who was a very large and apparently well-muscled Black man who had come to live in the city from Nova Scotia. He was apparently a person with some history of criminal ac-tivity. Out of what I call madness, he grabbed the night stick of the police officer standing nearest to him and allegedly beat him over his head with it. As the police officer, dazed and obviously hurt was going down, he instinc-tively, I believe, drew his service revolver and shot the patron. The man shot remained alive for sometime, but the police allegedly and in a collective man-ner, delayed calling an ambulance to take the badly wounded man to the hos-pital even though he was apparently begging for someone to do so. The other patrons looking on in alarm dared not do what the police officers should have done. By the time the police finally called and the ambulance arrived, the young man had succumbed to the gunshot wound and died at the scene. His death, I believe, was what the police wanted—maybe not necessarily because he was Black, but because in this case, he dared to beat one of their own in their very presence and in the presence of other patrons of the night club. This led to another investigation and, of course, another inquest.

As with the Albert Johnson affair, the police were found to be "acting lawfully" as is most times the case even if the evidence from the perspective of Blacks clearly points in the other direction. On this occasion however, there was no uproar over the night club case in the Black community. For my part, I concluded that the ambulance should have been called immediately and the man could have gotten his just desserts behind the iron bars of a jail-house. Notwithstanding, it was mighty stupid of a Black man to beat a White police officer with his own night stick in Toronto at that or any subsequent time and expect to receive a gold medal from them for his efforts.

Then there was the case of a police officer being shot by a White patron at a Richmond St. night club not very long after. I happened to be the fare in a cab not many days after the incident. The White driver told me how glad he was, not because the police officer was shot, but because the killer was not a Black individual. In his opinion, all hell would have broken loose at the time. I was also very glad the killer was not Black. I believe the situation would have boiled over like an ocean of over-heated oil with no one being able to tell of the repercussions which could have followed.

The killer in that case apparently refused to listen to the dying pleas of the police officer whom he had shot, as well as the promptings of the police personnel on the outside speaking through a loud speaker to him imploring him to allow ambulance personnel and other police officers to attend to the badly wounded one inside and get him to the hospital for medical care. I have wondered why they on the outside did not storm the place and get the dying officer. The poor, unlucky policeman succumbed to the gunshot wounds on the way to the hospital after the shooter finally allowed the ambulance attendants entry. It was only human for me to think back to the Albert Johnson affair, but I could not allow that incident to over-shadow my sympathy for the now dead police officer and his family, who had lost a father and a husband.

These were very sad moments indeed in Toronto's history. It left a pall of blackness and depression over the city for many long weeks. As a Black person, I felt so responsible and guilty when Blacks had at last become involved in ciminal activity, and as I went about my business it seemed, maybe to me alone, that the city was on the verge of an apocalypse. I was terribly saddened by the atmosphere pervading an otherwise very good city. No one seemed sure of what would happen next. Deep down in my heart, it was a place I was growing to love even though I was sometimes made to feel very unwelcome, and even though one could see the obvious hatred for Blacks. I consoled myself that at least there was no open violence against us as that was not the "Canadian way", and for the most part people went about life without much to worry about until these things started to happen. After a while, the blackness ended and life slowly returned to normal.

Bad police relations with Black people continued for quite some time, and as such were given much publicity, probably to the embarrassment of Blacks for complaining about almost everything and making it sound racist, as well as to the police for not letting up on their harrassment of Blacks. It was alleged in the Black community that there was some co-operation between the Jamaica Constabulary and the Metropolitan Toronto Police that the Jamaican police were requested because Jamaicans were the ones responsible for most of the crime, and as the Toronto police were not oriented toward the Jamaican mindset, their own kind would do a lot better job. The Jamaican cops, it was further alleged, would barge into the homes of Blacks, breaking down doors and committing violence against them with reckless abandon. I feared a lot when I heard this because they did not seem to care about innocence or guilt. No one I spoke to felt that the situation warranted such a drastic measure at that time, and let me hurry to say that the allegations were never officially confirmed by anyone in authority.

To the shame and alarm of law abiding Blacks, there was a bank robbery by some young Black men where a White pregnant teller was roughed up and made the conduit whereby these very wicked and very evil young men got the loot they wanted. I was so ashamed about this event that I hardly wanted to show my face in public. Imagine putting a pregnant young woman through the traumatic experience of armed robbery! How emotionally detrimental it must have been for her and her unborn child! To the best of my recollection, they had even physically assaulted her. It made me wonder what kind of demons these fellows were. Luckily for the police, and for us the Blacks too, one of them took a cab as he was leaving the area where the crime was committed, and paid the driver with a very crisp and clean $50 bill. The cab driver, when he heard about the robbery which had taken place in the early morning and near where he picked up this passenger, became suspicious and tipped off the police to where he had dropped off the passenger. Because of this the police were able to apprehend these thugs in a relatively short time before they could have a repeat performance.

Then there was the murder of a young White woman shot by Black gunmen at the Just Desserts Restaurant on Davenport Rd. This was a most alarming and disturbing development for most everyone, especially because this happened in one of the most celebrated areas of the city, very close to the prestigious and upper middle class neighbourhoods of Forest Hills and Rosedale, and the celebrity haunt of Yorkville. Many conscientious Blacks, including myself, were much embarrassed and very shocked at the boldness and utter recklessness of these young men who would dare to do such a thing and in such a place. There were musings by some Blacks I know wishing they were White in those days, and there were Whites who told me that they were glad they were not Black. Those mutterings helped to put a human face on the problem and said in a way that Whites and Blacks were feeling the effects of these crimes together, even though we were on opposite sides of the racial divide.

Later on, there was the incident when a previously deported Black Jamaican shot and killed a White police officer. The immigration officer in that case lost his job over that incident because he had not enforced the deportation order. I was living in Toronto when the restaurant killing and the other noted crimes took place. I felt like leaving the city in a hurry to get away from the shame and disgrace of it all. I also feared a White backlash. Thankfully, I was not in Toronto at the time of the shooting of the police officer. But I had kept in contact with relatives here and was told that the atmosphere then was chilly cold and extremely volatile. I feared for them. And if the police had gotten over-enthusiastic, it could be understood somewhat. This police killer could have gotten the Black population of Toronto into a lot of trouble. Thanks to the intelligence and self-control of the Whites, especially the young White males of Toronto, who did not take the law into their own hands and seek revenge.

From the start, I was never comfortable with Blacks committing crimes in Toronto, and every time a Black person did, I would be incensed. It seemed so inappropriate and ungrateful that a group of people who had arrived on the scene so recently should begin to impact the community so negatively so soon. The fact is I was and is of them. This situation was made all the more disconcerting when looked at from the historical stereotype of Black crime. It looked bad too from the perspective of us being as visible as Blacks are. We stood out so conspicuously. It cannot be denied that the society started to dislike us from the beginning and would not do much in terms of jobs, and other facilities to make changes that would accommodate a wave of new people with a different outlook and background. But they did not bring us here. We came on our own and should have oriented ourselves toward life requirements as they existed in the new homeland. One could reasonably have expected that a society would take a while to face up to the idea that a "new kid" was in town. It made it more awkward when that "new kid" was Black and the society was White. They saw us as unwanted newcomers arriving to take their jobs and enjoy the benefits of their society - benefits such as health care, which their tax dollars had provided for. I don't know that it wasn't human of them to think that way. Other people of other nations would probably have felt the very same and acted worse.

I consider Black new-comers at the forefront of criminal activity to be very ungrateful to a society that had allowed us to live among them in relative peace despite racial overtones. There were no lynching mobs, no burning of Black neighbourhoods, no Hardy Boys gangs roaming the streets looking for and beating up Blacks in Toronto. Except for bad police relations, some employment inequities, and being socially ostracized, Blacks were left to live in peace. By and large, we are much-marginalized, much-ignored people and unless we threaten society in some way or become a criminal element, people don't really care about us except when politicians are seeking our votes, etc. Our most important need is to find a job where we can "eke" out a living and carry on with our lives in silent obscurity as we sometimes must. I am being contextual here and not saying that we must necessarily be content to be mediocre. However, a number of Blacks decided to be revengeful because they were treated badly and started to commit crimes.

Interestingly, we were not the only immigrant group to suffer discrimination at the hands of the Toronto establishment. I spoke to an Italian gentleman who told me that when they came to Toronto they had to fight discrimination also, but they took it silently and allowed their worth in work and talent to speak for them. In time, they earned some respect and admiration, and now they are not so much the butt of jokes as they used to be. He was a bit disappointed that some Blacks chose violence and revenge to voice their dissatisfaction with the society. Subsequent to our coming to Toronto, the Brown people will say that they have suffered much discrimination also. But they are proving themselves to be productive members of society, and so can more of us Blacks if we wish to.

For some Blacks in Toronto, the rule of law and those enforcing it may not have been given their due respect in the early days of our existence here. And to understand the attitude of West Indian Blacks toward law when they came to Toronto, one must understand that a lot of them are free- spirited, were not used to the idea of contending with police officers on almost a daily basis, and would rather be left alone to lead their lives without interference and intrusion. They hate to deal with law enforcement personnel whom, as I pointed out earlier, they neither respect nor like. They also got very angry when they were stopped by the police for no apparent reason. There was no under-standing or appreciation for a "police line-up" where cops bring people of similar physical appearance together to fish out the guilty. So in the beginning, when some Blacks were stopped on the streets by a White police officer saying that "a Black man had just 'committed a crime' and they were trying to find out if this was he", their responses were loud complains about being stopped only because they were Black. They also felt very humiliated because other people, usually White, were looking on. West Indians are some of the smartest people on the planet streetwise, and they know when rubbish is rubbish.

I was stopped a number of times by the police also, but I always greeted them with a good morning or good day, answered them politely, and promptly showed them the documents they asked for. To my mind, even if stopped just because we were/are Black, the police's right to stop a citizen for whatever reason is almost inherent in the job. What is the big deal about being stopped? If there is no law that one has broken then there should be no worry, even though some of the police who lacked sophistication and good breeding were immediately condescending and deprecating.

But maybe if we had behaved in a more civil manner and if our attitudes had been cooperative and somewhat respectful of the police, things probably would not have become the problem that they became in Toronto. To make us stand out even more than we already did, a lot of Blacks did not dress like the rest of the society and even back then some Some Black men wore dread-locks and the traditional colours of the Rastafarians. This was something quite new to the Canadian society and might have helped to alarm the people. Imagine our manner of dressing making us look like we were wearing Joseph's coat of many colours and that too without proper co-ordination. The hair was sometimes uncombed and our beards were scruffy. Even when we were going to church we did not always dress conservatively. Some of us were loud and bold and as one media person said to me, – "aloof and arrogant". These things did not endear us to the Toronto establishment of the time. They did quite the opposite, they made us targets of fear and people did not really know what to do with a group of people they did not understand. Now-a days, even in the heat of summer, it is so very common to see young Black males dressed in heavy winter coats with the hoods pulled over their heads. I feel like chasing them off the streets and out of the malls every time I see that. We really do not need to try to be so different from everyone else.

One of the reasons I think we could have been called arrogant or ungrateful for the privilege of being in Canada is an attitude that a lot of non-White immigrants take to the country. I have heard it said that Canada does not belong to the European. The same is said of America and of South Africa. The opinion is that America and Canada belong to the Natives or the Indians who were here before the Whites came. As a result they argue that it is the Indians who should have the preeminence, not the Whites. I can recall Glen Cole of CITY-TV fame asking Charles Roach mentioned before in an interview if (West Indian) immigrants should not be grateful for the privilege of being in Canada. Mr. Roach was adamant that they should not be and that being in Canada was not a privilege. (There was no indication from Mr. Roach that he was one of those who thought that Canada belonged to the Indians). Personally, I share the sentiment about North America belonging to the Indians even though a higher power than man has the final say. However, I believe that immigrants, nonWhite, White or otherwise, ought to be grateful for the privilege of being in Canada. If we cant be grateful we should not continue living here. And in truth, we probably would not be here if the Natives were still in charge. As hinted before they did not do anything with the continent which would have attracted us to it. The White man is here and it may not be by simple happenstance. "The earth is the Lord's and the fulness thereof, the world and those who dwell therein. He founded it upon the seas and established it upon the waters." He has even determined the boundaries of the seas and all the bodies of water. It is He who gives stewardship over the planet to whoever He wishes, and if we are not able to use its resources in a way that benefit others, He will give it to those who will. I will not disagree that Europeans have destroyed a lot of who and what they saw in North America and also in Africa. But it is probably not just the inclination of Whites to destroy others and what they think stands in their way. Shaka Zulu and other conquering chiefs of Black Africa did the same. In retrospect, Whites have benefitted much of the human race by their conquest/occupation of the Americas. If we did not see a benefit to coming to Canada and other countries "recently" occupied by the White race, we would not be in them. So we should be grateful for the privilege.

The Present Situation in Toronto

In the Toronto of the twenty-first century, the crime of Blacks especially against other Blacks has sky-rocketed. There have been many murders using guns as drug dealers and gangsters eliminate each other. Gangs in Toronto are a fairly recent phenomenon for a city not known before as a place for such, except for motor cycle gangs. But even with them, the level of violence and criminal activity can be considered tame in terms of publicity when compared to the activities of the gangsterism of some Blacks. There have been many killings of some otherwise fine young Black men who found themselves members of these gangs. Sometimes innocent bystanders, who unfortunately just happened to be in the way of the bullets, have also been killed. A case or two have had people killed in their homes by stray bullets intended for others. And who Black or White will ever forget Jane Creba, the young 16 year old who was gunned down by the stray buttlet of Black criminals in the Dundas/Yonge Streest area of Toronto? Can you imagine gangs taking their fights on Boxing Day to the downtown area of a city full of people with no consideration about their lawless activity? Those responsible should not have had time to go before the lenient court system that is in Canada. The service revolvers of the arresting officers should have just accidentally misfired into them.

There is talk in some circles that some people don't care, and indeed people have called into radio talk shows expressing their pleasure at seeing the bad guys killing each other as opposed to killing innocent, law abiding citizens by way of criminal activity. I cannot say that I totally disagreed with the sentiment.

Interestingly, the police force has never been better in their efforts to serve the entire community. They have not chosen to make it a Black crime issue and do nothing about it, as was so common in some other large cities on this continent. They fight it as if it is their professional duty. And they rightly arrest these criminals whenever they can. They have recently arrested a lot of the gang members and had them placed in jails where they belong. They continue to hunt them down and I hope they succeed in rooting out this unwelcome element in the society. Sometimes, due to the strange laws in Canada, a lot of these people get back onto the streets in practically no time at all and continue their criminal activities.

There is the issue of racial profiling, which upset a lot of Black people. But a lot of the young criminals are known to drive a specific kind of vehicle as their trademark. In their efforts to fight crime, it seems logical that if the police are doing spot checks, for example, and they see that kind of vehicle being driven by a young Black male that they would be quick to stop it, and question the occupant/s. In some cases, that is how they get their men and sometimes they get others for other criminal activities other than gang-and drug drug-related offences. Even though some Blacks may be upset with this type of police procedure, we are mostly the ones involved in the crimes in Toronto lately, and the law-abiding ones, of which there are many, should appreciate what the police are trying to do. This kind of police work, I believe, is of service to the community in the context in which it is done and can save lives, etc. if a person stopped had criminal intentions and was by this means prevented from carrying them out. Some innocent Black males, unfortunately, have been "roughed" up by the police because of suspicion and paranoia based upon the vehicle they drive. It is, therefore, up to everyone including the police to be objective and not jump to conclusions as they do their work. The Toronto community in general is not as openly bigoted as it used to be, and is also interested in seeing crimes solved even though the victims and most of the young men committing them are Black. The politicians as well are very keen to rebuild and protect the now tarnished image of the city. To stem the tide of gang warfare and drug-related crimes, the police in and around Toronto have made great strides infiltrating these gangs and bringing lawbreakers to justice. I say more power to them for that.

Blacks and Crime in the United States of America.

In this segment, I will take a look at the state of things in America as it relates to criminal activities involving Blacks. I will address the historical social ills, which I believe are the likely reasons for Blacks committing crimes in America in the numbers they do. I will address who and what I think were and are responsible for initiating these criminal activities, while calling on Blacks to take responsible action to cease and desist from these criminal activities. I will also make mention of two high- profile cases where celebrity Blacks have been implicated for crimes committed, citing subconsciously the effect on the Black community. Lastly, but just as important, I will close with some damning statistics on the incidents of Black crime in that country today. Though Blacks are just above 11% of the population of the United States, they commit more than 50% of the crime in most or all cases. America, it seems, is going the other extreme where the issue of Black crime is concerned when one takes into account the present reaction of civil and police officials in regards to this epidemic.

Taking a look at the situation in the United States in regards to crime, it could be said that Blacks have been a target of the law enforcement agencies from the moment they were forced to be a part of that country. Not even being considered as persons in the first place, their entry and stay was with hostile intent, the sole purpose being servitude, and it seems that the hostility was so widespread that only if the individual White slave owners wanted to, would they be shown the slightest bit of kindness. While early on there were Blacks in the U.S. who were free to some extent, they were looked upon as a breed of a different sort. Needless to say, most wanted these "non-persons" kept in line. Seemingly they had a brain, could probably think, and may have begun to show some kind of resistance to some of the evil treatment they were receiving. Even dumb animals are known to strike back when teased or treated with violence. So why would'nt humans?

In a country where most everyone hated them primarily because they were Black and because they were slaves, how would things play out? The stage was set for them to be deprived of every bit of dignity that a human should have, if they had they been considered humans under the laws of that country. These laws had already existed for the protection of its White citizens, with much of the privileges reserved for the male of the specie. The very ant on the ground would be treated better than Blacks, and that would be for a very long time. There are stories and stories and countless cases where Blacks in the United States have been treated worse than dogs before the law. And while things are changing—thanks to the advent of the Internet and 'media outlets' like YouTube, MySpace, and so on—some things I've heard happening to Blacks in that land goes beyond nightmares and are discussed so openly and in such a matter-of-fact manner that it is appalling that there are not widespread opposition to the order of things and calls for the authorities to make changes in regards to the callousness with which they were treated, and even now continues though to a somewhat lesser extent. For many Americans it was just business as usual with nary a thought about the effects that their treatment may have had on such a large, though in most ways politically and socially insignificant segment of that country's population.

Even in these postmodern days, the stereotyping there is nothing short of incredible. A White woman kills her children and blames it on some non-existent Black man she "came" across. White women cry rape to put Black men in jail; Black men are accused of crimes, and though found to be totally innocent, are put in jail for decades just because they are Black. White males commit criminal offences and blame it on whatever Black person they can find. White police and district attorneys anxious to "solve" crimes allegedly plant evidence on innocent Black people, and then get them convicted and thrown in jail for very long sentences so they can "move up the ladder of success". Can you comprehend that, readers; superior White men and women "moving up the ladder of success" by lying and cheating to convict the innocent? Sometimes the innocently convicted are executed, even though the ones who arrested and convicted them know in their hearts that they were innocent. At the same time, those really guilty of the crimes are left free to continue their criminal activities. White drug lords get rich by poisoning Black neighbourhoods with the free flow of drugs, while law enforcement goes only after the poor Black idiots who fall into the trap of marketing the poison for these rich White criminals to the detriment of their own people. And the list goes on!

Now, this is not to say that Blacks are not guilty of terrible crimes in that country. They are guilty a lot of times and it makes well-meaning people feel very uncomfortable. And they continue to commit crimes with reckless abandon. I watch *48 Hours* and shows like that all the time, and I just keep wondering if some of these young men walk around with concrete in their skulls instead of the usual grey fleshy matter that is supposed to be there. Sometimes too they are handsome, promising, and fairly intelligent young men. I can tell of the intelligence because of the jobs they hold sometimes

But let us examine the stereotype that Blacks alone are the perpetual criminals of society, especially in America. It is one of those nonsensical conclusions that should be carefully looked at nonetheless, because on the surface it does seem to have a ring of truth to it. And like we say in Jamaica — "You never see smoke without fire existing somewhere." In almost every nonBlack country on earth the stereotype exists and is most times consciously or subconsciously promulgated. One does not have to be Africoid to earn that label. Being dark-skinned is often good enough for those who love to label. When did society first start thinking of Blacks only in terms of committing crimes and casting this undeserved label at us? I have been reading the Toronto *Sun* for a very long time. It first came to my attention in 1972 when I migrated to Canada. There was a columnist for that newspaper whose feature on Sundays and Mondays was called "Crime Flashback." Though I read that section for years and years, and learned about some of the most heinous crimes in human history, I can count on one hand the number criminals in his column who were Black.

I watch *American Justice, Cold Case Files, City Confidential* and others of the kind on television. They also tell of very terrible crimes. The number of White criminals involved far outweighs the number of Blacks most times in those episodes. Do these producers simply refrain from doing episodes on Black crime on their shows, or do they show them as White when they are really Black? I know that on *America's Most Wanted*, Blacks are featured very often and for some really terrible deeds. I know also from reading the newspapers and listening to the news that Blacks do commit a lot of crimes in America as I said before. But I am now seeing that they are not the only ones who do. I see that Whites, Hispanics, and Orientals also commit a lot of crimes. When I was growing up it was quite rare to hear of White criminals in America.

Some of the blackest deeds relating to crimes have been committed by Whites. From what I have learned, they are usually more prone to be the serial killers, serial rapists, the sexual abusers of small children or the pedophiles, and the pornographers. Jeffrey Dahmer, Ted Bundy, Jack the Ripper, John Casey are names that immediately come to mind and are names that have made whole nations tremble. These men were/are White. The trouble is that Blacks have been getting most of the coverage in the spontaneous media such as daily newspapers, television news reports, and radio. Reporting on criminal activity in America was tainted with such bigotry that mostly they were portrayed as criminals. Because of Americans' penchant for keeping statistics on Black crime it makes it seem that Blacks were the only ones committing crimes. I have also noticed that of the developed Western countries, America possesses the greatest number and the most hardened and depraved criminals—White, Black, or Hispanic. Some also come out of England.

I am wondering if Blacks started their careers in crime with the idea of just getting by in mind or as a revenge mechanism because of the ills they were suffering? But even as I write this, it does not mean that I excuse any crime committed by Blacks in any way, shape, or form. Breaking the law is breaking the law, and a crime is a crime. I am merely saying that White emphasis on Black crime especially in America is quite hypocritical given the fact that they may have set the stage by denying them what they needed to survive, as well as the fact that so many White and Hispanic Americans are also such hardened criminals. As mentioned above, if you don't feed all your animals, some will slink away and die, and some will become hostile and take by force what has been maliciously denied them. White legislative and corporate America had a responsibility to take care of Blacks in the beginning because they brought them there with only a loincloth to cover their behinds and their genitals, and that was barely so. Then after they worked for them for centuries they would not even give them a piece of land in most cases to even build a hut.

It is very noteworthy that as Blacks were being labelled for every conceivable crime in America, that even some White governors and other high officials were themselves criminals. Some were plotting and facilitating the demise of Blacks, were taking bribes, and were supporters of the Ku Klux Klan who murdered so many Blacks in cold blood. It is alleged that the KKK even cut out unborn babies out of their expectant Black mothers' wombs without the slightest concern, and has mentioned before. Some of America's White leaders were themselves members of this wicked organization, dedicated to the total and brutal annihilation of the Black race in America, and practiced their evils while disguising themselves under the hoods of the KKK. So while White Americans were penning Black crimes, they should have penned their own right beside those of the Blacks. They were pointing to the little specks in the eyes of Blacks while beams were in theirs.

In America, Blacks are under this perpetual canopy of infamy, labelled as criminals from the time they are born till the time they die, even if they have never committed a single crime in their lives. It is believed that no matter how exalted the Black man in America may be, he is never beyond the accusing hand of a White society of one of its favourite pastimes, that of keeping statistics on Black crime. While the figures that I will produce later will agree that the incidents of Black crime are certainly disproportionate to the Black population where such is true, I can also say here that even corporate America, owned and run by Whites, is not above the miasma of criminality. But sometimes they call theirs "white-collar crimes," giving them a "human" face. In the late 1990s, America did not make the list of the 100 least corrupt countries in the world out of the 216 or so included in the United Nations count. So it would seem that every segment of the American society, Black or otherwise, rich or poor, stops at the feeding trough of criminal behaviour of one kind or another, even though till recent years, aside from the celebrities of crime like Jesse James and Bonnie and Clyde, Blacks were disproportionately called out.

The passion then for White America keeping statistics on Black crime committed there seems to require an object much more worthy of this misuse of time and energy—including that of looking for their own reflection in the same mirror that they set up for Black people. What kind of satisfaction can a dominant White society such as America gain from gloating that its Black citizens are "criminals"? Are they so happy that their conquered "former slaves" are still impeded by lack of progress even in the very elementary basics of self-control? Can they not see their own culpability in setting in place the delinquency which caused the social and emotional trauma precipitating this aberrant behaviour for most of that country's Black criminals? This is especially grievous when one realizes that they are not using the information gathered to help these criminals in any positive way. Though the statistics are there, to me those who compile them are acting like a little boy who though himself a participant in the antics with his siblings starts adding up only the things that they did so he could run home and tell his mommy on them in the hope of getting his naughtiness overlooked and save his little behind from the spanking it deserves.

And why do Blacks continue to commit so many crimes in America after all the adverse publicity and shame earned because of it? They still have a choice in what they do, in spite of very unfortunate circumstances, and even though we all expect that a certain segment of any society will grow up and commit crimes no matter the colour of their skin. While I strongly believe that the bulk of the blame for the problem of Black crime in the American society lies at the door of the neglectfulness and almost complete disregard for the plight of Blacks that the Whites practiced, I also believe that Blacks and the Black leaders need to do a lot more than they are doing to end this pattern of destructive behaviour.

Apparently there were reports of Black crime in America even in the very early post slavery days. These crimes I imagine were crimes of revenge committed out of frustration for being treated so poorly by those who must have started to become alarmed and afraid of a group of people so underprivileged yet still willing to break the law. The White society was creating a monster but was too indolent or incognizant of its responsibility to address the problem. And where did Blacks find guns and other weapons used by them back then? They were never known to own shares in the Smith and Wesson gun manufacturing company. The Whites should have known all along that if they provided help for these people such as gainful employment, education, and made them useful members of the society, that fewer and fewer of them would become criminals. But they continued to ignore the problem until now it is much more than they can handle. As one White fellow who used to live in America said to me many years ago, "Maybe if America had known how much of a problem a (neglected) Black populace would become, the leaders would never have brought them onto their soil as slaves in the first place". According to him the sentiment was a water cooler discussion across much of White America at the time. That sentiment was in hindsight, however. The concentration should then have been placed on solutions as soon as possible.

Nonetheless, the troubling factor is that the criminal bent among a lot American Blacks now almost seem like an inherited trait because of the sheer number of the criminal activities committed by them. It could be seen that way, or it can be argued that the sons have been suffering from the same dis-affection, hate, and the same social ostracism and detrimental stereotyping as the fathers, foisted upon them by their White captors which have caused the mental trauma, and behaviour disorders leading to a diminished mental ca-pacity to function as healthy positive human beings and causing them to even-tually turn to crime. Leaving others over whom we have control and power in neglect, isolation, and poverty has never resulted in self-esteem, productiv-ity, or any other real benefit to society. As pointed out earlier, Blacks looked up to Whites back them as their masters and "caretakers." But most Whites care little for these ex-slaves. They brought them in when they needed then for forced labour, but now wanted to discard them like they would a piece of rug that had spent its usefulness. In short, they hated Blacks. If you have sowed hate dont expect love. In all the years I saw my father planting crops, he has never reaped tomatoes from the beans he planted.

But if the Blacks who went to America as slaves were so docile that they were not even able to resist capture, where then did they learn the violence they now are practicing, and where and why did they learn to become crimi-nals? I believe it can be logically concluded that they learned all about violence and how to become criminals from White people right there in America. There is no doubt that they learned all the cruelty they started to practice from seeing the many cases of beatings, lynchings, and hangings with other forms of cruelty that their White masters and civil and law enforcement personnel practiced against them. Having witnessed and experienced all that cruelty, it was logical for them now to be very cruel themselves. They turned to crimes, self hate, and other forms of destructive behaviour as a natural outcome of what they had seen and learned. It was and is hardly any different from chil-dren doing what they see their parents do.

Any group of persons of any colour or race will eventually turn to aber-rant behaviour when they have been mistreated with cruelty and unfairness, and because the basic human nature has in itself its own sense of right and wrong it will extract from society that justice it should have been rendered. Most times, this takes the form of unlawful revenge, and even former slaves, still considered to be non-humans, have this disposition and know when they have been pushed to the limit. Sometimes turning to crime is viewed by those who commit crimes as an act of self preservation, or as a display of the last vestige of their misguided definition of self esteem. It is also some people's way of feeling good about themselves. Thankfully, most Blacks have chosen a different way to express this same spirit of self preservation. If this was not so, how else could Nelson Mandela have gone from a beaten prisoner of almost three decades in the jail cell of one of the world's most cruel and repressive regimes to the presidency of his native country without extracting the penalty he should have from those who were responsible for his ill treatment? Also how else would we have had a Dr. Martin Luther King and others like him who refused to use crime as a way of changing the mindset of the society that hated them? More Blacks can learn a lesson here that Whites should have learned. Dr. Martin Luther King's approach of non-violence has accomplished more good for them than all the crime Blacks are committing in America today.

It is to White America's discredit that they can now "boast" that roughly 30% of young Black males in their country are in jail at any given time. They ought to be ashamed of themselves in this context. Instead they seem to be ever so happy as if they have just won a platinum record for their endeavours. And as long as White America continues to sweep reality under the rug and consider itself oblivious to the situation, it will be building more jails to house an ever-increasing Black criminal population. Unless White America pays a different kind of attention to this problem it will continue to exist. The problem cannot just be wished away. Just because the ostrich has "put its head in the sand" so it does not see its predicament does not mean the lion is not closing in on its tail.

On my first trip to New York City where my sister once lived in the mid-seventies, I happened by a bridge one early morning, just about sun-up. People were emerging from under the bridge where they sleep in quite astounding numbers, at least to me. I could not believe I was seeing this in America. Those people were not only Black, there were White ones also. Because it was around Christmas time, the temperature was very cold, I saw one man in the street whose pair of shoes was newspaper first folded around his feet and up to his ankles. He then wrapped plastic around the newspaper and tied it with some strings to keep his street-made shoes in place. He was just standing there in the cold. I gazed for longer than was necessary at this sight of human neglect and tragedy while at the same time admiring his genius. Not even in the deep country of Jamaica had I seen anything quite so intuitive. But the overwhelming thought in my mind was, "How could this happen in America, the richest country in the world?" I understood at the time that New York was the richest city in America.

When I discussed this with someone, the person said to me that America's leaders probably know of these people's situation but may be too unwilling to address it for fear that such would then become publicly known and would disgrace the country. He said for them to speak of the problem would be an acknowledgement of its existence, and that they would rather not do. I concluded then that the leaders of America probably thought the same about Black social problems and their crimes, only in this case they were trying to blame the crime on the "inferiority" of the Black mind. It was baffling to me to learn that Washington DC, the very seat of the government of the United States was such a crime-ridden place. Surely America must know that foreign diplomats and others would see and hear about the plight, poverty, and crimes of Blacks as they come and go from a place as popular as the nation's capital? Is the American government so keen on showing the world that Blacks are criminals that it would make little or no attempt to clean up the problem right there under its nose? It is so very typical for White Americans to hasten to their jobs in the skyscrapers of their cities by 8 a.m or so in the morning, then rush back to their homes in the suburbs just before sundown, leaving just before the Ides of Crime move in to do their lawless deeds under the cover of darkness. As long as their offices are still there in the morning when it's time to work again they seemingly don't give a damn about what happens overnight.

As the crimes committed by Blacks in America increases, the justice system turns even more harshly against them. They are given longer and more unreasonable jail terms; they are charged with crimes they sometimes have not even committed; and they are sent to the death chambers much more frequently than the other races who commit similar crimes. Even some White Americans are forced to admit that because most Blacks are poor and cannot afford to defend themselves, they are treated much worse than others. And this from a country which runs all over the world trumpeting the abuses of human rights by despotic regimes that they target, and sometimes, except in the case of the former South Africa, would even press economic sanctions against those nations because of what it calls human rights violations. What injustice to treat the poor so unfairly from a nation so "enlightened"! These things reinforce in the minds of some Blacks that White America has no use for them, that they are not a part of that country even though they were born there. This probably serves to make Blacks even angrier and more disposed to be disruptive to that society. And the price the society pays is the continued detrimental criminal behaviour of Blacks. Some White Americans might say it is no concern of theirs, especially when the Blacks are segregated in their own neighbourhoods and commit their crimes there. But in the final analysis, does this not reflect badly on the entire nation?

Politicians would rather spend lots of money building jails, and hiring prison staff. They will feed the Blacks and clothe them, get them a little of the needed medical attention, provide them with entertainment, and may even let them study, but all this is being done for them only when they are in jail. The governing bodies put few or no remedial programs in place for these young Black criminals, nor will they provide them the alternate opportunities early on for them to grow up with a different perspective. America seems too pre-occupied with its capitalist status to have too many social programs for its Black and ethnic population other than the building of jails. Welfare payments, as I understand it, are now much curtailed and had accomplished very little anyway to enhance the standard of living and opportunities for Blacks. In all, welfare was and is a poor attempt to remedy social problems because young men and women who sit around collecting welfare money find lots of mischief to get into with so much spare time on their hands. People are simply being paid to be lazy and unproductive and to plan evil. Poverty translates to insufficient funds needed to get the proper nourishment needed for healthful living, and the proper state of mind. Then medical America runs around with another finding: that Blacks disproportionately prone to diabetes and other diet related diseases. Could that be caused by the stress and poor diet because of the poverty that those ones are kept in which may be the cause of that?

It would be much better to spend money to train them for usefulness. It is much better to have people doing something to help themselves. Perhaps the government should make the people on welfare go out and clean up the many dirty streets and neighbourhoods of the nation. This would at least give them the oxygen their brains need to aspire a little to a better existence. It might even inspire some to get off welfare to start with.

America's pre-occupation with attributing criminal activities, real or imagined, to its Black population is so pervasive that even the Blacks who make it professionally still suffer from the stigma of being seen as criminals. I read an American newspaper article some times ago about Blacks riding in elevators to their office with Whites. It went on to say that some of the White women have the habit of clinging tighter to their purses as soon as a Black man enters these elevators. I brought this up to a White American woman from Georgia. She had a lot to say about the plight of Blacks in her former state as she then lived in Texas. She found stories and episodes of Blacks being chased out of some White neighbourhoods in her former state most amusing. When I mentioned to her about this stigma attached to us, she simply smiled her pretty smile and said that this was something "Blacks just have to learn to live with." She offered no apologies and said what she said not only with the smile on her face but almost with a note of triumph. If only she and the others know the shame and belittlement this brings, and the animosity and hate that grow in the hearts, and how much self-control law abiding Blacks have to exercise just to make it through each day, they would not utter and live such sentiments. It also does something else. It precipitates a desire in the hearts of those who suffer, to hurt those who practice these infractions against them. We all need to become a bit more discreet and change our attitudes if we want other people to change theirs. Imagine the animosity of people who know that they are hated by so many around them. If some Whites were placed in the same situation as Blacks and had to live our existence, then they might begin to understand. A nation might have the best armed police services to combat crime, but if they don't learn about the human psyche and show some consideration for the fact that the people they despise see themselves as deserving of respect and will wreak havoc on society for despising them, the problems will continue. Force and neglect does not put an end to crime, but kindness and civility may. White South Africa's massive brute force and neglect of the Blacks finally led to its downfall. They use to go out against unarmed and harmless Black civilians with enough fire power to take out the Third Reich, but where are they today?

But how are affected Blacks to combat this problem of neglect without turning to crime, and how can such a large number of them be turned from the present mindset to live law abiding lives? Someone, somewhere will have to make a conscious effort to effect a real change from the "normal" way things have been going for so long. Most likely, those Blacks will have to take charge of their own lives and make a serious and deliberate effort to do things differently. There are enough intelligent and professional people among the race who should look beyond themselves and see the plight of their own people. Black professionals and businesspeople need to collectively address this problem. They have the money and the wherewithal to help out. They can't hide, because no matter how insulated we think we are because of our success and our wealth, and the prestige of our addresses, the colour of our skins puts us all in the same boat. Sometime from our "Ebony Towers" we have the tendency to mostly ignore the plight of our people because we have "arrived" When I visited Soweto in South Africa, I saw there the homes and automobiles of the well-off Blacks. They drove Mercedes Benzes, Audis, BMWs, and other luxury cars as if they manufactured them. But on the other side of the same township I met Black mothers who fed their children sometimes when they are hungry with only a cup of water. I saw that with my own two eyes. Those did not even have electricity, a sewage system or running water. Both groups are Blacks, and both live in Soweto. When I gave a few *rands* to three of these poor mothers and to some of the others just watching I was told not to do so by the tour guide who was also Black but who was well-off enough to live in her own house among the comfortable in Randburg. I learned further that the only contact that the richer Sowetan Black males had with these poor women was when they came on their side to buy sex from them. Hopefully that is not always the case, but I am writing what I heard. As Blacks, please dont give the Whites the impression that you dont care about your own people. More than a few of them have told me how divided against each other and how discombobulated they know us to be. While I point out White culpabality in the situation we too must do our part to combat whatever disfunctionality we ourselves have identified or caused.

When I questioned the logic of having children when they are not able to afford them, these women told me that those men who bought their bodies did not want to wear condoms. They wanted the "natural feel" of the womens genitals and insisted that they were paying customers and should get it the way they wanted it. This gave birth to children that were not being properly cared for. So in this instance these well-off Black men were adding to the problem of these poor Black women. As far as I am concerned, it is men like those who should be made infertile.

We must help our own when we can. We can start just where we are. Even if we start with one individual such is progress. One might wonder out loud about what will be the benefit of changing one individual. The answer is that it can become a good habit which others can emulate. If the effort is continued, eventually there will be so many changed individuals that it will start making a real difference. Start with responsible parenting. Let each Black mother and Black father decide that his or her child will be the focus of positive stimuli. Cut out the excess television and bad movies. Teach your child to respect the rule of law. Make yourself your child's best friend as well as a sensible parent. From the time of its conception, think of the unborn child as someone who will make a very important contribution to society. As the child grows up, tell that child that he or she can one day be someone well-respected by society. Encourage the child to seek a respectable profession. As long as he or she is a useful contributing member of society, it hardly matters what they choose to do for a profession as long as they are productive. Let the child know that God considers him or her to be His child and loves it as much as He loves everybody else. Give your child the greatest sense of value possible.

There is a better way for our young men than just to copy and perpetuate a life of crime. Maybe we can introduce them to better role models than presently occupy the space reserved for such idols in their lives. Where are the mothers and fathers of these young men? Where are the community leaders? Where the government and law enforcement bodies are absent by design, we need to step in. Unless it very negatively affects the economy and social well-being of the White-run state, no one in government will be addressing this appropriately for us, and most times when they do address it, the result will not be remedial. It will be more jail cells, longer jail time, and the continued incarceration of even the innocent. We owe it to ourselves to dispel the negative stereotype, which for so long has been most deliberately and successfully used to keep us from improving.

One of the most disturbing things to me is the committing of a crime by a celebrated Black. I have often wondered if these people placed in such glare of prominence ever think that their actions are carefully scrutinized by most everyone. While it may be true that the number of Black celebrities who commit awful crimes is very small, the potential negative effect is enormous. I have also noticed how eager the media is to make a very big issue of celebrity crime. Usually the crimes of Black celebrities receive more publicity than those of their White counterparts. Not that this should come as any surprise. However, if we know that we are made the subjects of this scrutiny, we should do much more than our best to ensure that we are law-abiding. As indicated earlier in this book, and on more than one occasion, Blacks should recognize our position in White and other non-Black societies and make an effort to avoid criminal activity even when we are not celebrities. It is just that the crimes of Black celebrities are much more detrimental to the Black community as a whole. There are those ready to point fingers and say "I told you so," when popular Blacks mess up. They are happy to see the "great ones" among us fall because it reinforces the stereotype in their minds that we will forever have a criminal problem even among our celebrities. Some of the Whites say in South Africa to our detriment, — "It's in the genes." Let us get it out of the genes.

I would like to use two cases by which I will make my point about the effects of criminal activities on the part of Black celebrities. One might say that I did not make any specific mention of the detrimental effects of White police brutality on Blacks. To this I will say, read all of the book.

The first is the case of Rae Carruth, a prominent former member of a few years ago of the Carolina Panthers. My first exclamation after hearing the story was, what would make such a promising young man the architect and planner of such a despicable deed? His girlfriend was six months pregnant with his own child. It is alleged that they had just spent an evening together watching a movie at his house after which he decided they would go to hers. He had arranged with three other men to kill her on the way to her house. He pulled his car in front of hers at a given spot on the highway to slow her down. The other men moved into place and did what they were contracted by him to do. Fortunately for justice, she had a cell phone and called 911 to report the crime while she was still able to do so. This phone call and her subsequent statements from her hospital bed, along with the confessions of the actual killer, were able to convict Carruth of this very {black} deed.

How could this young man do such a thing! And what made him think he would get away with this crime? It was pointed out by his accomplices that he had no plans to marry this woman and no intentions of paying child support for the child soon to be born. As is so typical of so many Black young men, he liked the fun but was unwilling to take the responsibility for the child. I have wondered if this young man had ever considered the outcome of what he planned, or if he ever weighed the cost of his misdeed against all other costs before he committed this crime? As he was earning millions every year, what was the problem paying out fifty, sixty, or even a hundred thousand dollars per year in child support? It might have been a big price to pay for having sexual relationships with a woman without protection against pregnancy, but it would still be a small price when compared to losing the much greater income of a lifetime, embarrassing himself and his family in front of the world, losing everything he had achieved and had hoped to keep, and then spending the rest of his life in jail. On top of all this there is the death of an innocent young woman. I hope that others might read this and learn the poignant lesson that it contains. The hit men themselves, in this case, displayed the same lack of wisdom as the planner, Rae Carruth. For a few thousand dollars they agreed to snuff out the life of this promising young woman and her unborn child. In their minds, the life of this precious young woman must have been very cheap indeed. Where are common sense, compassion, and pity when needed? And what a very gullible bunch of nincompoops they were to do what they did! Sometimes I think that every Black male celebrity in America, should immediately upon their rise to stardom, appoint for themselves a good moral counsellor if they dont already have one to advise them. Some do need to spend the few dollars it takes to keep themselves from making bad choices. As well a decision to abide by a sound code of moral conduct would really help.

I live here in Canada and read about these things or see them on television, and even from my location, I feel embarrassment and shame for these activities, much the same as I feel chagrined at the treatment meted out to Blacks by the society in which they live. Here was a successful young man with the world at his feet and yet he was still unable to unshackle himself from the dictates of a criminal mind, and see the larger viewpoint of acting responsibly for the good of himself, his family, and race. And he, with the spotlight on him, seemed to have had no embarrassment and apparently felt no remorse for what he did. How sad!

Another case that comes to mind is that of one of America's most celebrated Black former football players. This very foolish man! If he had just allowed his wife to leave him peacefully, or if he had just chosen to leave her himself without incident, how differently his life story would have read, and how celebrated his life could still have been, and how much grace as a race we could still have been enjoying because of him? He could have gone, I believe, into a lot of homes in that country, and pretty much the entire world, and request the hand of any unmarried young woman and the answer would probably been positive. Instead, he allowed jealousy and insecurity to cause him to murder his beautiful wife, the very mother of his very lovely children. It was too bad that for all his physical stature and his international fame he possessed so little self-esteem, and was so devoid of self-control that he brought himself down to the level of a cold-blooded murderer. As a Black individual, I used to be so proud of this flashy young man dashing through America's airports to catch his "rented" car.

I watched his criminal trial with very keen interest indeed, hoping that I would find some reason to believe that he could not have been guilty of doing such a thing. There was enough doubt in my mind with regards to his guilt when I watched the criminal proceedings, even though to my searching mind there were still holes in the story. But at the civil trial, I could no longer believe that he was innocent. The defence then was almost non-existent, which led me to conclude that if he were really innocent it would have been as vigorous as at the criminal trial. I later read the book written by his former house-mate about the matter, and that reading solidified the guilt of this man firmly in my mind. After reading it I was left wondering who else could have done it. The most astounding thing to me about this case is the total lack of presence of mind he displayed when he was planning his crime. I find it hard to believe that he was so blinded by his desire to kill that he had no thought for his social stature and prominence in the American society, which had accepted him so well and loved him so much over the years. He also should have been thinking about the effects of his crime of the Black population.

We have to start looking at the larger picture of societal responsibility. I learned this from an older gentleman I knew when I was growing up. He was an avid reader of the newspapers and listened frequently to his radio. In the deep hill country of Jamaica when I was growing up, these were to us indispensable means of learning about the world. Though most unlikely himself to ever commit any wrong act, he would always recite the likelihood of anything wrong he might do being reported on the radio or be written about in the newspapers, and by his imagination gauging public opinion. Sometimes I would laugh at the idea of his being so unnecessarily panicky, but I began to see that there was some logic to measuring one's course of action against likely outcomes. The more celebrated one is, the more reason to be careful. If our station in life is humble we should still be discreet and tactful. And I know we can all make mistakes, but premeditated crime is not a mistake. It is a purposeful and wilful act.

I want to include here a very disturbing bit of information where actual statistics on Black crime are concerned. It is believed that Blacks in America are seven times more likely than people of other races to commit murder, and eight times more likely to commit robbery. When Blacks commit crimes of violence, they are nearly three times more likely than others to use a gun and more than twice as likely to use a knife. Of the nearly 770,000 violent inter-racial crimes committed every year involving Blacks and Whites, Blacks committed 85 percent % and Whites 15%. Blacks commit more violent crimes against Whites than against other Blacks. Forty-five percent of their victims are White, and 43% are Black. Blacks are estimated to be 39 times more likely to commit a violent crime against a White person than a White person against a Black person. Blacks are also 136 times more likely to commit robbery, and are two and a quarter times more likely to commit officially designated hate crimes against Whites than is the other way around. While only 10 percent %

of youth gangs are White, Blacks are 15 times more likely than Whites to be members of youth gangs.

Between 1980 and 2003, the US incarceration rate more than tripled from 130 per 100,000 to 482 per 100,000, and the number of prisoners increased from 320,000 to 1.39 million. Blacks are seven times more likely to be in prison than Whites. In almost every category of major crime classification in America today, Blacks are the leaders, and it is believed by some that in a lot of cases some Blacks who commit crimes are not arrested or prosecuted because the police and civil officials are now becoming sensitive to the cries of Black activists who are never unwilling to publicize their views on police brutality, racial profiling, and the inequities of the legal system in America. In 2001, there were 600,593 Blacks in state and federal prisons in America out of a population of 35.4 million Blacks. This fits an incarceration rate of 1,695 Blacks per 100,000. While this figure is alarming, it means there were nearly 35 million Blacks living out of jail in America. So they should not really, therefore, refer to all American Blacks as criminals.

Something to think about at the same time: it is unlikely that all White police and civil officials in the United States are racist. Some do their jobs without racial taint or bias. Where that is the case, their hands should not be tied where arrest and prosecution of criminals are concerned. And if Blacks are as prone to crime, as indeed it seems to be, it should be understood that the police officer on the beat is not there to go into instant historical recall of Black disenfranchisement when he sees a Black person committing a crime. His job is to make a justifiable arrest in such a case. The point that I am making is that the statistics do speak for something, and it is up to those Blacks so affected to change their focus and start living good and responsible lives. It is really very difficult for me to believe that some of us can be such dunces that for all the news and shows on television pointing out Black crime that it cannot penetrate our minds to conclude that we should change. As my mother used to tell me; two (2)wrongs dont add up to one (1) right. We cant live the present life and plan the future actuated by revenge for the injustices of the past.

I believe that a grave responsibility rests upon the shoulders of the members of the American Black community to endeavour to make contact with Blacks wherever they can find them, and give them advice and counsel in regards to curbing their criminal behaviour when such is the case, and teach them to conduct themselves as if their behaviour is truly reflective on Blacks all over the world. This is especially so when they are celebrities. The same practice probably is needed in other countries too.

I am aware that some will wonder who or what gives me the right as a non-American Black, and as a non- American more specifically, to write on issues pertaining to that society. When I was living in Texas, I met a Black woman who said she was one of those children who was a pioneer for bussing in the Little Rock, Arkansas school integration. She was spat upon by White students in the school and hated by practically the whole state, not to mention much of White America in general. Yet, when I commented on the racial injustices of the American society she was quick to tell me that I had no right to make negative comments about her country. I really wanted to ask her in sarcasm about when America decided that the country was the domain of Blacks, but I held my tongue because I did not feel like getting into an argument with her. In Texas, every White person I met thought I was a Black American until I spoke to them. They found out by my voice signature, otherwise called my accent, that I was not. However, when I lived in the Philippines for a while, they thought for sure that I was a Black American and referred to me as such. The accent, (voice signature) did not make a difference to them because they did not know any better, and certainly my skin colour and hair kinkiness could not fool either group about the fact that I was Black. The point that I am making is that this "mark that has been set upon us" sets us apart from anyone else, and people believe that we are all the same. Whatever issues concern Black people anywhere, in my opinion, concerns Black people everywhere and specifically do concern me. I have been a conscientious observer of the Black experience to use a Jamaican phrase, "ever since my daddy was a boy," or "ever since my eyes were at my knees."

Maybe some of the successful ones among us now think themselves suddenly removed and insulated from the stigma placed on the backs of ordinary Blacks. But now, let's not kid ourselves. We should not ever cease to be aware that we will always be Black, and that this is more than just a skin colour description in the minds of some. To a lot of them, this is a label and a very negative one at best. When we start to really built our own engines of wealth and prosperity, and educate ourselves appropriately, then we can start opening our mouths in arrogant self-pride and vain self-adulation. It will even be better when we start working to eradicate crime and social angst from among our people and our ranks to the improvement of all.

So if I should be taken to task for meddling in Black American affairs, I would answer by saying that this world is a global village and that some of us humans are wired to have emotions and opinions about any issue that affects the lives of other humans anywhere in the world, especially when they are racially linked to us. I may not be speaking for some here, but I may be speaking for others. And this is not to say that I have no concern for others not of my race because, as I said before, I am of mixed ancestry and hates no one, and as a matured and somewhat mellowing human being I try to love everyone. In this book I simply am a defender of the helpless and the innocent underdog in every case. God has endowed me with this inviolable privilege. I was angry with Idi Amin when he took advantage of the few Whites in Uganda, and when he kicked out innocent Indians out of his country where I find such was without just cause. I was angry when I read about what the Nazi's did to the Jews in Germany, and what the Japanese did to the innocent babes in the Philippines in the Second world War. I was mad at Iran when they held innocent Americas as hostages in the late 1970's, and I will continue to be angry with those who treat Blacks cruelly. When Blacks kill innocent Whites I will continue to be angry with them too.

Given the space and time, I will speak on any issue that I think concerns the Black race, good or bad, and from any location on planet Earth. And given more time and space, I will speak out against any mistreatment of any group of people-White, Black, Brown, or Yellow, as long as such is defending their rights to live and prosper on this planet.

CHAPTER NINE
Apartheid and the Blacks of South Africa

In this chapter, I will be talking about the apartheid system of South Africa, my visit to the country and the changes it made to my feeling and understanding of apartheid, my visit to Soweto, the former home of Nelson Mandela and still the home of Winnie Mandela and Bishop Desmond Tutu, my visit to the Apartheid Museum, the arrival of the White man in South Africa, the rise and probable reasons for apartheid, and what I feel may happen to South Africa in the immediate future. I will include an example of the Chameleon Dance of the apartheid system—one of the many things I learned about at the Museum, and as well explain why apartheid was really not a twentieth century idea but one that had been brewing ever since the Dutch arrived in Africa in the mid- 1600s. I will bring to light the fact that religion played a major role in the Boer mindset, which engendered separation between the races and the eventual enactment of apartheid, even though initially there had been sexual relations and even marriages between the early colonists and the Khoi and the San, which has resulted in the largest group of Coloureds in that country ,who now live mainly in Cape Town, South Africa.

When I first considered the inclusion of the 'fairly recent' history of apartheid in South Africa, I had no intention of giving the subject matter a chapter of its own. However, after visiting South Africa and discovering information not readily available elsewhere, I made the decision to address the subject of apartheid on a more prominent basis. I have also decided to address the subject from a different perspective - that of bringing to light the initially, near "benign" intentions of self-preservation initiatives of the Boers. Although hard to accept from those who were directly affected by apartheid, I believe that a balanced view of the subject is the best option for them as well as for those who, like me, reacted from the perspective of an interested outside observer. We must resolve in our minds to forgive so we can move on with our lives relative to this grave injustice done to a segment of the human specie, which we can actually call our contemporaries. I discovered also that apartheid had been on the brew in one form or another ever since the Dutch came to what was to be eventually called the Republic of South Africa.

Interestingly, the Dutch who first inhabited the southern tip of the African continent thought of themselves as dedicated, Bible-believing Christians, and even in the cruel days of apartheid they practiced

"Christian principles" of no television, no prostitution, no adult sexual material, and no sexually suggestive advertising publicly or otherwise during their rule of South Africa. A person could have been imprisoned for owning a *Playboy* magazine or any such immoral material, for example. All these rules came with a full serving of total hate for Blacks and the wish of nearly all of those Whites for the complete and total annihilation of the race; maybe except for those who served their slave labour requirements.

I grew up hearing about the evil system that was South African apartheid and developed tremendous dislike for those who enforced and practiced such a system of government (if their system of rulership could thus be dignified to be called government), placing such a large segment of the population of that country; people who themselves were and are indigenous South Africans into the abject misery, poverty, and denial of the basic human dignity which God gave to every human being. "The Rule of the Brutes," even though some people may hate the label, in my opinion would be a better description than government when it came to apartheid, even though this description might apply not just to the former South African system but to a few existing Black governments even now in power on that continent. At the end of the chapter, you the reader will make the decision about whether or not the term is justified.

The mystery I had always hoped to solve was what caused the relatively newly arrived Whites of South Africa to put in place such a system of rule on the indigenous Blacks. I thought that if I could find the reason then I would be able to better work with what had become for me an obsession, and being the type of person who tries to forgive and get hatred out of my heart towards those who I am sometimes tempted to hate, it had become my objective to find a reason for it so I could come up with a reason to justifiably forgive it. I learned of the apartheid system almost in conjunction with slavery in America for Blacks, and had already decided that hate and evil treatment by Whites of Blacks was something Whites from those countries delighted in practicing. In the American situation, I understood that they confined Blacks to absolute slavery. In South Africa, they seemed not to have applied the same rigours of slavery as such in the days when apartheid was made official,even though their treatment of Blacks was not much different. I concluded however, that there must have been another reason for them putting their system in place.

As more information became available to me I discovered that there were two distinct colonial nationalities of White people settling what became known as South Africa. These were the Dutch and the British. It seemed to me, however, that apartheid was enforced by the Afrikaners or the Boers as the Dutch farmers came to be called. At the Apartheid Museum in South Africa I learned that the two nations schemed together to enforce apartheid after they "had kissed and made up" about 6 six years after the war with the Boers ended. My grandmother had often told me about the Boer Wars which was fought against the British in South Africa. Because of that bit of information I always thought that the enmity between them had remained. It would take a visit to South Africa to finally figure out what really happened between these two former enemies so far as the apartheid system was concerned.

Although my planned trip to South Africa had nothing to do initially with the writing of this book, I thought that once I was there I would seek to find out some information relevant to the apartheid era. After deciding that, one of the first places I wanted to visit was Soweto. Before going to South Africa I sought by way of the Internet to arrange some accommodation instead of scrambling to find a place upon my arrival. I was told beforehand that South Africa was rampant with crime and the unprepared would be taking a huge risk not having things like accommodation and transportation from the airport properly arranged ahead of time. Mostly I sent emails to places advertising Bed & Breakfast establishments. One person answered who could provide me with the accommodation needed. When I later called to confirm, I was told that the Internet cables had been stolen. There was no possible way for me to survive in South Africa or anywhere else without the Internet. It was/is the third most important thing to me. With just a couple of days to go before I left, I again took to the Internet to locate somewhere I could stay. Instead of sending emails I decided to make phone calls, which would be quicker and could produced immediate results.

One of those calls was answered by a gentleman who had such an accommodation in Randburg, a city slightly east-northeast of Johannesburg. He turned out to be one of the best things that could have happened to me on the trip. In my search to find accommodation in South Africa, I wanted everyone to know that I was Black. He told me that such information was no longer necessary in the new South Africa. I believed him but told him however, that it was important to me to pass on that bit of information because I am wise enough to know that simply because a government has changed it did not mean that discrimination was not still in the hearts of the Whites there in regards to Blacks, and that as individuals they still had the right to offer their services only to those they chose.

This gentleman, who I will refer to as George, turned out to be a "walking encyclopaedia" relative to the South Africa past, the South Africa present, and was not afraid to speak his mind about the South Africa to come. He saw things from the White perspective like most Whites do, just as most Blacks see things from the Black perspective. When I booked in, I saw he was very helpful to Blacks. His recommended tour drivers were both Black—one—was a Xhosa (pronounced kosa) woman from southern South Africa, and the other was a Zulu man from the province of KwaZulu-Natal. I was most elated to meet them because meeting various peoples is a pleasure I enjoy even if I do not get to know them too very well. Gordon employed only Blacks at his Lodge, I suppose because they were the labour force there, but he treated them very kindly, even providing lodging for some of them. All his workers, however, were from Zimbabwe because he preferred them to Black South Africans. He thought that they had better work ethics and were more educated on the average. Later, I met another "walking encyclopaedia," and he told me how efficient the Black South Africans were at their jobs. So I concluded that such an overview depended on the personal experiences of the one being spoken to. George had also adopted the Zimbabwean daughter of one of his workers and was paying her way through private school, which was the same school his own White child attends. He and I had some very interesting conversations about the new South Africa. He was scared of what he was looking at and what he thought was coming and felt he had very good reason to be. Toward the end of my stay at his lodge he was planning to migrate to Thailand. He planned to sell his lodge in the middle of a buying frenzy he expected to see just ahead of the 2010 football World Cup, which is to be held in South Africa.

The female tour driver he recommended was arranged to take me on a tour of Soweto the first Sunday I was in South Africa. Along the way, she stopped at a hotel to pick up a young woman who was visiting from England, which was her home. This young woman had come to South Africa with a young White British couple, with whom she shared a flat in London. As she was fair-skinned, I asked her racial mix. She told us that her mom was Australian White and her dad was Nigerian Black. She gave the distinct impression that she thought that she was White, and I told her that here in North America even if people were White as snow, blue-eyed and even if blond—if it could be proven that they had one single drop of Sub-Saharan African blood such as she possessed, they were considered legally Black. I dont think I swayed her one bit with that piece of information.

Ah well!

Our driver had earlier taken a number of other people to the Apartheid Museum, which is on the way to Soweto, before she picked us up and was supposed to take them from there to a tour of Soweto also. Her car was small and there would not have been enough room for all of us to ride in comfort, so on the guise of adding what to her was a most important tourist site, she practically demanded that we stay and visit the Museum while she took the other people on to Soweto. She promised us that we would never be the same again after the visit. She bought us the entry tickets (with our own money, of course); one for the "Whites Only" entrance—the other for the "Non-Whites Only" entrance and this young woman unabashedly decided that she would use the former. I was intrigued but not surprised. Now this was only meant for us to feel firsthand what it was like to have lived in the South Africa of the past. In retrospect, I am amazed that some of the Whites, especially of South Africa past, so much as 'consented' to live on the same planet with Blacks. Maybe they are chafing that they, like the rest of us, do not have a choice and lived here against their will. Anyway, the driver promptly increased our touring fee by about 40%, charging us R650 instead of the R450 that we had settled for, even though it was her plan to include this venue, and even though the Museum was directly on the way to Soweto. But why worry? The Museum was well worth the trip, as I was soon to discover.

Incidentally, from information I gathered, it seems that a large majority of South African Whites have never visited, and will in all likelihood never visit the Apartheid Museum even though when I was there a lot of White people were all over the place. I concluded that they were most probably for-eigners and had no need to feel shame or guilt about being there. Incidentally, the Museum was set up after 1994 and, as one can imagine, was the brain child of the Blacks who were now in political power.

It is also most likely that very, very few of South African Whites will ever visit Soweto. They believe that the place is swarming with criminals, and so they avoid it. But Soweto may also credit them with shame because of the poverty in fair abundance there. It was in Soweto mostly that the White South African security forces murdered Black people in cold blood, and carried out a lot of their evil designs against defenceless Blacks over the years. Other townships were not necessarily exempt. But anyway, one could understand the attitudes the Whites adopted in regards to Soweto as it was offering them the most effective resistance against their unjust rule. My visit to Soweto did not confirm any criminal activity at the time however, even though there is crime, and it is as likely to find crime there as in any place else in South Africa. Criminal activity is considered a plague all over South Africa, and even the rich enclaves of Sandton and Bryanston are pregnant with concrete walls, security gates, and electrical wire fences - and not becasue of criminal activities taking place in Soweto. Quite frankly, I found the people very pleasant and curious. The children were as curious and as friendly as children from any other place wanting their photographs taken and grabbing on to my hands in gestures of friendliness and warmth. My heart opened up to them and I felt quite good to be thus liked and just wished that I could go back there to give them a bit of love and care because of their poverty and lack of opportunities.

At the Apartheid Museum, I gathered both in writing and mentally every bit of information that I could obtain. I read as much as I could of every caption, every newspaper clipping, and every bit of history that was displayed there. I pretty much learned about the founding of Johannesburg and discovered that at one time both Blacks and Whites got along somewhat, and that the Blacks and the poor Whites even lived together in the "slums" of the city till some Afrikaner idiot began to take advantage of the ignorance and naivetÈ of the poor Whites, and were able to set them against their Black counterparts with talk of White superiority. Although this was not the main reason for the modern apartheid that they practiced, it did not help the situation. The museum's exhibits made it clear that this was not a new idea but one that had been around for centuries. The impetus for racial segregation and some kind of political isolation of and by the Boers was born long before apartheid was actually put in place.

The tour guide had promised that we would never be the same after going to the Museum and as it turned out she was absolutely correct. I know that I will never be the same again. I saw pictures and watched movie clippings of Blacks being savagely beaten by the Whites and read story after story of how cruel they were to the Blacks who were mainly wanting to be treated with the dignity that human beings deserve. Only a few times did it seem that the Blacks ever had the ability to retaliate in any meaningful way, and a very heavy price was paid by those who chose to do so. I am here referring to incidents related in the Museum, as there could indeed be others not recorded and of which I know nothing presently. It amazed me that the White ruling class would call the Blacks terrorists when they were the ones practicing terrorism and atrocities against Blacks. When apartheid came to an end, as opposed to truth and reconciliation, those people who committed their heinous deeds should have been charged with crimes against humanity just like they are now charging Blacks from Rwanda, the Congo, and Darfur. Chief among the demons was P.W. Botha, that monster of cruelty, who seemed to have wanted to be re-incarnated as King Herod, allegedly ordering the murder of Black children at birth in hospitals. I don't believe that he was called *Die Groot Krokodil* for nothing. Neither did Helen Suzman, one of the few Whites to take up the Black cause against apartheid, speak of him as a "bad-tempered, irate debater, and a bully" for no reason.

Helen Suzman was a Jewish woman who was born in South Africa. She was a brave and fearless anti-apartheid spokesperson who even visited the jail where people like Nelson Mandela were incarcerated. Her life's work won her many friends among South Africa's Blacks, as well as others from around the world. She, along with other Jewish people, who understood the hatred levelled against Blacks in South Africa having themselves suffered hate, should long be remembered for taking the position they did at the peril of their lives and livelihoods to help the Black cause in South Africa.

How quick the UN is now to prosecute Blacks when for decades they did nothing about those who practiced apartheid, killing even little innocent children. The Blacks were, by and large, practicing non-violent opposition against the evils of apartheid, but instead of understanding that, the White rulers were determined to be as brutal and murderous as they could possibly be. I was told of Black children being thrown ten stories down to their deaths and little girls who had the heads of bottles shoved into their little virgin genitals by the security forces of White South Africa as lessons to the others to remain docile, and in an attempt to make the little girls sterile for life so they could not bring any Black children by birth into South Africa which I guess the Boers thought would be theirs forever. A lot of this, it was alleged, was carried out under the P.W. Botha administration which, at the same time, wanted the West along with the rest of the world to believe that he was a true reformer. A few Whites protested the harsh treatment and some of them were executed as mercilessly as were the Blacks. Anyone who had the audacity to oppose them were targets for the security forces.

I was lucky enough to go and sit in one of the armoured vehicles I had seen on television driving through Soweto. I saw the damage on the bullet-proof glass enclosure that the vehicle sustained when the people started pelting it with the only weapon they had—stones. Interestingly, the security forces needed not even have gone into Soweto. The government did not really care about the people who lived there. They went because they saw it as a place of resistance to their evil schemes and would have loved to totally annihilate the residents in their brutish and demonic anger. It could have been any of the many Townships of Poverty that surround the rich enclaves of Gauteng. All they did when they went to Soweto was to murder innocent little children, women, and unarmed men. That was what they delighted in. The first person to have died in Soweto in the last pogrom conducted against the township by the Afrikaners was an unarmed ten-year-old boy on his way to school. I was privileged to visit and took a picture at the memorial site set up for him.

In the early days of the apartheid system, a few groups of White South Africans protested against its evils but as a whole, almost the entire population of Whites accepted and practiced it with impunity against the Blacks. The modern movement started with the uneducated and gullible and poor Whites, some of who still exists. But later the teachers, office workers, civil servants, and other professionals accepted it with relish—most likely very happy that they, the small minority, would now be empowered to have complete mastery over the vast majority. While it may be fair to say that they could not all have been in favour of it, there was no evidence anywhere of White opposition, except in very few cases where those who opposed it did so at the peril of their existence.

The Boer Way of Life and the Rise of Apartheid

In addition to the very natural aversion to people of a different race, colour, or nationality, which the European is known for, I will document here what I think were the probable reasons for the rise of apartheid or what might have helped to fuel the flames of hate, malignancy, and exclusivity which gave birth to it in South Africa. But I believe that in order for readers to fully comprehend the issue, it is necessary to give a brief rehearsal of history relative to South Africa going back as far as the fifteenth century to Bartholomew Dias and Vasco da Gama, and the time when these explorers set out to find a new route to the Spice Islands of the East Indies. I will review how and why the European first set foot on the shores of Southern Africa and how he subsequently was able to rule in this Black African country.

There are those who believe that later the nations of Europe sat down at some table and discussed how the continent of Africa should be divided up between them. While I have not come across any officially recorded document to authenticate that event, we probably all know that there was a peaceful occupation of sorts of various parts of the continent by agreeable various European colonialists, and that this went as well as if it had indeed been planned. The only information I have of conflicts was the fight between the British and the Boers over South Africa. The Portuguese, the French, the British, and others seemed to have had the continent nicely carved up to serve their various purposes. Come to think of it, Europe is mostly a drab, overcrowded, and with very little natural beauty really. These colonialists lived in relative peace in paradisaical Africa except for the British and the Boers who for a long time had many conflicts. They went on with their lives and plans, which suited their national agendas, without reference to, or consideration for the Black inhabitants of Africa, seeing them as dispensable, just like the natural resources which were and still are their only interests, namely the gold, diamonds, copper, platinum, and other precious materials which were/are of value to them. It is interesting to note though, and just in case I forget this later, that in spite of their absolute cruelty to Black South Africans, though probably unwillingly, the Boers are the only ones who have left anything, of worth for the continent. The British, the Portuguese, the French, and others took all they could back to Europe on a regular basis and left nothing for the Africans.

Africans were never regarded by Europeans as human beings but rather as creatures just above the gorillas with the ability to carry out limited functions requiring very little intelligence and unworthy of the high estate of European humanity. With such a mindset, Africans were just a commodity to Europeans to be bought and sold at will and at their whim and fancy, or whose services could be obtained for the meager wages that were paid to them.

The European Entry into Sub-saharan Africa

The European trade routes overland to Asia had been thrown into chaos by Muslim expansion across North Africa and into the Balkans. Venice and Genoa had dominated this trade. Gold imported from Africa was minted in Italy and paid for profitable imports of spices and silk from Asia. Now, those land routes were in peril. The Portuguese sought to find a sea route around Africa to Asia, reopening the trade route interrupted by the Moors, and taking the profits so long enjoyed by the Italians. Each year, the Portuguese explorers were ordered to go farther and farther south down the continent of Africa.

In 1497, Vasco da Gama set off from Lisbon with four ships and followed the African coast. He may have been following the course of Bartholomew Dias, who had discovered what was later to become the Cape Colony in 1488, and what the king of Portugal at the time called the Cape of

Good Hope. Vasco rounded the Cape and stopped for Christmas along the southeast coast of southern Africa. He named it Terra du Natal (the Land of Christmas). At Malinda (Mombassa), he went east to cross the Indian Ocean and arrived at Calcut (modern-day Calcutta) on May 20th, 1498. He returned to Lisbon in triumph via the Cape after 26 months away and the loss of two ships. But he had not established any fort or colony in southern Africa. Now, however, at least the rest of the European nations with exploration ambitions were made aware that there was indeed another way to the Spice Islands and would not be afraid to make the journey themselves.

These long, dangerous, brave journeys changed the course of both Western and Eastern history forever and prepared the way for a settlement at Cape Town. The first settlement on the Cape of Good Hope was that of the Dutch East India Company. This company was an entity from 1602 till 1798 by the Charter of the States-General of the Netherlands to expand trade and assure close relations between the government and its colonial enterprises in Asia. It was granted a monopoly on Dutch trade east of the Cape of Good Hope in Southern Africa to west of the Strait of Magellan south of the mainland of Chile. From its headquarters in Batavia the company subdued local rulers, drove the British and the Portuguese out of Indonesia, Malaya, and Ceylon, and took over the trade of the Spice Islands.

In March, 1647, the *Nieuwe Haarlem*, a ship of the Dutch East India Company, ran aground in Table Bay at the Cape, which had already been mapped by the Portuguese navigator Vasco da Gama. The stranded crew built a temporary fort, grew vegetables in the fertile soil, and made contact with the local Khoi. After a year, they were picked up. Two merchants, Leendert Janz and Mathys Proot, were asked to write a report of their experience at the Cape. What they submitted contained recommendations that impressed the Amsterdam Chamber of the Dutch East India Company.

At that time, there was increased tension between the Dutch and the English, and the Dutch now saw the far-flung Cape Peninsula on the sea route to the Indies as a practical, healthy, and strategic area to take ownership of. The proposal to establish a meeting place and fortress at the Cape was approved. In June, 1651, Jan van Riebeeck was appointed as the first commander of the Cape. He was to establish a station at the southern end of Africa to provide passing ships with fresh food and water. A fleet of five ships set out, and three reached Table Bay in April, 1652. The other two arrived later. They had had 130 burials at sea. This colony at the Cape was to remain with the Dutch till its capture by the British in 1814.

The Cape became an important resupply depot for the Dutch East India Company as its ships travelled to and from the Spice Islands with their valuable cargo in the seventeenth and eighteenth centuries. The Dutch East India Company allowed Protestants from Europe to augment the Dutch Colony in order to promote its growth. Consequently, there was a large influx of French Huguenots to supplement the Dutch farmers. Over the course of a century and a half, the Boers would slowly encroach upon the lands of the Khoi and the San, the indigenous peoples of the lands around the Cape. They were looking for land to graze their cattle and to grow food for the sustenance of the Colony. In some cases, the settlers intermarried with the Khoi and the San. But the technological difference between these groups of people was wide, and the Khoi and the San were unable to resist the growth of the Cape colony.

The colony started in 1671 with the first purchase of land from the Khoi beyond the limits of the fort built by van Riebeeck. The first colonists were mainly lower working class people who were indifferent to development, but later a more dedicated class of colonists started arriving. The colonists eventually acquired all the land of the Khoi immediately east and north of their base. These Dutch, who were mainly Calvinists in their religious beliefs, exterminated large numbers of the Khoi directly while many others died in small pox epidemics, which naturally were European infestations. Some Khoi took jobs from the settlers as herdsmen, and in 1787 the Dutch passed laws restricting the nomadic Khoi and making them dependent on the Boers or forcing them to move further north. As they did this, they encountered their adversaries, the Bushmen. The Bushmen stole the cattle and sheep of the farmers prompting the government to adopt a policy of total annihilation of the Bushmen and large numbers of them were killed or captured.

The Dutch East India Company ran all the affairs of the Cape. It interfered with free immigration, monopolised trade, combined legislative and judicial powers into one body, told the farmers what crops to grow, demanded large percentages of each farmer's harvest, and harassed them. It was from this root that sprung a dislike of orderly government and the libertarian view point that has characterised the Boers for many generations. To escape the oppression of the Dutch East India Company, the farmers trekked farther and farther inland to find pasture for their cattle and homesteads for themselves. The trekking was to continue further under the impending British government which will be discussed a little later in this chapter. As they moved inland, they established governing bodies, however, and neither they nor any other European respected any African ownership of land, which to Africans was communally owned property handed down from their ancestors. The laws of the newcomers ensured that Africans had no legal title to their land unless they came up with the means to make purchases of their own property. The constitution of the Boer republic in April of 1844 further forbade African settlements near White towns unless they were given express permission by these governments.

But other forces would affect the life of the Boers as they sought to establish themselves on the southern part of Africa. Eventually, one of these entities would be as unwelcome as the intrusion of the Dutch East India Company into the way of life for these farmers who were seeking to unshackle themselves from the chains of any government and become a nation of their own.

The Netherlands fell to the French army under the leadership of Napoleon Bonaparte in 1795, and the Dutch entered the European war on the side of the French. This weakness of the Dutch did not go unnoticed by the intensely observant British. They sent out an army under General Sir James Henry Craig to Cape Town to secure the colony for Prince William of Orange against the French. At first, the Cape governor refused to obey any instructions from the prince but the British threatened to use force so the Dutch governor relented. The British gained control of the Colony but gave it back in 1802. War started again in 1803, and the British recaptured the Colony in 1806. The Khoi people were also deserting the Dutch and joining the British, and large numbers of Boers had already gone out on their own. The British now had a foothold on the Cape and became the government there. The Boers did not surrender until an army was sent against them, but in 1799 and 1801 they revolted. The arrangement to give the Cape over to the British in 1806 would lead to much friction between the British administration and the Afrikaner colonists.

When the British took control of the Cape, they confronted a society in which slavery was already well established as the Afrikaners had already held the Khoi in conditions not much better than slavery, and in 1807 the British parliament enacted the abolition of the slave trade. This made it illegal for British ships to carry slaves or for the British colonies to import them. An early English rule on the Cape called the Caledon Code required written contracts to be registered for the employment of tribal peoples and provided safety against their ill-treatment. But it provided that servants could not leave a farm without a pass signed by the employer. The British missionaries led by John Phillips fought against this and campaigned in Britain against it, and in 1828 the British House of Commons passed a law emancipating the Cape tribes. In the same year, the Cape government granted complete liberty to free persons of colour. For the Afrikaners, worse was yet to come when in 1833 Britain emancipated all slaves in British Colonies after a period of apprenticeship, which ended in 1838 for the Cape Colony. The Boers were feeling the effects of this alien colonial power. Their sense of isolation had already been heightened by other changes when, in 1820, British families numbering about 5000 people were brought to the Cape and given 100 acres of land per family.

English became the new language of the courts, and British teachers set up schools in villages with lessons in their native language. However, it was British interference in the relationships between the races in the Cape that gave the greatest offence to the traditionally minded Boers. It did not matter that in 1812 an ordinance was issued giving judges the power to bind and enslave African natives. This was overturned because of the emancipation act. Although the Colony was prosperous, the remaining Dutch farmers were as dissatisfied with the British rule as they had been with the Dutch East India Company, even though grievances were different. Moravian Missions had been established for the benefit of the Khoi, and in 1799 the London Missionary Society began efforts to convert both the Khoi and the Xhosa. For the missionaries to help the Khoi and the Xhosa was a big problem for the majority of the Dutch Colonists who had racist inclinations.

In 1815, a hanging incident had also caused permanent hostility for the British by the Dutch frontiersmen. A farmer, Bezuidenhout, refused to obey a summons issued to him after a complaint from a Khoi was registered. He fired on those sent to arrest him and was killed when fire was returned. This caused a small rebellion which had to be put down, and in the process five of the ringleaders, who had sworn to expel the English tyrants, were hanged in public by the British. The hatred was deepened when the scaffold on which the hanging was attempted was broken by the weight of the five who were then hanged separately. These deeply religious Boers believed that the breaking scaffold was an act of God and should have halted the hanging. This was not going to be the only time that these religious people would attribute events as an act of God, only the next time it would lead to religious bigotry, the slaughter of innocent Blacks, and the thought that they had a divine right to disenfranchise Black Africans.

An ordinance passed in 1827 abolished the Dutch court system and replaced it with that of resident magistrates, stipulating that all legal proceedings were to be conducted in English. A subsequent ordinance in 1828 granted equal rights for the Khoi and other free coloured people equal rights with the

White population. Another ordinance in 1830 imposed heavy penalties for the harsh treatment of slaves. Finally the end of slavery was proclaimed in 1834. Each of these ordinances made the Dutch farmers more resentful of the government. As well, the compensation awarded to the slave owners and the method of payment also caused suspicion, which further strained relations and caused further resentment. In 1835, the Boer farmers began their Great Trek into unknown country to escape from a hated government.

An Afrikaner woman, Anna Steenkamp, recorded the complaint of her people in this way, "The British placed slaves on an equal footing with Christians, contrary to the laws of God and the natural distinctions of race, so that it was intolerable for any decent Christian to bow down beneath such a yoke, therefore we withdrew in order thus to preserve our doctrines in purity."

It is said that when the Afrikaners are unhappy with their circumstances they apply one very proven, and traditional response—they move to some other place or they trek. In 1834, the Boer farmers sent out three groups of fact finders to determine what was beyond the Orange River. The party heading northwest came back with a bad report as they had hit the Kalahari Desert. The other two parties, which went north and northeast, came back with glowing reports of rich fertile lands and great herds of wild animals. With this, the Boers decided to strike out into new territories. It is reported that there was political turmoil in those areas because of the bloodthirsty policies of Zulu king Shaka, who by then had been killed by his half-brother, but the Boers were not aware of this,

In 1836, some 1200 people consisting of Boer families and their African servants crossed the Orange River heading north into the interior through the passes of the Drakensburg Mountains into Natal. The first party to cross was led by Hendrik Potgieter. It consisted of 200 people with their wagons and cattle. In the territory ahead of Potgieter and the others were the Ndebele people. The first sign of these tribesmen is was the massacre in July 1836 of a small group of trekkers who had pushed north of the Vaal River. This encounter is was followed in October by an extraordinary battle when Potgieter decided to make a stand with about forty men against an Ndebele army of about 500. He used circled wagons as a barricade, from behind which his men shot, proving from within the barricade more than a match for African wooden spears. The Boers had killed nearly all of the 500 Ndebeles with only two Boers dead and fourteen wounded. Potgieter then followed up with a brutal massacre of the other Ndebeles to prove who was now in control. The Boers rode into sleeping villages and destroyed about a dozen of them and stole around 6000 cattle. This sent a clear message that the European guns were the new master weapon on the battlefront of Southern Africa.

It took one more engagement to prove the point conclusively. In October of 1837, Potgieter led a commando group of 330 men northward in a final push against the Ndebele. In a succession of engagements over a nine-day period near the Marico River, the Ndebele were driven steadily backward until finally they retreated beyond the Limpopo River where their leader, Mzilikazi, established a new kingdom. At Vegeop, the Boers reported some 3000 dead Ndebele and not a single Boer casualty. But the coming months produced a sudden reversal in trekker fortunes. It involved Piet Retief, who had replaced Potgieter as leader of the Great Trek. Retief, rode north to join the main body of trekkers at their encampment near Thaba Nchu. There, they elected him their governor and commander-in-chief, angering Potgieter, who felt pushed aside. Potgieter wanted to trek into the veld, but Retief suspected that their best chances would lay in Natal. Scouts brought back news that five passes have been found through the Drakensburg Mountains. By mid-October, with a small advance party Retief descended into the fertile Natal. They found themselves in a beautiful landscape scarred by abandoned and destroyed villages left by fierce fighting between Shaka and his brother Dingaan.

Shaka himself was very cruel. Following the death of his mother in 1827 he literally became mad. He had 7000 Zulus killed to pacify his grief. No crops were planted and any pregnant woman was killed along with her husband. Finally, Shaka was murdered by his brother Dingaan, and it was Dingaan who, as the new Zulu king, confronted the Boers as they trekked into Natal. Retief made his way first to the region's main harbour of Port Natal or Durban where a few British merchants had settled. He heard from them that Dingaan had no problem with Europeans settling in the depopulated areas south of the Teluga River. Taking two settlers as interpreters, Retief and four of his men decided to visit Dingaan at his palace at Ngungunhlovu. They got to the palace in early November of 1837 and found it an alarming place with a hillside reserved for extremely brutal executions. The visitors were greeted with two days of martial dancing by Zulu warriors before they were granted an audience with Dingaan. Dingaan made a strange request: that if Retief could recover a herd of stolen royal cattle he would be given all the territory between the Teluga and the Umzimvubu Rivers. This was 200 miles of rich coastal territory, but Dingaan, who had promised this before to others, had no intention of keeping his word.

Retief, however, was interested and went out to find the herd, which he recovered by deceiving the chief who had taken the animals. The trekkers, meanwhile, were waiting in the Drakensburg Mountains, and hearing the good news, they descended into the plains in large numbers. By the end of November 1837, there were 1000 Boer wagons in Natal. Dingaan thought that it was a European invasion, and when Retief went to get his reward accompanied by 70 Boers and his own 24-year-old son, after several days of martial dancing, Dingaan signed the document granting the territory to Retief and his countrymen forever. Nonetheless, at a farewell ceremony on February 6th, the dancing warriors closed in on the Boers, overpowered them, and dragged them to the hillside to be slaughtered and left to be picked clean by the vultures. Dingaan now turned his attention to the trekkers who were camped near the Bloukrans River. Early in the morning of February 17th, 1838, Zulu warriors attacked the sleeping families. Nearly 300 Boers, mostly children, and 200 African servants were killed. The surviving Boers spent nearly all the rest of the year in fortified camps under frequent attacks from the Zulus. But things would change in November when Andreas Pretorius arrived.

Pretorius was a rich Boer who decided to join the Trekkers in Natal after hearing of their plight. About a week after he arrived, he was elected their commander-in-chief and he immediately began to organise the men to fight. His plan was to march on Dingaan's palace and on his first contact with the Zulu army to take a strong defensive position. He found the right place on the Ncome River. On December 16th, 1838 a Zulu army of about 15,000 warriors attacked the Boer position, which was guarded by muskets and three small, muzzle-loading cannons. By the end of the day, the Boers calculated that they had killed about 3,000 Zulus with none of their numbers dead. The name of the river was changed to the Blood River. When the Boers got to Dingaan's headquarters, they found it burned and deserted. They also found the remains of Retief and his companions who had been killed earlier. In a leather pouch with the bodies Pretorius claimed he found documents allotting to Retief the coast of Natal in return for finding the royal cattle. Some believe that this letter was a forgery.

A young Afrikaner with whom I had a discussion on the airplane on my way back from South Africa said that the reason the Boers were killed by Dingaan was because they were fraternizing with Zulu women who were wives of Dingaan and his men. He also told me how pleasantly surprised he and other Whites were of the docility of Blacks from a corporate perspective, when after apartheid finally ended they did not take vengeance on the Whites.

Pretorius and his group's next task was to set up an independent Boer republic, which they named Natalia. Pietermaritzburg became its capital, and 24 elected members become its governing body with Pretorius as its commander general. About that time, Dingaan's brother Mpane defected to the Boers with 17000 of his followers, which greatly helped the security of Natalia and the Boers. He was declared reigning prince of the 'migrating' Zulus. Dingaan was finally removed from the stage when his army was defeated by the efforts of Mpane and his army with the help of the Boers. Dingaan fled to Swazi territory and Mpane became king of the Zulus.

For a short time, the Boers prospered in their new republic. But a strong foe was already on their heels. The British greatly valued Port Natal as it was the only deep water harbour on that part of the African coast. The Boers also showed signs of treating returning Black African villagers with racial hatred and injustice, that they are known for as a result of their religious bigotry and superiority thinking. In 1842, a group of British soldiers sailed up the coast into Natalia and marched unopposed into Durban, as Port Natal was called by the British. After arguing for three weeks, Pretorius forcefully took the cattle from the British garrison. The resulting fight proved a decisive victory for the Boers who killed 49 British soldiers and captured their weapons. However, later reinforcements by the British changed things, and in May of 1843, Natalia was proclaimed a British colony, and a garrison was sent to take charge in Pietermaritzburg.

This ended eight years of Boer efforts to escape British rule. They again found themselves in a colony where Black Africans were to be treated as their equals. They reacted in their usual way. They packed their wagons and went back over the Drakensburg Mountains. Andreas Pretorius was among the last to leave as he was hopeful he would find some points of compromise with the British. Finally, in 1847, he led the remaining Boers—about 300 families—into the northern plains, and for a number of decades the British left the Boers on their own. The Boers had kept a presence in the area north of the Orange River, and it was to this region that between 1843 and 1847 that they returned to. And although there were many quarrels between groups of them, they there developed what would become the heartland of the Afrikaner tradition.

True to form, the British always followed the Boers into the hinterland and for two specific reasons. The first was humanitarian—to ensure that the Boers, with their penchant for racial superiority, did not employ Africans to work for them and keep them in conditions of servitude in British territory. Second, the British needed to keep the trade links north of the Cape opened. On two occasions, the British annexed one part or the other of the Boer heartland. Each time they withdrew, leaving the region once again under control of the Boers. The first intervention was in 1848. The newly appointed high commissioner of South Africa, Sir Harry Smith, annexed the land between the Orange River and the Vaal River. He called this new province the Orange River Sovereignty, and not surprisingly there was a Boer uprising. Even though the Boers successfully drove the British back over the Orange River, Smith marched with a reinforced army and defeated Pretorius in August 1848 at Boomplaats. After this, the Boers retreated to safety on the far side of the Vaal River.

The British government got tired of administering the distant and landlocked Orange River Sovereignty, which was occupied by troublesome Boers and bordered by the lands of powerful chieftains, and in 1854 the British withdrew, leaving it as an independent Boer republic, which was called Orange Free State. The Boers then established their own constitution combining elements from Boer tradition and the Dutch and American political models. Dutch would be the official language, and the Dutch Reformed Church would be the state religion. For Whites, the constitution was good, allowing adult males to vote and establishing a free press. Three years, later the land across the river—Transvaal—declared independence as the South African Republic. Their leader was the son of Andreas Pretorius, who had died in 1853. In 1860, Mathinus Pretorius was elected the first president of the South African Republic and remained in office till 1871. Pretoria, which was named in 1855 in memory of his father, was the new nation's capital. The Orange Free State proved the more stable and prosperous of the two states. Because of financial mismanagement the South African Republic became bankrupt and offered little opposition to Britain's annexation of the Transvaal in 1877. This caused another Boer uprising after Paul Kruger made little progress negotiating with the British. This happened in 1880. The Boers inflicted a series of defeats on the British culminating in victory at Majuba in February 1881. The British Prime Minister, William Gladstone, decided on a colonial entrenchment and after lengthy negotiations in London in 1884 confirmed the renewed independence of the South African Republic.

Native African Land and the Boers

As the Boers were colonizing various regions of Southern Africa, there were areas where Native Africans retained their land in other areas. These African areas were important to the British in South Africa. The first to become a British protectorate was the mountainous area of the Sotho tribe. Previously, the Sotho people had been weakened and displaced by conflicts with other tribes especially the Zulus. However, they benefitted greatly by the leadership of Moshoeshoe who united them into a nation in the 1820s, accepting other displaced tribes as well. He also proved himself capable of dealing with the Boers and the English. Moshoeshoe decided to form an alliance with the British in the interest of the Sotho people. He received British protection in 1843 although it was withdrawn in 1854 because of the breaking down of the Orange Free State, which left him in conflict with the Boers. However, he lived long enough to see his territory annexed by Britain in 1868. Its boundaries were fixed in 1869 by agreement with the Orange Free State. Moshoeshoe died in 1870 having secured the hereditary kingdom of Lesotho, which gained independence in 1966.

Bechuanaland, to the west of the Transvaal, had no such clear identity. It was ruled by many rival chiefs, and its sovereignty was often violated by the Boers to the increasing alarm of the British who were never afraid to engage the Boers in battle. The Boers had established two small republics there, putting pressure on the vital trade route north to the Zambezi, which was prized by the British. German colonial activity also threatened the territory from the west. The Cape entrepreneur Cecil Rhodes was determined to keep the route open. This placed pressure on the British government until in 1885 when Bechuanaland south of the Molopo River was made a Crown colony. It merged with the Cape colony in 1895 while the other part of the territory, north of the river, was also declared a British protectorate. It remained under British control until it achieved independence in 1966 as the republic of Botswana.

Swaziland, which is east of the Transvaal, followed a harder route to independence. The Swazi people moved north into their region in the early nineteenth century as they were pressured by the Zulus. They, however, established a stable, well-protected monarchy. Bordering on Natal to the south and Transvaal to the west, Swaziland was of concern to the British as well as the Boers. However, they all got together—the British, the Boers, and Swazi officials—to form a three- party government. The British took control of the area after the defeat of the Transvaal. In 1906, the region was entrusted to the newly appointed high commissioner for Basutoland, Bechuanaland, and Swaziland. Swaziland followed the other two into independence in 1968. Zululand, the most powerful of this group of four regions of native land, was the only one to engage the British in military conflict. As a result, the independent Zulu kingdom ended as suddenly under Catshwayo as it had begun under his uncle Shaka.

A few wars between the British and the Zulus were all that it took to sub-jugate these African peoples in southern Africa. Because of superior weaponry, the Europeans were able to outmanoeuvre the wooden spears of the Africans who just threw themselves into battle without respect for the ef-fectiveness of guns and bullets. For the next few decades, the wars for control of South Africa would be fought between the Boers and the British. Outright warfare between these two groups of Europeans came out of the tensions of the 1890s due to British expansionism and Afrikaner fear of being sur-rounded and absorbed. Following various raids by the British, especially the Jameson Raid, which had been intended to foment an uprising in the Boer territory, the Boers were very distrustful of British intentions. Before the Boer war of 1899-1902, Paul Kruger, who was president of the South African Re-public, took steps to prepare for war, which he saw as inevitable. He concluded an alliance with the Orange Free State, another Boer republic, in 1897. He began a program of rearmament to improve his republic's readiness for mil-itary conflict.

On the British side, new factors made war increasingly likely. In 1895, Joseph Chamberlain became the British secretary of state for the colonies. In 1897, he appointed Alfred Milner as southern African high commissioner. They were both strong imperialists. Milner urged an assertive and vigorous policy against Paul Kruger, who had been elected to a fourth term as president of the Transvaal.

It is said also that Milner wanted to favour Queen Victoria on the occa-sion of her Diamond Jubilee by stealing and giving to her the lucrative gold mines of the Transvaal and the Orange Free State.

But the most inflammatory issue between the two sides this time was the Uitlanders or migrant workers. These were the non-Boers who had come into South Africa after the discovery of gold. They were very heavily taxed but had no political rights. At a conference in Bloemfontein in June 1899, Milner demanded that the Transvaal give them the right to vote. This Paul Kruger refused to do. In the next few months, half-hearted but ultimately unsuccessful attempts were made to find a solution. In October of the same year, the Boer republics demanded that British troops withdraw from their borders. The re-sult was war. At first, the Boers whose forces out-numbered the British, had the advantage. The Boers, moving rapidly to lay siege to important British bases even beyond their borders.

A British army unit that landed at the Cape in December of 1899 did nothing to reverse the trend, and the British forces were soundly defeated in three battles on three fronts between December 10th and 15th, 1899. In each case, the British lost between 700 and 1100 soldiers while the Boers lost only a few men. Frederick Roberts and Herbert Kitchener arrived in January 1900 to take command and things began to change in favour of the British. The British regained Kimberley and Ladysmith in February and Mafeking in May. Lord Roberts occupied and annexed Bloemfontein, the capital of the Orange Free State, later the same month. On June 5th he occupied Pretoria, the capital of the Transvaal, which he also annexed. The president, Paul Kruger, ran away into Mozambique.

While the war seemed over, such was not the case as the Boers resorted to commando-type tactics to war against the British. The British, in turn, adopted three ruthless but very effective measures. The most effective was a "scorched earth" policy, which destroyed the crops and farms of the Boers. This led to a large group of homeless and starving women and children whom Lord Kitchener provided for by placing them in concentration camps. By the end of the war in 1902, about 115,000 people were living in these camps. Roughly 4000 women and 16000 children had died in them from various illnesses.

The British had been winning wars for the past 50 or more years quite easily because they had been fighting against ill-trained and ill-equipped natives, and this gave the generals much confidence that the war with the Boers would be won and over by Christmas. But they had not fought the Boers before, and the Boers had a lot to defend. They proved tougher, and it took two-and-a-half years for the British to prevail. The Boers had been preparing for war since October of 1899, but by June, 1900, the British had taken the two cities. The Boers were bested, but, known for their stiff resistance, they started a guerrilla commando-style campaign, which wreaked havoc on the British who eventually resorted to a scorched earth and concentration camp policy against the defenders. They carted off women and children to these camps. However 22,000 British soldiers had lost their lives, while only 6000 Boers had been casualties of the war. A treaty ending the war was agreed to in May 1902 at Vereeniging, interestingly a name meaning Union in Dutch. British annexation of the Boer republics was confirmed but there were also important concessions with no recriminations.

Among the Boers, defeat in the war promoted a new commitment to Afrikaner culture where language and politics would go together. They formed a language union to promote the use of Dutch rather than the use of English. There was a campaign to take more seriously the written language of

Afrikaans, which was a colloquial version of Dutch spoken by the Boers, in poetry and prose.

Political organizations accompanied this development and parties committed to Afrikaner self- government were formed. Though not specific, there was a promise of internal self-government for the Boer colonies of Transvaal and Orange Union in the Vereeniging treaty. Notwithstanding, the promise was fulfilled with a change in government in England from the Conservatives to the Liberals, who were more inclined to offer concessions.

All this time, the region was prospering, and Arthur Milner was busy integrating the economies of the British and Boer colonies, bringing them into a single customs union and railway systems. With increased economic cooperation, a greater degree of political union became attractive, even though both communities had just ended a harsh war. Australia had just been given dominion status in 1901, New Zealand in 1907, and the possibility of a united and independent South Africa free of any interference from Britain began to look more attractive to the leaders of both the Boer and British communities. A national convention of delegates from the four colonial parliaments met in 1908-1909 and drew up a new constitution. This passed almost unanimously in referendums in Cape Town, the Transvaal, and the Orange River Colony, and in Natal by a large majority in a referendum.

There was one thorny issue, that of the local traditions in the new "provinces." Cape Town had eliminated race as an issue in its franchise, being still under direct British rule which did not favour racism. It was allowed to keep its policy. In the other three colonies, there was a point in principle that the electorate become exclusively White and so the colour bar remained. The British parliament passed the South Africa Act in 1909, and South Africa became an independent dominion within the British Empire in May of 1910. Some of the Boers had retreated to the central part of South Africa near Pretoria, and so Pretoria became the administrative capital of the new nation. The legislative capital or the seat of Parliament was to be Cape Town. The stage was being set for institutional racism in the new nation.

Racial Distinctions between 1910 and 1934

The new Union of South Africa now implemented clearly defined racial groups, something which had always been an obsession of the Boers. In 1910, there were about 1.3 million White citizens in South Africa, and the majority were Afrikaners of Dutch descent. The British were the smaller minority, but the two groups had much that separated them, and the Boers hated the British who for two hundred years had displaced and harassed them. By far the largest group in the new union were the Black Africans, numbering some 4 million people. The Boers and the English disagreed on the level of rights that these indigenous peoples should have, but with one mind they saw them as a vast supply of very cheap manual labour.

There were two smaller communities consisting of about 500,000 Coloureds and 180,000 Asians. Most of these Asians lived in Natal, to where they had been taken in the 1860's as indentured labour from India to work on the colony's sugar plantation. In individual provinces different restrictions were placed on these various racial groups. In the Cape Province, the Coloureds had the same status as the Whites and could vote it they had the property qualifications, but elsewhere they were classed with other non-White groups. Asians suffered particular discrimination in Natal where they outnumbered the Whites. They were subjected to a special head tax and to humiliating measures such as an act in 1906 requiring all Indians in the colony to register their fingerprints. The law was withdrawn when Gandhi developed his policy of non-violent resistance which South African Asians apparently became aware of and may have been prepared to use it.

At the level of national politics, the Afrikaner majority over the British, plus the law restricting voting to Whites, only meant that from the beginning the Afrikaners dominated. The first Union cabinet in 1910 was headed by Louis Botha as prime minister with Jan Smuts as minister of the interior as well as defence. These two men had distinguished themselves against the British in the Boer wars. Even so, the party they formed was committed to cooperation with the British government and to partnership between the two European communities in South Africa. This accommodation proved very offensive to the radical Afrikaners who were always fearful of their identity being eroded by the British influence. They were even more excited when Botha brought South Africa into the First World War on the side of the Allies. In this atmosphere, the Nationalist Party was founded in 1914 by J.B.M. Hertzog. This party had started to set the national agenda. The National Party won the election of 1924 and began to put in place legislation to protect the privileges of the White minority population. Over the next 15 years, laws were passed to prevent Africans and Asians from taking skilled trades, to limit African access to towns, and to enforce segregation upon the White and non-White communities. With all that, Afrikaners still wanted Hertzog to go further.

Then in 1934 Daniel Malan formed the "Purified" Nationalist Party. Its attitudes prefigured the ugly and bad days of the future apartheid policies of

South Africa.

Bad economic times in the mid 1930s caused Hertzog to form a coalition with Smuts, and in 1934 their parties merged as the United Party. Hertzog remained prime minister with Smuts as his deputy. The Second World War divided these two men and Hertzog resigned as prime minister making room for Smuts to return. South Africans rallied behind Smuts, and in a general election in 1943 returned him to power. But every seat lost by his party was won by the Nationalistist Party of Daniel Malan. Five years later, Malan's party, which was now the Reunited National Party and subsequently just the National Party, won a narrow majority in the Assembly in partnership with a smaller Afrikaner party. The period of strict apartheid and of South Africa's international isolation was about to begin.

The Afrikaner word "apartheid" was much in use after 1948 and as a central policy of the South African government. Although it was not that different from the segregation of the races practiced by Hertzog and Smuts, it was pursued with much enthusiasm after 1948 by successive National Party prime ministers such as Malan, (1948 to 1954), Strijdom (1954 to 1958), Verwoerd (1958 to 1966), and Vorster (1966 to 1978). In addition to segregation, new elements were devised and imposed. A population register was established to fix the racial classification of every citizen of South Africa. Interracial marriages and interracial sex between Whites and non-Whites were criminalized, towns and rural areas were divided into zones and property ownership was limited to people of specific racial groups as they were placed, and Black Africans traveling into White areas for work had to get passes. Universities were reserved for White students only, while extreme apartheid was applied to the education system. Each colour classification and tribal people was given schools and colleges of their own. There were separate facilities and separate areas in buses, trains, post offices, libraries, cinemas, and theatres. The non-White population was progressively excluded from the political system, and the Coloured citizens of the Cape were finally deprived of their voting rights.

Those who advocated apartheid claimed that these restrictions were balanced by a separate political system designed for majority Africans and created Bantustans with limited self-government. Because of international censure, South Africa withdrew from the British Commonwealth in 1961 and became a republic. The U.N General Assembly condemned South African apartheid in 1962 and called for an economic boycott. Most Africans states did so, but western governments, especially the United States and Britain, were reluctant to take such steps. Reagan and Thatcher were complicit with South African apartheid. However, in 1986 public pressure against apartheid was so strong in America that congress over rode Reagan's veto and imposed trade and financial restrictions and banned air travel to South Africa with other western governments following suit. Eventually, hatred for apartheid led to the isolation of South Africa in matters of international sports, culture, and the arts.

However, the most significant opposition to apartheid came from within through non-violent protests, but probably included the 1966 assassination of Prime Minister Hendrik Verwoerd in parliament by an immigrant of mixed mixed-race ancestry. As the White regime became more repressive, violence escalated with the African National Congress and the Pan Africanist Congress. The African National Congress was founded in 1902 as the South African Native National Council but took its present name in 1923. Its first purpose was to defend and extend the voting rights of the Coloured and African citizens of Cape Province. As conditions worsened after the National Party won election, the ANC became radical under the leadership of Nelson Mandela, and Walter Sisulu. They organized boycotts, marches, strikes, and other forms of passive resistance to apartheid.

In 1955, the ANC convened a mass public meeting and proclaimed a Freedom Charter, which emphasized democratic non-racial credentials stating that South Africa belonged to all who lived there. The ANC leaders and their supporters –Coloureds, Asians, and liberal Whites, faced increasing harassment by the police. Yet even at this stage, the ANC remained non-violent. This fact was recognized when in 1960 the ANC president Albert Luthuli won the Nobel Peace Prize. Then, in 1959, Robert Sobukwe formed the Pan Africanist Congress, a breakaway group from the ANC, which he believed was weakened by the ANC's association with other races. The PAC was quite confrontational. In March 1960, tens of thousands of Black Africans presented themselves at police stations all over the country without passes, which was against the law, challenging the police to arrest them. At Sharpeville, near Johannesburg, the police over-reacted killing 60 and wounding 180, most of who were shot in the back as they were running away. This was a turning point. Thousands marched and went on strike. The government reacted with utmost severity, outlawing the ANC and the PAC and arresting 11000 under emergency measures.

The ANC formed a guerrilla force to carry out acts of sabotage. Nelson Mandela was captured in 1964 and sent to jail for life at Robben Island in Cape Town, and Oliver Tambo escaped to Zambia. Because the leaders were in jail or exile, the rest of the 1960s were relatively quiet. But, a new generation in the 1970s began to demand changes, and a group of students including Steve Biko formed the Black Consciousness Movement to encourage pride in African culture and traditions. In such an atmosphere, school children in Soweto staged a protest in 1976 against a new government rule that lessons be taught in Afrikaans. The demonstration apparently turned to looting and police fired on the crowd of students. This caused nationwide riots and unrest, and at the end of three days, 100 were dead and more than 1000 wounded. A government crackdown led to the execution of many by the Afrikaner police and Steve Biko was murdered in police custody. By this time, internal problems and international aversion to South Africa made it evident that apartness could no longer continue it the form that it was.

In 1978, P.W. Botha became prime minister of South Africa, and under his administration much of the practices of apartheid came to an "end." Laws that required Black Africans to travel in the country were done away with. The laws banning interracial sexual and marital relationships were rescinded. Segregation was quashed or much reduced, and skilled jobs were no longer reserved for Whites only. As well, Black unions were allowed to function legally and be registered. While all this seemed progressive, there was still no place in the nation for Black Africans to have political rights and the roots of discontent were still intact. Botha increased the nation's armed forces and sent his troops into Angola, Mozambique, and southwest Africa to destroy the ANC and destabilize those countries. He also authorised aggressive brutality and intimidation of Black townships. Because of rigid press censorship, the rest of the world knew very little of this, but a few people continued to speak out. One such person was Desmond Tutu, then the rector of an Anglican church in Soweto. In 1984, Desmond Tutu was awarded the second Nobel Peace Prize of the apartheid era.

A decline in the economy of South Africa in the latter half of the 1980s was further damaged by strikes by Black workers in gold and diamond mines, which were and are the main source of income for the nation. Botha was in a fix. In 1989, he became ill and was forced to step down making room for a much younger man, in F.W. de Klerk. In 1990, de Klerk shocked the world and the South African parliament with the announcement that he planned to dismantle apartheid, free political prisoners, lift the bans of the ANC and the PAC, and introduce a new era of consultation and dialogue. Nine days later, Nelson Mandela was released from prison, and before the end of the year Oliver Tambo returned from exile. White apartheid had officially ended.

Until the 1990s, it seemed impossible that non-violence and a peaceful transfer to majority rule would ever come to South Africa. However, Mandela and de Klerk accomplished just that and collected the third Nobel Peace Prize of the apartheid era. Mandela was greeted with enthusiasm by Black Africans when he was released from jail and became the official leader of the ANC, replacing Oliver Tambo in 1991. He and de Klerk worked on getting their followers to make sufficient compromise for a feasible transition to Black majority rule. This was made easier by Mandela's generosity of spirit. In spite of spending almost 30 years in jail, he harboured no bitterness. He was even eager to talk with those who were most belligerently opposed to what he had fought for. He personified the hope of a shared multiracial future and the spirit of reconciliation.

Mandela's greatest obstacle was the Zulu chief, Mangosutho Buthelezi. The Zulus had stood apart from the rest of the other Black tribes of South Africa, and Buthelezi had become their chief minister in KwaZulu-Natal, collaboratingating with the apartheid government of the Afrikaner saying that the advancement of the African cause was best served by forming an alliance with the apartheid regime. He had broken ranks with the ANC. There was disagreement leading to a brutal power struggle between the Zulus and other Black South Africans, in which and thousands were killed as a result. Despite this, a free election took place in April of 1994. The ANC got 63% of the popular vote, the National Party, 20%, and the Inkatha under Buthelezi, 10%. An interim constitution in late 1993 provided for a proportional share of the seats in the cabinet. There were twenty ANC ministers, seven from the National Party, and three for the Inkatha.

On May 10, 1994, 45 heads of state and millions of viewers from all around the world witnessed the extraordinary and unbelievable spectacle of the swearing in of Nelson Mandela as head of state for the new democracy of South Africa. He had many problems to deal with, but the two most pressing were the past and the immediate future, and the past had its distrust of the Afrikaner. He had to build trust and allay the fears and bitter resentment of apartheid. He also had to confront the unrealistic hopes of the South African poor and unemployed for instant remedy to a centuries' long problem. This hope was fuelled by the slogan of the ANC –A Better Life for All.

The Chameleon Dance of the Apartheid Era

Apartheid had been the most emotionally distressing element in the lives of most of the people of South Africa who were completely confused about it all. Even the leaders were so confused that they sought to make radical changes to their racial classification of the people. When it began, eleven million people had been racially classified. There were 3904 objections to apartheid and 2823 successes by 1966. As South Africans began to challenge their racial classifications, the ludicrous nature of such identifications became obvious, especially in situations where members of one family had been classed as belonging to different races. In order to survive the ramifications of apartheid, some people had changed their racial classifications.

In 1985, Stoffel Botha, who was in charge of the matter at the time, reported that in that year a number of people did the "Chameleon Dance," which meant they changed their racial classifications. The following figures applied: 702 Coloureds became White; 19 Whites became Coloureds; 3 Chinese people became Whites; 80 Indians became Coloureds; 43 Coloureds became Indians; 21 Indians became Malays; 30 Malays became Indians; 249 Blacks became Coloureds; 20 Coloureds became Blacks; 2 Blacks became Other Asians; 1 Black became Griqua; 3 Coloureds became Malay; 1 Chinese became Coloured; 8 Malays became Coloureds; 3 Blacks became Malay. Zero Blacks became White, and zero Whites became Blacks. In all for that year, 1155 people changed racial classifications.

Apartheid caused another long-lasting problem. There are Black Africans today who will never embrace the Christian religion for the simple reason that the people who were so brutal and inhumane to them considered themselves Christians. Most Afrikaners of South Africa were members of the Dutch Reformed Church, and as such claimed Jesus as their Master. They, however, did not represent Him when they treated others that He also created with so much cruelty that it defies human comprehension. Repressive denial of the basic rights and dignity of human expectations cannot be called Christ-like in any way. But Whites of other faiths did not do any better. I was told by the tour guide that Nelson Mandela was once a Seventh-Day Adventist, others say otherwise, and still others believed that it was his first wife who was. However, he apparently left the religion when he experienced the utter malignity that the organization spewed out. Even today in South Africa, White Seventh-Day Adventists hate Blacks and refuse to worship with them. Apartheid not only caused grief among the Blacks, Coloureds, and Indians. It also did not have a place for the poor Whites of South Africa. The leaders were so confused that they forgot the plight of their own people because they were poor and uneducated. Today these poor Whites are taking their place among the most marginalized and economically disadvantaged among South Africans as it becomes apparent that the new government because of its Black Empowerment agenda may be replacing apartheid of the Whites for apartheid of the Blacks. They complain, and rightly so, that the new government campaigned under the policy of inclusion for everyone but is now favouring the Blacks. That is just too bad. No government should despise or marginalize any group of people over whom it has jurisdiction.

Present-Day South Africa

I was fortunate to visit South Africa roughly 14 years after apartheid officially ended, and when Black rulers were in power in the country. I was even more fortunate to hear personally from a number of people who were not afraid to speak their minds on what was then transpiring and what they thought the future of South Africa would be as the years went by. While the answers depended on who was speaking, it was evident that there were two schools of thought as far as the Whites were concerned. During the apartheid years they had kept the Blacks so impoverished that envy, greed, and covetousness was evident everywhere on the part of the Blacks.

Then there is the subtle White arrogance and the expectation that Blacks should still be what they had been before. It was as though they thought that Blacks had no entitlement to anything beneficial and should still be their maids and yard boys which a lot of Blacks still are. The arrogance can be seen in their faces and demeanours as they go about their business.

My visit to South Africa came with an unexpected but very pleasant surprise. I saw very many Blacks there in positions that I never expected. They managed many stores, were waiters in some of the best restaurants, were cashiers in all the grocery stores, worked in high fashion clothing stores, jewellery stores, and appliance and furniture stores, and drove some of the best cars on the roads. In many banks there was not a single White face to be seen among the cashiers and bank managers. This shocked me. I was mainly in the province of Gauteng and around Johannesburg, but I saw much of the same in Durban and Port Elizabeth, parts of the province of KwaZulu-Natal. It was much the same in the Northern Province where I went.

When I mentioned to some of them that I would be very lucky to see a Black person working in a high-end restaurant in Canada, they seemed incredulous. Managing jewellery and high-end clothing stores would even be more of a rarity I told them, because in Canada, and I suppose in America, they treat us as if we have not yet "attained" to such a status. And so far as television was concerned, young Blacks in South Africa were hosts and hostesses of so many shows it was as though they were born for it. More surprisingly, their skills and acumen would match anything I have seen on American or Canadian TV. Their programs were well-planned, well- choreographed, well-executed and well presented, and were of very high quality. They had their own versions of soap operas, and very talented and sophisticated actors and actresses in movies and programs that rivalled anything in the West.

I was also very shocked to see and hear the kind of professional singing done by Black South Africans. Their opera singers need not be afraid to take on the best in the West. All through my stay I wondered why Africans have been presented as of so little talent. Maybe they are more fitted to this than creating economies and forging material progress, but it is certainly not true in the arts. After coming back to Canada, I began to reflect on the importance of having people of ones own colour and culture properly represented in these areas of public exposure. When that is not the case there can be a loss of identity and lack of self esteem. Being very religious, church was a place I went every week. Whereas in Canada my religion might criticize us for driving luxury vehicles, in Soweto, supposedly a place of extreme poverty, I saw more luxury cars there than in probably all the parking lots of all the churches of my religion in Canada. These comprised BMWs, Audis, top of the line Toyotas, and other Japanese cars, and Mercedes-Benzes. I counted more than 60 in the one parking lot. Luxury American cars were not visible even though mid-range ones existed.

Interestingly, the Whites are now leaving South Africa at a rapid pace. Depending on whom you speak to it is either because they are unwilling to live under Black rule either in government or in business, or because of the increase in crime. It is fair to say that the government acted too quickly and too unwisely setting up a Black Empowerment division where Blacks are put in positions they do not yet have the training or experience to fill. This is not to say that there are not very capable Black South Africans. I have met a lot of them there. Some of the Black people are as educated and intelligent as to astound anyone. They are distinguishing themselves in many areas of professional life in South Africa, but no one who is inexperienced or untrained to accomplish a certain task should be given a position of important responsibility, no matter what colour they are. However, government's penchant for appointing its own people is not a new thing in South African politics. When the British first took over the Cape they replaced the government with people of their own. When the Boers gained control of the government in the late 1940s, they kicked out the British and appointed their own. So, as one can see, the ANC is only doing something that has been the norm for South

African politics for hundreds of years.

The major difference, however, was the fact that as Europeans both the Boers and the English had much experience in governance, as it would then and now apply to a system that they themselves had set up. In this scenario, it would have been more insightful if the ANC had partnered with the former government for a co-management of the systems of government that they are now responsible for.

What Black Empowerment has done is create many situations where services and functions have and are suffering because of lack of knowledge, and misuse of funds that would otherwise be used for maintenance, and in many cases the government is calling back the White people to retake their old jobs. Some of these people are no longer available having gone on to other jobs in the private sector or their own businesses. Others go back as consultants.

There has been a steep increase in crime in South Africa. The freedom to go anywhere and everywhere has enabled Blacks to traverse South Africa as they never were allowed to before. A lot of them have targeted Whites as the people to rob. There are many tales of excessive brutality in terms of the crimes perpetrated against Whites. The dwellings of Whites are more like fortresses as they build high walls around their homes and put up electrical wire fences to prevent thugs from getting into their homes. The Blacks, mainly coming from the Townships to commit their crimes, do succeed however in causing terror to Whites. Several of these criminal acts were committed while I was there. I spoke to a gentleman who said that if I went to his church, which was in Sandton, and asked how many people had been affected by crimes directly or indirectly, I was sure to have more than 95% of respondents raise their hands. I was told also that some times the armoured money deliver vehicles were robbed and that such was probably done by an elite group of Black criminals who had been trained for paramilitary activities against apartheid but as that was now gone they turned to crimes using AK-47s and sophisticated tactics and were so efficient that not even the police services could match them.

These crimes are causing them to flee and South Africa will not be better off when they go. It's like a brain drain on the country. Thankfully, some emigrants are now going back to South Africa because of the global economic slowdown. They should be welcomed back with open arms and be requested to keep creating an economy, something which Blacks know nothing or very little about. The Whites should then be encouraged to create opportunities for all the citizens no matter the colour of their skin. Let me make it perfectly clear that I do not support crime against the Whites in South Africa or anywhere else. Those who are victims of crime are usually people who have themselves done nothing wrong and should not be targeted for revenge by criminal Blacks. Blacks there should still be grateful for the contribution of the Whites in South Africa. When they arrived, there was not much but warring tribes, wilderness, lots of wild animals, and people who did not know what to do with the minerals and natural resources that were just sitting in the ground. Now, there are beautiful roads everywhere, also beautiful buildings and malls, and all kinds of places of interest. If the Whites had undone all the good they did in South Africa when they gave back the country, what chaotic conditions would now exist!! The Whites, too, need to appreciate the service of the Blacks and realize that Blacks have contributed their labour and efforts to build up the country. The Indians too should also be appreciated. They contributed to the wealth of the country taking care of the vast sugar plantations in the early years. Those vast sugar cane fields are still there. Driving up the eastern coast of KwaZulu Natal they stretched as far as the eye can see in many places. Each race should be grateful for the efforts and contributions of the other where the contributon has been for the improvement of the country.

In relation to the corruptness of the government, which the ANC is now rightly getting a lot of discredit for, it must be pointed out that there was government corruption under the Afrikaner regime also. A corrupt government is also standard issue for most of Africa's nations, and indeed for a lot of other nations as well. This includes the nations of the Middle East, the Far East, Eastern, Central, and Western Europe, North, East, West and South Asia, North America, the Caribbean and Central and South America. Just this Spring of 2009, 12 of England's cabinet ministers have been found to have violated the graft laws of that country taking funds for their personal use.

The Infrastructure

In many places, the streets of the new South Africa are becoming in ruins already. A lot of the sidewalks in the city of Randburg, for example, where I spent most of the time, were made up of cobble stones, and in many places they were being disassembled and were not being put back together. There were places where work was attempted but never completed. Parts of the city were strewn with garbage, and one could see the general decline as Blacks moved in on certain areas. People, White and Black, told me that under the White government this would never have happened. It was distressing to see that there would be empty garbage bins everywhere on the streets, but the

Blacks would rather throw their garbage on the street rather than in those bins. In one section of the city of Randburg, the authorities have allowed a flea market of sorts to be set up. All the vendors were Black. Refuse was strewn all over the place with nary a care about sanitation. How Blacks would do that is always a big point of concern to me. It is a shameful display of what one young Black woman called the "Black mentality." On one occasion, as I was walking up a fairly nice street I saw water oozing out of the ground and was actually walking in it. Then I asked the person walking with me where the water was coming from. I was told to get away from it; it was sewage water. This sort of thing happened all the time, said my companion, and no one does anything about it.

In one issue of the *Sunday Times*, a leading newspaper in the country, one Black editor wrote about a pothole in the nation's oldest and leading city Johannesburg. He claimed that this pothole had been opening up since October of the previous year. It apparently started off as a very small breach and then grew to a size where cars were being damaged, and finally, he said, it had become something everyone knew about. It was then mid-February, and no one had chosen to do anything about it. He went on to say that that was only one case and that there were many more things to fix. We could say that potholes are incidental, and most other countries have infrastructure issues like this. However, due to the number of things going bad in just such a short time, South Africans were really worried about what would be next. And especially so when they concluded that funds that should have been used for such repairs were being siphoned off into the bulging pockets of undeserving friends of the government. Apparently, the government would rather spend the money to enrich their personal interests and that of their friends. I spoke to one Black woman who said that she was part of a group that could have benefitted from the free flow of government funds to local officials, who had become very rich on government money. But she said she could not do that because of her conscience. She told me of one occasion where one of her former colleagues had just received 500,000 rands for awarding a contract to a close friend of his. This, she claimed, was happening all over.

The city of Johannesburg where prior to 1994 Blacks were not allowed to live now crawls with Blacks. When I went there I could not believe the number of Black people all over the city and in the banking institutions that I went into, but it was not hard to see that there was general decline in that city. A former five-star hotel was now cordoned off with concrete blocks and wire fences. When I asked why, I was told that there were so many rapes and other crimes taking place around it that they literally closed it down. White businesses had fled the city. It's as though wherever and whenever the Blacks dominate, watch out for dirty cities, a callous attitude, and a general decline around anything that was good previously. One could see that although South Africa is a beautiful and totally enjoyable country, that a dark day is coming if the government at all levels refuses to take drastic steps to stem this tide of decay settling in. When the Whites see this they are very eager to take flight in as much as it personally affects them. Most Blacks just don't care about clean cities and proper working systems because they are used to living in dire poverty and will make do with just about anything and in any condition. Like a pig returning to its mud wallow, some of us Blacks would turn a sparkling diamond into rubbish overnight. I was told that it was quite typical for a number of people from Nigeria who migrated to South Africa to dispose of their garbage in the middle of city streets, sometimes throwing them down from their apartments. They chose to do so whenever there was some kind of celebration such as New Year's Eve. I was told that at times people actually got killed because of this. As well I was taken into neighbourhoods which were formerly occupied by White South Africans. It was amazingly sad to see that the new Black occupants had thrown old sofas, mattresses and other household furniture just outside their dwellings on the streets, sidewalks and backyards. It is such a shame! Thankfully not all the Blacks are like that.

It is quite distressing to see the large number of street vendors selling all kinds of articles on the streets. They are usually Black and wherever they go they leave a pile of garbage behind them or keep it for company. In any case it is awful to see and to conclude that that will probably not get any better anytime soon. Another very unpleasant sight throughout much of Gauteng and also of the city of Durban is the amount of Black beggars who ply their trade in the cities. I do see a few young White men doing the same, but the overwhelming majority are Blacks. Usually its a woman with a number of children. They place themselves on the islands of boulevards and at 4 way stop streets and under the glare of the sun they can be seen with their very small children. It is a very a very pervasive and visible spectable and one that ought to put the civic leaders to shame, if shame in this context is a word they can incorporate into their vocabulary, for not putting an end to it. I could not help but feel pity for the children, but it is the foolish parents that I have anger toward. They keep having sex and bringing children into the world who they are not able to support. Most alarmingly, they would be seen even in the most exclusive neighbourhoods. I went to see the residence of former Preseident

Nelson Mandela who lives in a really upper class neighbourhood and even there they were present. Both Whites and Blacks I had conversations with tell me that before 1994 one would never see anything of the kind. They are very unhappy seeing their once beautiful and very clean streets becoming what they are.

A Final Word

Despite the negative aspects, South Africa is a very beautiful country. It is the most beautiful country I have ever seen. The mountains are majestic, the plains scenic, the people mostly wonderful, and mostly kind. The flora and fauna make the country a literal paradise. Everywhere are sights to feast the eyes. Around Port Elizabeth are the gentle breezes floating off the Indian Ocean and there are places where beautiful palm trees line the streets. I understand its even better around Cape Town.

The songs of the birds around the facility I stayed were pleasant sounds to be awakened to. The stores are filled with many wonderful things and many people who serve you with pleasure. Most people have not lost their sweetness and lots of them when they perceived I was not South African wanted me to come back for more visits. And from the poverty of Soweto, a city of about 5.5 million people, to the super-rich enclave of Sandton, it is worth the sights and the time and effort to go there. The food is good and people serve you gracefully. The place is rich in Zulu culture and their martial dance is something to see and enjoy though it seem quite mystical. I just hope that this beautiful country survives all the onslaughts and remains as beautiful as ever. I hope also that it remains the home of all who are a part of it, whether they are African Black, Indian, Oriental or European White and everyone in between. There indeed is ample space for all. I am hoping too that the government will do its best to maintain the infrastructure and that the Blacks will start cleaning up their streets and neighbourhoods.

Chapter Ten
DEALING WITH HATE

In this chapter, I will use a religious illustration to show that reverse racism, or the concept of hating those who hate us, is the wrong thing to do. In so doing I will rehearse somewhat a bit of what I previously wrote in this book. The conclusion may be drawn from this that Blacks can be as racist as anyone else. I also discuss the possibility that we practice self-hatred. This self-hate seems to be almost an epidemic among us.

I belong to what I think is one of the most fundamental of Christian organizations in the world today. Although it is worldwide, it is relatively unknown, and is not considered mainstream by most people, and though the organization began here in North America, and has been legally formed into a corporate body since 1863, many people here have no knowledge of the denomination's existence. As written earlier, one of the things this organization was known for, was its poor treatment of Black people. In some instances, though not with corporate approval, this attitude still exists. Not surprisingly, it was in the United States that the organization began and where it is presently headquartered. Not surprisingly, it is from Americans that most people take their cue so far as relating to each other is concerned.

The racist/class-conscious attitudes of its White people have spilled over into other parts of the world. And where racism has not been a part of the psyche of its people, it has shown itself to be class-conscious where the people are otherwise homogenous in terms of colour or nationality. It really is not surprisingly that it has been in America mostly where Blacks have been made to feel the keenest hate this "Christian" organization has been able to dispense. Blacks can tell of being called "niggers" even as little children in its schools by some of its teachers, and they have been made to feel that they were of little or no value. In the not-too-distant-past, it would not treat Blacks in some of its hospitals, and even in its churches where they worship Blacks have been made to feel like non-persons, if they were allowed in some of those churches at all.

There are legal divisions comprising this organization, and these divisions have been racially split between the Whites and Blacks in America. When I lived in Texas I went to churches of both persuasions, but my church was under Black leadership. The congregation I attended there was made up of predominantly White members when I first got there. But surprisingly, the church was under Black leadership. The White members were professionals and earned lot of money, part of which was paid in tithes and offerings to the headquarters. They quickly became the "crown jewels" of that leadership. This church congregation was never given a Black minister. He always had to be White. For the first three years I attended there, they changed ministers about three times. The third pastor was a gentleman from Minnesota. Things were not going well for this particular congregation, and it is alleged that he was asked to come in, clean house, and set things right. A little more on him will be discussed later.

A few years after I had began attending church there, we had a visit from one of the corporate leaders. At that time all their leaders, including the President, were, naturally, Black. Before he preached that morning, he stood in the pulpit and complained that no one had welcomed him. He chided the Black people in particular for not making him feel welcome and at home. He named them by colour, seemingly wanting nothing to do with the welcome from the White people. A number of the Black people went up to greet him. I sat there in stunned silence! Did he not see that half of the members were White? Did those Black members who went up to greet him forget that they were doing something that, if taken out of context, could injure the feelings of the White members among whom they worship? This leader was only going to be there for one day.

Until then, there had been no visible signs of acrimony between the White and Black members of the group. Everyone got along fabulously as far as I could tell and very frequently socialized together even in each other's homes. I hoped hard that this would not damage the heretofore good relationships the members seemed to enjoy. We normally had potluck lunches when such high-profile people came to the church. It was no different this time, but the atmosphere at lunch that day was quite subdued as the Whites stayed by themselves. I could not help but feel very embarrassed, and I sympathized with them, even though I said nothing. I thought that they might think I was insincere if I joined them or expressed my sentiments verbally.

My family and I got to know the minister from Minnesota and his wife very well. We often talked about race relations in the context of his position, him being the only White minister of this Black led division in America where everything seems to have race attached to it. He had quite a surprising story to tell. Every so often the ministers and leaders, and their wives would gather for important meetings. Once a year, they gathered for the annual camp meeting, which this church organization has for all its members here in North America and in other parts of the world where it exists though I don't remember hearing about camp meetings when I lived in Jamaica. These meetings are held in the various places owned by the various Conferences and Regions. He told me that at these meetings his presence was not a factor for them to take note of. His contemporaries rarely spoke to him. He said they told him verbally that they were only concerned for the Black people. He would be required to help with the physical setting up of platforms, chairs, and so on, but he would never be allowed to address the sessions.

I found this most disconcerting!

I asked him, why he would continue going? What about the White people whom he was there to represent? Did they not have a voice and maybe issues of concern? I couldn't help thinking about all those tens of thousands of dollars his church, coming mostly from the White people, was sending to the corporate offices every year. As indicated before, a lot of the Whites there were highly paid professionals and some had their own businesses. He told us that he went because it was his obligation so to do and because he was paid by them. His wife did not attend these sessions, even though ministers' wives were supposed to be a part of these gatherings. She stayed in a room by herself. She apparently was too hurt to show herself after the first session. All the other wives, who were Black, were made a part of the activities but not her. They expressed no desire to have her be a part of what they were doing. It was as though she did not exist at all. I am talking about the late 1990's here. Not the 1800s.

Reverse racism? You bet! I personally would have complained loudly about this arrangement, and if nothing were ever done, I would not hesitate to give up the job. But as I did not know his personal circumstances I could not really speak for him.

There may be those who read this and say that there was nothing wrong with this action, given the treatment of Blacks in similar situations. I will admit here that though I have been discriminated against racially more times than I choose to remember, I have not personally experienced the same mindless, hateful, lifelong racial ostracism that American Blacks and other Blacks from places like South Africa, Brazil, and India have suffered. But to those people I would still say "Shame on you." My question was and still would be: "How could people who have suffered so much humiliation and hate because of the racist passions of others now perpetrate the same acts on those who were as innocent as themselves, at least in this situation and in this, a religious context?" Are they not proving to themselves and to others that they are of the same hateful stock as the people who treated them in such a manner? Why would anyone allow such lust for revenge to dwell in them when they profess to be better? And why do this as a matter of policy in a Christian church? (I use the word Christian in the context of following Christ whose practices were not hateful and vindictive).

Earlier I said that this new minister had been hired to "clean house," and because his views on most things were diametrically opposed to those of a lot of the members of the congregation, eventually there was a showdown between the Charter Members, who felt that they had the God-given right to do as they pleased, and the new minister, who felt that as the "under shepherd" of that particular flock he should have a voice in the affairs of the church. This happened about a year after he took over leadership of the church. About 40 of them left to do things on their own. Interestingly, none of the Black members opposed the White minister. Those who left were all White, and as time went on more of the White members left the church and more Black members came in. The main reasons were the membership which remained were now mostly Black, and they got a Black minister to take over pastoral duties because the White minister left to continue his work in the White conference in a nearby state. His leaving was due in part to interference in his personal life by a Black, female busybody in the congregation, but though he did not say so directly, I believe the treatment from the Black leadership had something to do with it also.

One of the new Black members was very strong in his opinions and was very unreasonable in his sentiments with reference to the remaining White members. Thankfully, he did not express his sentiments to them directly and there were never any confrontations between him and any of them. This was something that I would personally have gotten involved in to prevent any hurt to the remaining White members. As I said earlier in this book, I am for the disadvantaged and the underdog, and the skin colour to me then is unimportant.

One of this man's talents was the gift of music, and he was given a musical position in the church. He and I would sometimes have conversations, and especially in matters relating to music, he wanted to have his way entirely. As the music leader at the time, I told him that whenever he led out as a song leader, he needed to ensure that his music included that which the White folks liked also. After all, they had just as much right as we did to be blessed by the worship service for which they came. They were participating and supporting members of the church, and to add to that, many times they dropped off something in the offering plate when this member did not. He insisted that his music should just be for the Blacks. He could not understand my line of reasoning. He asked point-blank who cared about the interests and likes of the Whites? I told him that I for one sure did. But it didn't matter to him. He, being an American Black, did not trust my sentiments anyway because apparently, as far as a lot of Black Americans are concerned, West Indian Blacks are not of the same stock as they, and could in no way appreciate their experiences.

It is true that West Indian Blacks have not suffered the same as they did, relative to racial discrimination as I mentioned earlier. But I do not hate American Blacks at all. On the contrary, I very much admire them, even as I find it despicable that such a large number of them commit so much crime, notwithstanding the reasons why that may be happening. (Incidentally, a lot of West Indian Blacks (especially my countrymen), commit a lot of crimes too, are the culprit criminals in the West Indies and do contribute to a lot of crimes in other countries including America, Canada, and England). But as I was saying before, I greatly admire Black Americans for their successes and achievement when such is the case, believing that it takes much more than what the average person possesses for them to get anywhere in mostly White and very racist America where so many doors are closed against them. Yet some of them have gone on to do so very well. I enthusiastically applaud those.

In further conversations with this young man, I observed that he seemed to think with an entirely different mindset. I asked him on a couple of occasions who provided him employment and why he wasn't working for some Black corporation or the other. As there were no Black corporations or businesses in the area to provide him gainful employment, he realized that I was just trying to point out to him that he needed something more tangible than words to justify his lack of concern or appreciation for Whites, who if for nothing else were obviously the employment providers for him at this particular time and maybe even other times in his life. He simply refused to or just couldn't get it, but I tried to prompt him to see that despite the history of the past we have to move forward; that we should still be grateful to the White folks for such things as employment, etc., and that we do not have the wherewithal to dispense with the direct or indirect benefits of the expertise of the White race, even if we wanted to. But something else about him puzzled me. Though he was legally Black, his hair and physical appearance indicated a mixed racial background of the White and Black races. I concluded then that he hated a part of his ancestry, and in reality also hated himself.

By the time I left, nothing with him had changed, and later on I learned that he left that congregation for one that was entirely Black. Though I didn't like his attitude, I could not hate him either. I am as willing to empathize with his mindset as I am willing to work with the White folks who are uncomfortable for us because of whatever reason. Even those Whites who lynched Blacks in the American South, cut out the unborn babies out of expectant Black mothers, raped little girls and boys, and roasted Blacks at the stakes right there in "blessed" America need sympathy and forgiveness. And since God is willing to forgive them if they ask such of Him, I, His professed child, should be willing to do the same. If I don't forgive and try to love them whenever I have the opportunity here on earth, then when I see them in heaven I won't be on speaking terms with them either, and since heaven is a place where we will all have to be on speaking terms, those of us who continue to harbour hatred, revenge, and unforgiveness toward even those who have done us wrong historically and in the present will certainly find the gates closed against us.

Over the course of many years, I have heard sentiments of hate against members of the White race expressed quite a number of times by Blacks. A lot of Blacks think it is their inalienable right to hate and despise in return those who have hated and despised us. From time to time, I cannot deny my anger and dislike with Whites and other races for their hatred and ill-treatment of Blacks. With my sense of justice, this is just natural. It seems a part of human nature to hate those who hate and love only those who love. But I have never taken any anger out on them, and has never tried to hurt nor disadvantage them in anyway. I also had no general hate for them. If we always did what pertains to hate and revenge, we would not be much good to ourselves or anyone else, and the cycle of hate would be never ending. We could become like the Middle East with its cycle of attacks and counter-attacks.

In the past, the people I hated the most were the Japanese. I don't know why. Maybe it was because of the way they acted in the Second World War. I knew that I especially hated the fact that they bombed America, because odd as it may sound because of its chequered past in race relations, as I was growing up, America was a place I idolized. I always said to anyone who would listen that I did not believe that America dropped enough bombs on Hiroshima and Nagasaki to avenge the attack on Pearl Harbour. This hatred had become an obsession with me. But one day I was sitting in my church in Toronto, which by the way was a multi-racial church. Visitors were welcomed, and there was this beautiful young Japanese couple visiting from their church. They looked as sweet and as amiable as any couple I'd ever seen. Then it struck me. If I make it to heaven and they make it to heaven too, I will have to love them there. I knew instinctively and intellectually that I had to love them here or I would not get the chance to love them there. From that moment, with God's help, I have successfully erased my hatred of the Japanese people and by extension hatred for every other people from my heart.

Should Blacks feel justified practicing reverse racism and hate against Whites and others in situations where they have the upper hand? I would answer that question by stating that not all Whites and other people are racists, and that not all White people practiced racism and discrimination against Blacks, even in the American Deep South in the days of slavery. So, speaking from a religious and social standpoint, the answer is unequivocally, NO. Reverse racism will not do any Black person a single ounce of good. It will only make us as bitter and as unlovable as those who have hated us. Having suffered so much wrong because of discrimination, those who have been through this fire should be the first to rescue other unfortunate humans from this most evil malady, and the last to practice it on their fellow men.

People on both sides of the divide should try to walk in each others' shoes. This way we might then be able to be tolerant of each other, especially where we share the same space, etc. Hateful people are probably not always born that way but were made so by upbringing. Blacks are born into our physical being without any choice of our own. We should, therefore, not be hated on sight by others because of our physical appearance. This is where the trouble starts. By the same token, Blacks should not hate those of other races. Maybe if we can open our minds a bit we can then see beyond the skin to the person in it. Sometimes, it is a person hampered by circumstance and misfortunes not to mention a biased upbringing. In some parts of the world, the population consists almost entirely of people of one race. What great lack of experience those people must have in working with people of other races? It is not their fault that from the cradle to the grave, most of them have never been outside their racial group. If they hear only the bad about others they will think that is all there is, and they will be unwilling to work with or appreciate others.

Growing up, I loved(good looking) babies and(good looking) little children a lot. I still do, but now (good looking) is not necessary. There was this very handsome, and sweet little boy who I always wanted to be my little friend. However, he would always run away from me, so eventually I left off trying to get acquainted with him. One day some years later, I learned the reason for his behaviour. His mother told me that she used to frighten him with my name whenever she wanted to get him to listen to her. I was very disappointed when she told me that. I was only about 14 or 15 when the child was old enough to learn to be afraid of me. I still wonder how she was able to get him to learn how to do that. Mostly everyon else liked me including children. Anyway it shows how easy people can learn to react one way or another to others.

Sometimes this is what happens to us as Black people—causing other people to hate us. They are told that we are criminals, are no good, and that they are to stay away from us. We ought then to be understanding of their blindness, and still go on, and get rid of the chips that we carry on our shoulders. When I first came to Toronto I met this young mother and her three young children in church. The father and husband had long gone. The oldest child, a girl took a liking to me maybe as she had lost her father. She was sitting with me one afternoon and other children were chatting and laughing around myself and other adults present. She pulled on my jacket to get my attention telling me that some of the other children were talking about her. From where we were sitting she could not have overheard their whispers so I asked her how she knew. Her reply was that she thought that was what it was. Realizing the potential for turning her little mind in the wrong direction I had to quickly tell her that unless she can prove clearly that others are talking about her she should never come to such a conclusions. She told me that she would try. The moral of the story is; don't contribute to what will cause hurt to anyone mentally or otherwise.

Do We Hate Ourselves?

Sometimes, we seem to hate ourselves. How else can we explain some of the dysfunctional behaviour patterns that we display! This self-hatred, wherever it exists, is probably the biggest hate problem that Blacks have to overcome. Our skin colour has placed us in the spotlight of negativity and makes us as obvious as a spotted calf. Because of this, we are led to think that the first thought others have about us is something bad or suspicious. This has made a lot of us very sensitive and insecure. Many Blacks, sometimes including me, have wished they were White when seeking to escape from situations where they are singled out because of something bad that a Black individual may have done. Such a wish may just have been a temporary self-preserving thought. (I wrote about this earlier) If this is because we sometimes have very little appreciation for ourselves or very little self-respect, then that is not good. Self-image may depend on where we live and the degree of racial adversity we have faced. Some of you may remember Brook Benton, the Black American rhythm and blues performer. He went to Jamaica in the late Sixties or very early Seventies. I cant recall for sure, but I know I was there then, and I left Jamaica in 1972 for Toronto. At the time he lived in America where Blacks were treated much worse than they are today.

In Jamaica he saw Blacks going about without the daily dose of deprecations he received from some Whites in his country. He also saw Blacks in positions of government, etc. His remark was that in Jamaica he saw the "pride and dignity of the Black man." When I visited South Africa, I saw Blacks in almost every capacity- managing stores, working in fancy restaurants, working as political commentators, newsreporters, and so on. Though I was not a South African, I felt right at home and proud to see so many Blacks of whatever shade of skin in such visible positions. When I got back to Toronto I realized why I have felt so little self esteem all these years. I have not seen Blacks in many positions here which would say we are going anywhere socially anytime soon. It really does something for the self image when people see their own in good jobs. (Now I am not blaming White Canadians for this. I am simply making a point). I had the same feelings of self actualization when I went to Atlanta Georgia in the late Nineties on a business trip and found so many Blacks working at the airport and in other public places. I supose we could say that if all Blacks in America lived in Atlanta and see other Blacks in such visible places doing what Whites would normally do, they might feel less self hating. We may have to direct our minds inwardly and change the barometer which we use to decide what will make us like ourselves.

But of our own; why might it be concluded that we sometimes hate ourselves? We sell illegal drugs in our neighbourhoods to the detriment of our own people, and become gang members of nearly the worst kind. We shoot up our own people and others, rob the stores of innocent immigrants, destroy our own peoples' businesses in race riots, and refuse—in noticeably large numbers—to educate and improve ourselves. Sometimes even those who hate us expect better of us. They wonder why we do the things we do. Even decent Blacks are ashamed of some of us and ashamed because of us.

When I lived in Texas, there was a community in Dallas where it is alleged that a lot of the young Black men did nothing more than just collect welfare cheques, commit crimes petty and otherwise, and gathered in public places for no visibly productive reasons. Some of the White citizens were so angry, they complained through a spokesperson about the bad behaviour of these young men and said they were nothing more than "purveyors of poverty." That remark struck me like a bolt of thunder. It could only be said of a group of young men who did not like themselves enough to seek to improve their lot in life. But at the same time there seemed to me from the individual speaking a note of hope that it could have been different for these young men if they had only made the effort to change things in their lives.

We need a healthy dose of self-love and self-appreciation to change the "loser" destiny some of us have carved out for ourselves as indicated by our self-destructive behaviour. This may be very hard for some to do because for generations we have been fed and have also fed ourselves the poison of self-hate, and failure. God loves you so much, He sent His Son to redeem you from a life of self-hate and self-destruction. God Himself values us, therefore we should love ourselves and others to the point of making them and ourselves better. We cannot continue to hate ourselves and yet expect to be successful.

CHAPTER ELEVEN
BLACKS AND COMPENSATION
FOR SLAVERY

In this section of the book I would like to agitate the concept for compensation to Blacks on this side of the Atlantic for all the evils they suffered at the hands of others because of slavery. I would like to discuss what I think is the responsibility resting on all groups that have enslaved Blacks. Certainly this includes the responsibility of Black Africans themselves for the part they played in the slave trade. The method of compensation for those responsible will be looked at. Every time this subject is broached, the emphasis seems to be placed only on the United States of America as being solely responsible for compensating the descendants of the slaves. In this chapter, I will propose that many more nations than just the U.S are responsible for compensation.

The issue of compensation for Blacks whose recent ancestors suffered enslavement is one I feel I must bring up in this book. In contemplating this I would like to explore what form, if there ever is compensation, this should take. Should there be an apology to begin with? And if there is one, would just an apology constitute compensation? Should it be financial compensation, something already touched lightly upon in this book? I believe that in order to find a suitable answer one has to go back over several centuries to when slavery began to discover not only the appropriateness of compensation, but also any and everyone responsible. I would like to go back to the mid 1400s, starting at a time most people should be comfortable with. This was when the European connection to the African slave trade was initiated.

This is not to say that those responsible before this should not be held liable for compensation. Such a conclusion leaves out the Arabs of North Africa, for example, who kept Black Africans as slaves for many centuries before the Europeans of the pre-modern era.

The first Europeans to bring slaves from Africa were the Portuguese when, in 1444, they brought some from northern Mauritania. History reports that Europeans had been trading with nations of Africa in gold and salt before the Atlantic slave trade began. As they explored farther and farther down the west coast of Africa, the Portuguese established contacts that later helped in the business of slavery.

In 1483, they began what they wanted to be looked at as an exchange of diplomats from the Kongo Kingdom. Diogo Cao sailed down the Atlantic to the mouth of the Congo River. Reaching the Kongo Kingdom he established a relationship and brought back citizens of the Kongo with him to Portugal. They later went back to Africa with soldiers, priests, and goods to trade. This was the start of a strong trading relationship by which the Portuguese received slaves and ivory in return for goods and guns from Europe.

History records that the Kongo already had an ongoing system of slavery which the newcomers merely toused for their own benefit. However, the increased demand for slaves from the Portuguese brought pressure on the Kongo to fill the ever increasing demand. This seems to have led to raids on various others by the Congolese to supply this demand. It is said that this caused violence in the region, and by removing workers from the Kongo Kingdom it led to an economy based on slavery. This weakened the Kongo and caused it to become dependent on the Portuguese for their economic support. Elmina Castle, an early trading post in Ghana, began with the same "noble sentiment" of African trade in gold and other types of goods but it soon became a place synonymous with the slave trade, especially after it was captured by the British from the Portuguese. It became a holding cell, so to speak, for millions of captives who would become slaves as they awaited the voyage to the West. Other European nations followed Portugal's lead and gradually joined up in what would become a very lucrative business for both government and private enterprise. This leads to the right conclusion that Portugal bears the greatest responsible for the slave trade.

We know that no one involved in the slave trade for direct profit is alive today. We know also that no African who suffered the injustices of those times is alive today to receive compensation. But the concern is that historical wrongs should be set right for the descendants of those who were wronged, and the unfairness of the past should be addressed by the descendants of those who dispensed the cruelty and injustice of slavery. In this sense, the children become responsible for the wrongs their fathers committed. And while we hear of no Africans being enslaved today by Europeans to the same extent and as mindlessly as it was in days gone by, it can be concluded that, should those days return, the people alive today would probably do just what the others did.

When considering compensation for the slavery of Blacks Africans, we must think of all those who should be held responsible. Following the Portuguese, were the Spanish who needed slave labour for their plantations in the Americas and the Caribbean. The English were another huge purchaser of slave labour for their plantations in the wear Indies as hinted at before. They were not far behind the Portuguese and the Spanish. The French, the Dutch, the Germans and even the tiny Belgian nation were involved in the business of slavery becoming a very brutal and oppressive force in the Kongo. The Italians also were quite cruel to Black Africans though not quite as involved in slavery. There were also nations buying slaves that didn't go to Africa to get them. This would include America, whose citizens turned out to be one of the biggest purchasers of Black slaves. The purchase of slaves in America was started by the British colonisers. It is recorded that the couple of slaves which an American citizen actually went to get on the continent of Africa were ordered returned. In the American situation, some States wanted slaves and some did not allow it. It is an historical fact that earlier on the Arabs and Indians took slaves from Africa to work in their countries.

The African nations were themselves actively engaged in the slave trade. The first of those nations, as outlined above, was the Kongo. Others followed as time went on, either actively catching slaves or allowing the ships to dock at their ports to get their human cargo. In all those cases, the people of those nations were kidnapping their own countrymen and women for enslavement. This was done along tribal and religious lines. If these nations had not helped with the capture and forced enslavement of their fellow Africans, maybe we would not have had the problem of slavery in the first place.

The African nations involvement in the slave trade cannot and should not be overlooked when it comes to taking responsibility for compensation if that became the issue. As well, blaming America alone, as most people do, and expecting only America to be responsible for compensation is unfair because so many other nations in the Western Hemisphere, including nations in South America, Central America, and the Caribbean have enjoyed tremendous economic benefits from slave labour. Some of these countries, primarily in South and Central America, may say that it was under their Spanish colonial masters that slavery was practiced, and argue that Spain should be the country required to pay compensation on their behalf, even though the people now living in those nations are the ones enjoying the legacy of slave labour.

Is there one nation or one group of individuals that could facilitate this endeavour? It would certainly be a tremendous amount of effort because so many nations could be implicated. It would probably take the involvement of the United Nations to facilitate such an endeavour. It would have to determine the criteria, the procedure, the level of responsibility, and the amount of compensation. It would also have to identify the degree to which Blacks suffered in the countries named during and subsequent to slavery. Some of these nations have quietly silenced any reference to their involvement and there is not even a whimper of their past mistreatment of Black slaves. No one hears of Blacks having had harsh treatment in places like Mexico, Argentina, Costa Rica, as an example, but America, Brazil, England, and France, can absorb much discredit for this.

On this side of the Atlantic America and Brazil are the most notorious countries in the Western Hemisphere for Black disenfranchisement, even though America has forged ahead with changes that are beneficial to Blacks in some ways. In fairness to Americans, there is hardly any comparison between the fortunes of the Blacks in America and those in Brazil. Brazil has done nothing for its descendants of slaves, but quite a number of Blacks in America are successful and are probably the richest Blacks in the entire world. While some Whites in America can be credited for the present fortunes of some Blacks, credit should also go to American Blacks for all the hard work they put in to ensure some enrichment of themselves.

The question may be asked: what exactly are Blacks to be compensated for? They should be compensated for forced expatriation from their homeland, enslavement, denial of basic human rights, denial of the right to freedom of speech, education, deprivation, physical brutality, impoverishment, and denial of the right to family relations. They also need compensation for all the free labour they contributed to so many nations which even presently hold them in almost total irrelevance. Slave owners and governments perpetrated these evils against them, and now governments in those countries as they exist today should be held responsible for their actions and those of their now-deceased citizens. It is interesting that slavery ended in the 1860s in America, but well over a hundred years later there are still the same sentiments of disenfranchisement in many places. It is also interesting that when the slaves were "freed," all or most of the injustices they previously suffered were not redressed.

I may, at this point, be one of the few persons agitating this concept for compensation for the descendants of former Black slaves, and I do so knowing full well that my voice alone from my little corner of the room from where I am penning this thought might not be able to put it into action. My pen may just be stirring a tempest in a teapot. But nonetheless, the argument for compensation can be made. In my opinion the real question should be: what is taking so long? And why should compensation not be paid? The sooner the process begins, the better as it might take many long years to figure out the level of responsibility and the amount to be paid.

But I would like to insert here the benefits which accrued to only one of those nations involved. This will give you my readers, a slight idea of the riches that slavery brought to nations and individuals. I will do this for the nation of Britain.

British slave ship owners made profits on voyages of roughly 20 - 50%, so very large sums of money were made by ship owners who never even left England.

There were profits to British traders who bought and sold slaves.

Plantation owners who used slave labour to grow their crops made vast profits using these unpaid workers. They often retired to England with their riches and built grand country houses and lavish mansions for themselves. Some plantation owners used some of the money they made to become Members of Parliament. Still others invested their money in new factories and inventions, helping to finance the Industrial Revolution.

Factory owners in England had a great market for their goods. Textiles from mills in England were bought by slave owners to use as barter for slaves in Africa. It is reported that textiles from Yorkshire and Lancaster were bought by slave traders going to Africa in abundance. About half of the textile produced in Manchester was exported to the West Indies and the other half in Africa. Industrial plans were built to refine imported raw sugar. Glass containers were needed to bottle the rum made from sugar and that was done in factories which had to get people to work for them providing employment to very many.

Bristol and Liverpool became major ports for fitting out slave ships and handling the cargo they brought back. The population of Liverpool rose from about 500 to about 78000 in about 100 years. Bankers and finance houses grew rich from fees and interest they earned from merchants who borrowed money for the voyages and for the goods they purchased to sell on those voyages. The Transatlantic Slave Trade provided many jobs for other people in England who worked in factories which in turn sold goods to Africa. Birmingham as an example had some 4000 gun makers with over 100,000 guns per year going to the slave traders.

As for the government of England directly, through its own laws it established the Royal African Company and by 1760 England was the foremost European country engaging in the slave trade. The islands of the Caribbean became the engine that gave life to the economy of the British Empire. Because of sugar cane, these became England`s most valuable colonies. The

British government received millions of pounds from these West Indian plantations. It is reported than between 1750 and 1879 about 70% of the government`s total revenues came from taxes on goods from its slave colonies. The slave triangle was vast and poured much into the economies of England and much of Europe and changed their landscape forever. Many fine mansions were built from the wealth gained from slavery and it is believed that many banks were established and the fortune of even the Bank of England which was established in 1694 was greatly enhanced. James Houston who worked for a firm 18th century slave merchants wrote that slavery was a glorious and advantageous trade. He said of slavery that it was the hinge on which all the trade of this globe moved at the time.

In recent years, very quiet mention of compensationfor Black enslavement has only been discussed in America but far as I know, this has only been done by private citizens. Interestingly, this brings to mind the significant conclusion that some do recognize that something should be done to compensate the descendants of ex-slaves for all the hard work they performed, and the injustices they suffered. In my opinion, the passing of time and the wilful forgetfulness of the nations' chief executives do not lessen the responsibility of the leaders of these countries in regards to this. Since no one who can bear responsibility for compensation is addressing the subject, it is obvious that it will most likely never be addressed anytime soon. But if America were to settle, most other countries would probably follow its example.

Some time ago, there were musings that Blacks were going to ask that one of the states on the American mainland be handed over to them as compensation for slavery, and where they could have some kind of autonomy and feel a sense of belonging and independence. I personally think that such would be unwise. Some people might agree that a monetary compensation would be best. Others have considered education; some consider land, and some consider housing. Still others think that a fair and equitable society with true equal opportunities for all is the way to go. As a first step, I believe that an apology would be very appropriate because that sometimes goes a very long way to heal wounds festering for years. After the apology, other things should follow, maybe things such as money, land, or education.

It is obvious that there certainly would be differing opinions on the matter of compensation should that arise. And this may well be a very personal issue for some of the would be recipients. People whose ancestors were not involved in slavery will probably be angry at the thought of anyone being compensated and may strongly oppose the idea, even to the point of violence.

But should a compensation plan be initiated and some kind of opposition arise, this should not scuttle the process. The moral and legal obligations to compensate should far outweigh any anticipated negative outcome to any opposition. If the question of compensation ever reaches the action stage and national degrees of responsibility are apportioned, America would probably be required to pay the most because that country has gained a lot from slave labour. Nonetheless it is questionable that given the benefit to the British economy in the early days that America should pay the most. It is probably because that country has done so much bad things over such a long period of time against Blacks why it could be expected to do that. It is said that only 5% of Americans owned slaves and that only 7% of all slaves shipped to the West ended up in America. However that still amounted to millions of slaves, not including those born in America who remained slaves for life.

Following America is Brazil with its continued oppression of Blacks where they are practically denied even the earth they walk on, in a manner of speaking. Brazil should pay the same amount as America because they have done nothing for Blacks since the time they were brought there as slaves, inspite of all the many years of enslavement and all the work done for them on their farms and sugar plantations of that country during the 17th century. They seem to think that Blacks are only useful for a few soccer games if talented enough, or to be used when the police need to check to see if their pistols are still working.

On the other side of the world stands India with its *Dalits*. No nation on earth today treats its most helpless citizens as poorly as India treats the *Dalits*. Their situation has already been outlined earlier in this book. With its new found wealth there is no reason that India should not adequately redress people that have been despised for so many centuries. They should start by recognizing that those people deserve better treatment than the cattle that walk their streets. Hopefully one day their darkended minds will see that the Dalits are people who came from the hand of God just like everyone else and that they deserve to be given even the basics of human dignity. They owe those people untold Billions of dollars in compensation

England has had Black slaves, but its historical treatment of them has not been even faintly close to that of all the other countries where Blacks were enslaved. The British led the emancipation movement, but even before emancipation there were many illustrious Britons who sought and obtained a measure of freedom and protection for Black slaves both on and off its soil. Aside from its present day stand on Black issues, I would be tempted to forgive any responsibility the British would otherwise be liable for in regards to slavery. But they have profited so much from slavery that it would be foolhardy to let them go without paying anything for compensation for slavery.

Portugal ought to be held responsible as a primary culprit for the enslavement of Black Africans. It was Portugal that initiated the practice where Europeans are concerned. It gave the first and ultimate assistance to the slave market. They should not escape their financial responsibility but instead have their feet held to the fire for nothing less that the amount that the United States should be held liable for. The amount of slaves they took is not hard to estimate when one looks at how many Blacks are in Brazil, a former colony of Portugal, and one where the Portuguese took slaves to work in those massive sugar plantations in the 1700s.

The responsibility of the Spanish should not be overlooked. As the second power in Europe to join the slave trade they have profited immensely. They supplied slaves for all of Central and South America as well as parts of the Caribbean, and tapped into the trade to support the labour demands of their colonies. This brought them tremendous wealth and economic benefits. Their enslavement of Black Africans did not end officially till 1886, about two decades after America. It may be said that they may not have been as cruel to Blacks considering them as non humans as the Americans did. They even had Blacks travelling with Christopher Columbus and other Spanish explorers as they went out to explore new lands. Nonetheless reparations should not overlook them.

No one should forget the French, Germans, the Dutch and certainly not the Belgians in this. Of these four Belgium with its cruelty in the Congo and its continued raping of that nation's timber and diamonds should be held most responsible in terms of how much they should pay.

The Arabs held African Blacks in slavery much longer than the Europeans did and would have continued to this day had not France and England stepped in to end the practice of the last hold out - Saudi Arabia in 1962. They are able and should pay a very hefty sum not only for the enslavement, but also for the mindless butchering and mutilation of millions of Black Africans, and the sexual humiliation and exploitation of Black African female slaves. They have conveniently swept the details of their barbaric treatment of Black slaves from the pages of their history but it is inconceivable that they should bear no responsibility for compensation for Black enslavement.

Canada, as mentioned before had a few slaves, but in fairness to Canadians, they treated slaves more like respectable servants. In actual fact those who served in Canada could hardly be called slaves at all. They were allowed to marry, allowed to acquire good working skills, and were taught to read and write. We also cannot forget the role of Canada in the Underground Railroad story. There indeed were isolated cases in Canada of some unfair treatment by a few individual slave owners, but the ill-treatment of "slaves" in general was non-existent. The worst situation here for Blacks, as I understand it, was the unfair treatment they received from the Province of Nova Scotia, and the others mentioned previously. Even today, that province is still one of the worst places in English Canada for Blacks to live. Nonetheless, I don't believe this country owes anything to anyone for slavery.

Lastly, we have the African countries, which were involved in slavery from the very beginning. Black Africans themselves played their role very well in the marketing of their own people who they captured, and then sold them to the foreign slave traders. It would be more than hypocritical to leave them out of the list of nations responsible for compensation. They are right up there with Portugal where initial responsibility for slavery is concerned. Not only were they most instrumental in capturing and selling slaves, but they also enslaved their own peoplefor their own purposes. They still do in some cases Countries like Ghana, Senegal, Tanzania, Benin, and Mauritania are some of those African countries to be held responsible for compensating the slaves But how will they pay? For starters maybe their leaders could live on a lot less, stop robbing the public purse and redirect some of that money to their people. Anyway as this volume would be too long to read if every aspect of this subject were to be explored, it is best to leave things where they are for now till some time in the future.

CHAPTER TWELVE
LOOKING AHEAD

In this chapter, we are encouraged to get out of the historical lethargy and self-defeating state that we find ourselves in. I do this by pointing out things we can do to improve ourselves by making positive, deliberate, and meaningful choices, accepting things we cannot change, and changing the things that must be changed if we are to move forward. I accept the fact that some form of racial discrimination is here to stay and that an "enlightened" society now sees the need for changing to what I refer to as "discretionary racial discrimination" in instances which it may never escape racial prejudice.

Notwithstanding the negative effects of unfairness and hate that some of us the members of the Black race encounter on almost a daily basis, we must look ahead and make plans for a bright and even a prosperous future. We need to accept the fact that we sometimes can be our own worst enemies and change that. We should make plans to change our lives for our own good, for the benefit of our families, our friends, our race, the society in which we live, and for succeeding generations. All is not gloom and doom even if things are imperfect. The first glimmer of hope, which should brighten the path of every Black person, is the realization that we are beneficiaries of the goodness of God. Though we have suffered many grave and great injustices, we have not been totally abandoned to the whims and fancy of those who would like to see us completely annihilated. And if God is for us, who can be against us? Upon the strength resident in Him, every Black person can look in hope for spiritual and material prosperity, social progress, and survival. This is how many Black slaves survived and achieved a higher purpose for their lives. With this as a backdrop, let us look at the issues confronting us and plot our strategy, not only to surmount them but also to make progress and prosper.

One of the things we need to do is create a new outlook on this issue of race in our own minds. There are things that we will not be able to change or do anything about. One of them is the present established order of things. Whether by Providence, luck, or the evolution of thoughts, ideas, or opportunities, the Whites are the masters of enterprise on the planet presently and White people are in positions of economic leadership all over the planet. Japheth has certainly been enlarged in the tents of Shem. In terms of creating economies, employment, and businesses they have no equal. They are only superseded by the most prominent son of Shem - the Jews - who it is alleged are the real creators of money. This should not be surprising because God promised Abraham that in him would all the nations of the earth be blessed. The Jews are the direct descendants of Abraham.

Hating or disliking Whites will not make the life or lot of any Black person the least bit better, and as the saying goes, if you can't beat them, join them. Truthfully, I prefer the Whites than the other races to be in the position that they are in now. They have proven to be more generous than other people, and have proven that they are the most likely to share what they have. Most other races are quite selfish and very narrow with what they might have. Despite the negatives, they are the ones always helping Blacks with jobs and other opportunities for improvement though sometimes quite limited. This is especially true of the Whites in the Western world. I am not saying that they are all goody goody, but where would we be without them?

But can we do to change things? I personally do not believe that Blacks should seek social and racial equality with Whites. That should not be the focus of our energies, even though some will say that much progress has resulted from such initiatives. What I believe is necessary, and very right, is for Blacks to seek to persuade the governments of White countries in which they reside to provide a system of fairness from a moral, legal, and socio-economic perspective. If all are empowered, all can prosper, even though we sometimes must see prosperity in context. It should be obvious to governments that everyone in their jurisdictions needs to live. We all need the basic things in life—shelter, food, clothing, education, medical care, and so on, and we should be given the opportunity to obtain these amenities without institutional and government-sanctioned encumbrances. I see the government as a regulatory body of individuals, making laws to benefit the society over which it presides. That body has to make laws benefiting all the members of that society, ensuring proper schooling, good housing, and the availability of suitable opportunities for its citizens. It should also provide security from physical harm, and from the destruction of property and the other outcomes of hate perpetrated by one group over the other. No government should allow the racism and the hate that has been practiced by some people and even past local, state, and federal governing bodies of the United States, the apartheid system of the past South African government, the nation of Brazil, the sub-continent of India, as well as other countries where racism still exist. These nations,have missed and are still missing the mark so far as responsible leadership is concerned. Every governing body of men of whatever race should live above the miasma of bigotry. Blacks in these societies where fairness is lacking should attempt to bring the attention of authorities, business leaders, and employers to this imbalance in a peaceful and civilized manner in order to effect positive and lasting changes. Despite their short-comings, Western Whites are the most open-minded people in the world, and are the most likely to help to make changes to rectify bad situations brought to their attention. One can readily see that these are the people who never fail to help others, even their enemies in desperate situations whether they be famines, floods, or earthquakes. They are the most generous of people groups in my experience. This is true even of America, even though it did not do so well for the Hurricane Katrina victims on its own soil because they were mostly Black.

Blacks need not invade the space and personhood of other people in order to feel good about ourselves. We need not impose ourselves on others. We all make the best impressions when we conform to the established order of things and then seek to address unfairness with as little ruffling of the feathers as possible. Blacks seem to always be the most anxious of all the races to ingratiate ourselves among others. We initiate most inter-racial relationships, implying that we are not completely happy with who we are. I say that even as I myself have had a mixed- race marriage. We need not feel that we have to be in some other colour or have some other person's face or personality to change our circumstances and feel good about ourselves. No matter how much you feel that you have to be in some other skin colour to change yourself, it just won't happen, at least not on a permanent basis. Chemicals might help to change skin colour temporarily, but what will that accomplish in the long run? You have only one *you*. That is all God gave you to work with. Do the best with it that you can. Endeavour to love yourself every day. If you don't love yourself, no one else can love you. It is not wrong to love yourself. Does not the Bible tell us to love our neighbour as we *LOVE* ourselves? We are the first person we should love because we are the first person with whom we have to do. You often hear people say, "I cannot live with myself." But we must live with ourselves because we are the first person we see when we look in the mirror every morning.

Make an effort to become knowledgeable about the world around you. Knowledge is power. This is why others kept Blacks from learning. Success begins with knowledge. Some people might have been born with an inherent desire for knowledge, but most of us can acquire it if we desire it strongly enough. We can start with the little we find in our surroundings and expand from there. We can start by reading the daily newspapers. Even if one is on welfare, a newspaper can be afforded. Knowledge puts one head and shoulders above the rest, and sets such a one on a course of accomplishment. There are people who started on their path of knowledge just by studying plant and animal life around them, even in a non-scientific way. George Washington Carver started this way as a boy on the farm of his adopted White parents, and we all know what a success he became. God has put much in nature from which anyone can begin their acquisition of knowledge.

Those who seek to become successful in life will begin at whatever point they can. You don't need a university degree to be successful. It is alleged that Bill Gates did not yet have one when he and his friends founded Microsoft. Most Blacks who have become successful, started out with very little except the desire to succeed. More of us could be so inspired. Presently, the road to success is no longer as rough for Blacks here in North America as it once was. There are many successful Blacks everywhere, relatively speaking. Whether they made their success in sports, entertainment, or business is hardly the important issue. Even if they are just plain working-class people paying their bills and feeding their families, such can be considered successful. There was a time when Blacks could not be too successful and make much progress in White societies in some places here in North America, because their initiatives were sometimes maliciously and enviously destroyed. Now, however, the situation has changed, even if it will only be temporary.

This is the time to make serious and permanent inroads which will be very difficult to erase. Successful Blacks should buy into residential and definitely commercial real estate, construct apartment and office buildings in prominent areas, establish long-haul transportation companies, hardware stores and building supply stores, invest in grocery store chains, and develop construction and renovation businesses. We cannot always be at the "storefronts" of these establishments because bigotry may still identify and hinder us. Allow others to be visible and do not make it appear that these businesses are owned by Blacks. Nothing angers some members of other groups so much, and makes the hair stand up on their backs so tall, like seeing a successful Black person. So become silent partners if you must, with legalese protection for your investments. We can find capable accountants and auditors who can conduct investigations into business transactions, the hiring of such professionals should keep tabs on what is going on in your business.

We should invest in companies that are doing well by buying shares, stocks, and bonds. Foreign nationals invest a lot of money in American and Canadian real estate and other high performance companies and therefore are almost guaranteed to see their investments grow so their children can have a bright future. They operate trucking companies and manufacture things such as ATM machines, skids, kitchen cabinet doors, and so on. These industries are integral to the economies of today, and educated and wealthy Blacks who can should invest in these types of businesses and become players in such backbone industries. We should work together and support the business initiatives of our own people. I have seen Black West Indians in Toronto who are responsible for making others rich by shopping at their grocery stores selling foodstuffs and other articles indigenous to Black West Indians. The strange thing is that some of them would not shop at these same stores if they were owned by other Black West Indians. They just could not stand the thought of seeing one of their own become successful. They would rather keep their own people poor and make other people rich. These we know need to get a medical check-up from the neck up, and we hope they do so soon.

We need to make a stronger push in the education field. An education is more attainable now than it ever was for Blacks in North America. A lot of our women should stop resting on their laurels, lose some weight, and use the funds earmarked for excess calories to get to a school and learn something useful. They shouldn't just sit around and suck in nourishment like queen bees. If they were hatching worker bees this would be okay. But I will bet my bottom dollar that if they are hatching anything in that situation, chances are it will become like them. And this excess nourishment will only expand the waistlines and the already oversized behinds, while dulling the brain. A lot of our men, too, need to stop dealing drugs, which only poison the minds and aspirations of the young people in their communities, and get to a place of learning. This is no time for hanging out at the shopping plazas and hooting at every frock that goes by. Such behaviour angers other people, especially the women who are the objects of this unwanted attention. It would be much more profitable to turn that energy into accomplishing something that will change one's life for the better.

We may still face some hurdles in some situations where society may still want to deny us the opportunity of an education, but if you can't get one in person there are many accredited distance learning institutions that need not know that you are Black. We are lucky here in North America in that we can upgrade ourselves and get an education at any age, and if slavery gave us one permanent legacy which is sometimes helpful, it is the European surnames that we have. The Whites are sometimes fooled by this when they don't see us face to face. And you need not identify your race when you fill out the paperwork for these distance learning institutions if it is something they require. If you do have to fill in the race section, put it under "other" and write in "human." Do whatever it takes legally and ethically to get an education. Nothing is as important to raise the human condition from the doldrums of mediocrity and awaken the desire for success.

We should stop becoming a part of criminal organizations such as gangs. This is a dreadful way to waste a life. The world is large enough to accommodate everyone wishing to live a good, honest, productive life. Imagine going to bed every night knowing that the purpose of your existence is to kill, rob, steal, deal drugs, rape and hurt others. How can anyone live knowing that every morsel of food eaten, every drink taken, every piece of clothing worn, every enjoyment, every house lived in, and every vehicle driven is paid for from the proceeds of crime? What a dreadful existence that must be! Innocent lives are taken, young women and girls are raped and murdered, and are sometimes forced to become prostitutes, families are ruined, and communities are shattered because some of us have chosen to live this criminal existence. I wish every gang member and every drug pusher would see that their utterly selfish lives are ruining others. Not only do some people live this life but also they recruit others into it. Those who do these things may escape the arm of the law for awhile, or even for as long as they live, but in the final analysis such people will have to give an answer to the Judge of all the earth when called to account for all the evil they perpetrated on society? If there has to be such vagrants in society, why must they be Black?

Think clearly about the negative impact these things have on respectable Black members of society. Certainly one cannot be so dumb as to have no thought of this! We are already a group hated on sight because they think every Black person is a criminal, and yet some of us go on living the expectation, to the detriment of ourselves and other members of our race. For goodness sake, stop this life of self-hate, hate of others, and the revenge you feel you must wreak on society. Whether a petty thief, a white-collar criminal, a murderer, a rapist, a facilitator of prostitution, or a drug pusher, be ashamed of yourself and your lifestyle, and change yourself for the good of society. So many times I have watched on television many young Black men being arrested and charged with killing others. I am so disappointed to see, time after time, these young men who don't even seem to be on the radar where presence of mind is concerned ignoring the negative impact their actions are having on the people around them. They appear most times without shame or care before the public, the police, or before judges in courts of law. They display no embarrassment for what they do. They are in their own little world all by themselves.

Blacks who are able should start organizations that go into Black neighbourhoods and act as role models for the mentally and emotionally traumatized and dysfunctional Blacks who live in these places. We could yet rescue some from initiating and living a life of crime. If we don't help, who can we expect to help? There are so many young Black children with no reason for living. They exist from day to day without aspirations and aims, just passing the time in complete hopelessness. We must be able to offer them some hope. I am reminded here about where I grew up. In Jamaica, the Orientals were sure to take care of their own. While they were going about their daily business, if they came across another person of their race who needed a helping hand, they never passed them by. They would take such a person and provide that individual a new purpose for living. In all my twenty years of living in Jamaica, I saw only one Oriental person living aimlessly on the street and he seemed to have literally lost his mind. I wish we could be so caring about our people.

Begin every new day with a positive attitude. No one has ever accomplished anything worthwhile without that. The world never opens up for people with negative outlooks. You may have read of the success of George Washington Carver and how many setbacks he had. You may have heard of the time when he visited the US Congress to demonstrate the various products he could get from the peanut. At first, they looked at him with deep suspicion and disapproval, but he did not flinch. Because of his ability to remain positive, he eventually won enough of them over to his way of thinking and got the help he needed to do what he wanted to do. When there is a positive attitude, even the sceptics are influenced to see things in a better light. It may be hard to be positive when nothing is going well, but one can be happy if for no other reason than having life. There will always be people and circumstances unfavourable to progress. There will always be stumbling blocks, even for the best equipped. Use them as stepping-stones instead.

Make a conscious choice every day to find something to inspire you and make you a better person. There may be things about you that you are not completely happy with, and many of us may have a lot of issues with self-esteem. The lack of self-esteem is one of the most detrimental problems anyone can face, and I believe that we Blacks in particular have a lot of problems with this one because of how we view ourselves and the way we think others view us. We need to be reflective and see what we can do to prevent this from dictating our course of action. If you are unhappy with your clothing, then change the way you dress. If you think you are lacking in etiquette, then buy a book to learn proper etiquette. Practice boldness if you are shy. By this I mean the positive kind. If you make negative comparisons between yourself and others when you look in the mirror, stop that and tell yourself that you are the best looking person in town. It will amaze you how much your own positive brainwashing will make things better for you. God has not predestined any person to fail. Like the parable of the talents in scripture, He has given to each according to his ability. Find your talents and invest them for Him, for yourself, and for others.

As a child I was teased about my appearance and was very sensitive to what my peers thought of me. They used to laugh at me because I have a big head and because my forehead is wide. They would laugh at my very tight hair. When my father cut my hair, which was always a very low cut, they would point to my bumpy cranium and counted each rise as a separate head. Some concluded that I had six heads. Some said that it was seven. Every time my hair was to be cut it was a time of major trauma for me. They laughed at my mouth because they said it was too small, they laughed at my ears because they are small, and they laughed at my nose because they said it was pointy. In my little world, it was hell just to leave the house sometimes. To further complicate things, I was brought up to be harmless in word and action. (You may think I am no longer harmess in words because I have said some pretty mean things in this book, but at heart I mean no evil) I was not supposed to say anything harsh to anyone or cause them physical harm, no matter how badly they were treating me. But then, at a certain point, I realized that I had to do something about the incessant teasing because it was having a negative effect on my self esteem, and was making me very shy. I decided to become assertive about who I was and how I was going to deal with the issue for the long term.

When I was about twelve or thirteen years old, a number of us were at the local shop/variety store when one of the older and braver boys began the teasing. There was a showcase in the store with plain glass at the front, but the background was dark enough to reflect both of our images. I looked at him in the reflection then looked at myself and discovered that for all my physical "deficiencies" I was still more pleasing in facial appearance than he was, and I said, "I am better looking than you, though." Even that was hard for me to do because I felt I was insulting him. It was also the first time that I had seen any two of our reflections from the same "mirror." From that moment, on the teasing about my appearance stopped. I gained a new confidence, and I began to accept myself as I was. I am not trying to blow my own trumpet here about being goodlooking, but that day I did not look too unacceptable even to myself, and I realized that I had to live with what I looked like. So I say to you, accept what you cannot change, change what you can, and get on with your life. Don't let people make you feel bad because you are Black or because you have other physical detriments. You may not be able to change any of those things relating to your physical person, but you may be well able to change your mental perspectives which make you the person that you are. Develop a beautiful personality along with self-confidence. When you have succeeded in doing that, people of every kind will take notice and accept the person inside your skin.

Learn to live with dignity and class inside your Black skin. Be hygienically sensitive, especially when in public. How many people do you know who don't seem to shower for days and go among others smelling to the clouds, yet want to be accepted just the way they are. What about your breath? When you speak do people turn their nose in the other direction? Keep your head and or facial hair in a neat pattern despite the kinkiness. Don't use foul language even to to be part of the "in" crowd. When people insult and demean you, do not retaliate. It does not make you any better when you do. It actually brings you down a level or two lower. It is best not to respond in kind to negative verbal assauts from others. Just refuse to be drawn into any confrontation with angry and unsophisticated people. It detracts from your dignity. If you are reading this book and have gotten this far, it could mean that you are trying to do something good with yourself. So adopt some of these injunctions if and as they apply to you, and become a better person for yourself, for your spouse, your children, your parents, your employer, and even for those who dislike you because you are Black, or for any other reason

Avoid being drawn aside by the negatives around you. Think of all the outstanding Black people who have had to walk the same path of discouragement and encumbrances and still made a success out of life. Work hard to become the person you want to be, and remember that as long as you are alive, it is never too late to improve. Even those of us who are rapists, pimps, prostitutes, drug-pushers, thieves, adulterers, con-men and con-women, cutthroats and murderers in jails and prisons, can have a rebirth and start behaving like decent human beings should. Society may not be always willing to give us a second chance, and our past behaviour may require that we pay the price for our misdeeds to satisfy the requirements of the law. But God is always willing to return us to the dignity of a sound mind, even if we are on death row, if we will allow Him. Do not ever fight, neither verbally nor physically, and especially, never do this in public. It just makes you a little lower than the hyenas. And don't be loud and aggressive.

Do not run around having illicit sexual relationships with every man or woman you meet, disgracing yourself and others, and do not take advantage of innocent and gullible young women. I say this mostly to the men, even though our women can also be promiscuous and sometimes are indeed so. Such behaviour just cheapens the race and brings us down in the gutter a little faster. Until your last breath, give yourself the opportunity to make the needed changes and become a better person in life.

Some of you may have been hurt so badly that you have lost your will to make good use of the rest of the life you have in you. You may have lost a dream you once had. You may have lost the desire to aim and aspire. You still have the unique ability to fulfill your dream, but you are the one to believe in yourself and you are the only one who can do something about it. You have the power in your hands to effect the needed changes that will bring this about. We can become visionaries. We can become artists, scientists, scholars, inventors, and businessmen, etc. "Where there is the will, there is the way," is a saying we may all be familiar with, and it is true. So find the way to fulfil your dreams.

Sometimes, we cannot attain to our wishes because we are stuck in our comfort zone. A comfort zone in this context is a mental condition we have found ourselves in and have become satisfied with the way things are even though we see that we have placed a lid on ourselves. We feel safe and in control in this zone. We feel approved by those around us, whoever they may be. Most times, to fulfill our dreams we have to move out of this little mental state. As soon as we are out of it, we become very uneasy and unsure of ourselves. We then run back into where we are most comfortable, achieving nothing in the process. But our personal growth and the fulfillment of our dreams can only become reality when we cross this line of comfort and step right out into the unknown. We are not any longer little babies, totally dependent on our parents or the system. We have to depend on ourselves. The handouts might stop and the life of no achievement will lead to nowhere. Don't stay stuck in a mental rut. You must do something good with your life, and you might as well make it something outstanding. There is a saying we use in Jamaica, "When you aim, don't aim for the top of the tree, aim for the sky. If you aim for the sky and you fall, you may fall on the top of the tree, but if you aim for the top of the tree and you fall, you will fall to the ground." The logic of the saying is to aim very high, much higher than may be normal for you. If you fail to get what you really aim at, you may still get something worthwhile out of your new found desire and strength of purpose. With a bit of courage and a bit of willingness one can accomplish a lot, and remember that every big journey begins by taking that first small step. These steps are made one at a time.

This may never have occurred to you before, but you can have whatever it is that you really want. It may take a long time or a short time, and will depend on where you begin. Some of us will have to begin farther from the finish line than others because of circumstances over which we have no control. Coupled with that is the reality that the time-line of this achievement will depend also on what we have to start off with. You must first be true and honest with yourself about what it is you wish to accomplish. Once you have set the ball rolling, there are a few things to keep in mind:

1) Thoughts become things. The thoughts of your minds can indeed become your lifestyle and your experience. If you sow thoughts, you will reap acts, and the more productive your thoughts the more beneficial your acts will be.

2) What you believe will show up as factual to you. Remember the little train going up the hill. It got there by repeating, "I think I can, I think I can.". When you think you can, you will. But if you think you can't, you won't. Don't be your own worst enemy by consigning yourself to failure even before you begin your journey.

3) What you feel will become your reality. I have heard people say they want such and such a thing so much that they can taste it. You must feel and see yourself in a position of success or achievement before you can see it materially. When others started out with their dreams they felt for a certainty that they would make it a reality. If they didn't think so they would not have succeeded. Learn from them.

4) You must have great expectations. What you hope for happens. But along with your hope you must do something about it. No sense hoping to get to work if you will not wake up when the alarm clock sounds, get ready, and board the bus. Without taking the steps, you will certainly not get anywhere.

5) You have endowments with which you were born. You must use these to help you with your accomplishments. We all have the raw materials for success. This we must develop, improve, and finesse to our own situations.

6) You must align yourself to someone or something that inspires you. This becomes your stepping-stone to your success. Every successful person had a mentor, someone or something that inspired them to be successful. Find yours. It exists somewhere around you. It may even be above you so look up sometimes. You may find it calling you up to a higher purpose.

7) You need to create relationships with people and organizations that can help you to reach your goal. No one is an island, and even some of these successful White inventors had their Black slaves who stayed up with them all hours of the night to help and support them. These slaves never got any credit for what they did, but they were there all along. You may notice that even the religious people who knock at our doors come in groups of two and three? Create positive relationships. They can be your best resource.

8) When you think about it, there is a lot to help you achieve your goals. Nature is resplendent with resources to enable you to become successful. It will provide you with the right people, the right circumstance, or the right product. Have you heard of Microsoft, of Mary Kay, Noni Juice, or Himalayan Goji Juice and others? The world is there with its abundance to help you.

9) You have the equipment necessary to initiate your success. The equipment is the many billions of brain cells that you were born with. I have noticed that even the fish and the bird with their little pin-sized brains accomplish things. What are we doing with ours?

10) One of the means by which the cat learns is through curiosity. We all have that trait as well. If you are curious you will want to explore things around you. Use this inborn trait of curiosity to help yourself in your quest for success.

11) Develop relationships. It only takes a smile to begin one, and relationships can mean the difference between success and failure. Get to know those who are successful. Chances are you will find someone who can relate to your quest for success and is willing to help you.

12) Learn that life has meaning. Believe that you are not just here to pass time or warm seats. You can find a real purpose for living. Even the ant has a purpose. You should find yours also. Along with discovering your purpose, understand and accept the fact that you are a very wonderful and very powerful person, and never let your mind make you think otherwise.

13) Sleep less. Did you know that too much sleep can cause you to be a perpetual failure in life? When you have too much sleep you won't find time for accomplishing anything. In primary school I was taught this little gem,

"Heights by great men reached and kept were not attained by sudden flight, but they whilst their companions slept were toiling upward in the night." Reflect on this and work very hard to attain to something very worthwhile.

When I was young, the reason I was always a bit beyond my siblings and contemporaries in knowledge about a lot of things was because I did one thing that none of them did. I stayed awake at night and read every book I came across. When they were in their second shift of sleep, so to speak, I was still up reading. It used to upset my parents because they figured that I was wasting too much kerosene oil, but I had to satisfy my desire to read. I am much older now but one of the reasons I am writing this book is because of the love for books that I developed back then.

Avoid accepting the notion that being Black means genetic inferiority to other people. This is very untrue. The Bible reveals that every person alive today descended from Noah's three sons and their wives. The Bible also really recognizes only one race—the human race. Why then the uproar about skin colour? More particularly, why all the uproar about melanin? Though we have other physical differences, our skin colour is the most problematic for people seeking to highlight and promote differences. Since all people can intermarry and have children who themselves can produce offspring in spite of skin colour, this shows that the differences between us are not significant. It is said that our DNA difference is only 0.2% and of that only 6% can be linked to racial divisions. Even though we have so many different skin colours, white, black, yellow, red, and brown along with other shades, (Brazil counts up to ten), we all have the same colouring pigment in our skin. It is called melanin. This is a dark brown pigment and is produced in differing amounts in special cells in our skins. If we had no melanin, we would all be albinos. This is a mutation caused defect. If just a bit of melanin is produced, that person is European White. When our skins produce a lot of melanin we become very (dark) or Black, and differing amounts produce different skin tones. We can notice the melanin difference even among people of the same race and in my case, family. Ever heard of tall, dark, and handsome? They were not talking about the Black man. Notice that some Whites are almost milk white, while others are closer to a light tan colour. When I visited a Zulu cultural centre in South Africa I was surprised to find some of them almost slate black but others more like light chocolate.

God may have developed this just to see how we would react to each other as part of His overall plan to discipline and polish us. It could be part of the same reason He buried precious metals so deep in the earth just after the flood so that we would have to put some effort into retrieving them rather than leaving them on the surface of the earth as was the case before when precious metals were just on the ground everywhere. Life back then was so easy we took things for granted. You may notice also that God has placed people of different temperaments even in the same nuclear family, under the same roof, to teach us how to get along together. Before the tower of Babel, we all spoke the same language. I believe that before the tower was built there could have been plenty of evidence of this melanin difference among the earth's inhabitants already. Because the tower was being built in defiance of God, He decided to confuse our language so we could no longer communicate un-encumbered. It is conceivable that more than one persons spoke each of the languages into which the then known world was divided. God's plan initially was to get humans to live all over the face of the earth. Up until that time, they refused to do so and congregated at Babel to build this city and tower to stay together. As they were now forced to go their separate ways, it is obvious that the people divided themselves according to their languages. Seeking even more in common, they also most likely divided themselves according to other similarities they had; one could have been their skin tone. If this is true, it is then easy to see that their off-springs would have had the same colour, hence the different colours of people. People have other features we cannot explain, shape of eyes, nose size and shape, mouth size and shape, hair and eye colour, and so on. Except for pigmentation affecting some of the above, no one can yet offer a reason why these differences are with us today. Esau and Jacob were twins out of the same woman. Esau came out red and hairy. Jacob was plain. Can you explain that?

Some say that people from Africa with their large noses and mouths evolved such proportions so when they breathe they would take in enough oxygen, which is lessened because of the intensity of the heat in the air in the places where they live. Well, the people of Ethiopia and Somalia, the Bedouins of Saudi Arabia and the Indians of South America get just as much or more heat as any place in Africa, and they don't have large mouths and noses to the same extent as Sub-Saharan Africans. And the Whites who went to live in Africa have been there for many centuries and they don't seem ready to develop larger mouths and noses any time soon. The converse is true also for Blacks who have lived in the colder countries of the West for hundreds of years. They don't seem about ready to reduce the size of those body parts yet, either.

The melanin situation is a scientific fact. Nowhere in this has information been found to substantiate colour difference because of any inherent inferiority or superiority. The truth told, in some situations Blacks were worshipped as Gods earlier on in the history of peoples. This means that others considered them superior at one time. Even today, there is a Black God worshipped in Roman Catholicism called Jupiter who they call Jesus, and there is one in the Hindu religion as well. I don't think anyone worships anything of any colour they think is inferior to them. As pointed out earlier, I believe it was the Deity worshipped which in a large measure, made the difference in progress or lack of progress with people, and as humans descended further in degradation, the situation became worse and the mind became more and more darkened with an accompanying lessened capacity for progressive thought and action. It had nothing to do with skin colour (melanin).

A chain breaks at its weakest link, and humans will always find things to foster division among us. This applies equally to humanity without respect to colour or nationality. In my first grade at school I recall an incident when a group of older boys from our immediate area and a group from a neighbouring area decided to go to "war" over some wrong that had been done to one person from one group. The battle was to be pitched in the local village square. All that day, young men from both sides left school to gather "implements of war.". When they confronted each other after school that afternoon, there were sticks of various sizes and lengths, little pieces of twisted metal dug up from the ground, and stones many. The two "armies" faced each other, but there was no Goliath to defy either. Eventually, my older brother volunteered to "start the fight." He was soundly berated by an adult who knew our family and chased him home. The "battle" was never fought but it left a lasting impression on me. I could not figure out why they needed to fight. We were all from the same general area, of the same variated shades of Black skin, and why we wanted to fight I was too naive at the time to understand. As I thought about it later, I saw that we lived in two different locations and that was reason enough to differentiate us. The wrong done was only the catalyst that ignited this awareness. The point I am making is that it is better to find accommodation for our differences and seek to work together inspite of them.

As I grew up, I discovered that people will find anything to promote divisiveness. I live in Canada, an apparently peaceful country. But English-speaking Canadians hate the French-speaking Canadians and the French speaking Canadians hate the English speaking Canadians. Western, Central, and Eastern Canadians hate each other, even though they speak the same language. And the rest of Canada seems to hate the people from the Atlantic Provinces for socioeconomic reasons. Bear in mind that they are all White. Even those who live in the same areas suffer some form of discrimination if they have different sounding last names with ancestors from different countries. Hopefully knowing this will help you to see discrimination in a different light which might in turn lessen the stress you get from it when it comes your way.

In Texas, I lived in Travis County. Southeast of Travis County was Bastrop County. I was told one day of a service provided to people of both counties. This service was offered in Travis County. Well guess who got served first, and guess who was almost denied the service entirely? Then there was the young couple who lived below our apartment. They were Texans. They told us that they lived in Ohio for a short time. The wife became ill and needed medical attention. They told us that when it was known that she was from Texas she was neglected by the staff in the hospital. The young man said he had a car problem one day on the highway. When the police found out by his driving licence and car plates that he was Texan they refused him help. Hearing of these incidents left me gasping for breath. I thought only among "un-enlightened" people did these things occur, but I came to the conclusion that tribalism existed everywhere, only that in some places it changes its name. Now while these mentioned incidents may not be typical of every situation arising, I pen them in the hope that we may understand that it is not only in the direction of Blacks that the negatives of preferences are pointed.

Another interesting point is the fact that though we are refused jobs at a disproportionately high rate, we are not the only ones, and that jobs are not refused only because people are Black. Whites and others are refused jobs too, and sometimes feel the same rejection. From our perspective, a White job seeker is more acceptable to a White employer, and that is generally the case. But in my conversation with some Whites, they don't necessarily feel any affinity or entitlement to a White employer, nor do they seem to take for granted the fact that on this continent it is they who control 99.999% of everything economically. Some months ago, I was talking to a White female acquaintance and asked her if it made her feel very secure, when she looks at the infrastructure of downtown Toronto, and to know for certain that every piece of brick that make up those buildings, and every major corporation residing in those walls are White-owned. She said she never thought about it. I found her answer interesting because such a pre-occupation has rarely escaped my mind for many long years now.

Should this bit of information make Blacks feel any better or give them a little more self-esteem when they seek employment? Maybe the answer to that question resides with each as an individual. And if you are able to feel positive and motivated then that is the way to be. When, as a Black person, you are not chosen for a particular job or a promotion for which you feel you are qualified, you need to look at another possible reason for not getting it without feeling rejected. You need to also understand that even Whites are rejected for jobs for which they themselves feel qualified. Sometimes the very opposite of our negative conclusions might be where the real truth lies. Always remember that the mind will accept whatever you tell it to accept, and sometimes brainwashing, even by your own self, may be the only helpful resource you have to keep yourself from complete discouragement. I go back to one mental game I play on myself when I feel particularly insignificant and would encourage everyone reading this book to do the same. I tell myself that I am better than everyone else in the world. I start with being a million times better, then a billion times better, then a trillion times better. When the situation is really challenging, I raise the ante up a gazillion times better. I don't know how many zeros a gazillion has, but by the time my subconscious mind gets to that high a figure, I can take on almost anything and anyone mentally. The only other thing that has been as helpful to my self-confidence was the study of martial arts or self-defence as such is commonly called.

Try that mental game anytime you face a daunting situation such as going for an interview or when you need to go to a place where you'd be less than comfortable with the people.

Avoid over-eating no matter how strong the temptation. Over-eating clogs up the mind and uses up blood and energy needed to allow the functioning of other organs of the body. When there is food in the stomach, most of the blood surrounds it to help to digest this food. This means that the blood needed for the brain, for example, is much lessened and proper function is impaired. This is a real drain on the body. It is said that the average digestion time for food should be four to five hours, but when one eats a lot it makes for slow digestion. Add to that the cold liquids that we take in at meal times which must become heated in the stomach and digested before digestion of the solid food begins as the body digests liquids before solids. This lengthens the digestion time. Then some people have desserts an hour or two after a meal. This starts the digestion process all over again. Do this a number of times per day and the stomach is in a continual state of digestion. How then can the brain have time for functioning properly? It is constantly indolent as a result of over-eating, and poisoned food, which is just rotting in the stomach producing very olfactory flatulence and bad blood, resulting still further in a state of mind more fit for the dead than a live human. The mind of such an individual can have no desire to learn anything. Most times we, the poor, eat very unbalanced foods—pasta, macaroni and cheese, noodles, potatoes, frozen pizzas, and such, and in amounts reserved more for elephants than humans. And we continue this cycle of imprudence without end. You might notice that the wise do not eat as much as some of us do. I am amazed time and again by the scant amount of food consumed by those who seem to be achievers in society. They have figured it out a long time ago. Even at a pot-luck lunch or dinner, they will not go back for seconds. They then stay alert for conversations; meanwhile those who have had their stomachs filled to the point of squeezing air out of their lungs just want to fall over and go to sleep. Maybe there is a lesson to be learned here.

The preceding was just an observation by a lay -person, namely me. For any dietary advice, consult your doctor or nutritionist. Seek professional opinion for any bit of "advice" this book may seem to convey.

Finally, be patriotic and love your country, whichever it may be and whether you were born there or if you adopted it. You may be surprised that you have to learn to love its people even when you know they hate you. You might wonder why, as a Black person, you should love countries like America, England, India, Brazil, Canada, or any other country where Blacks are hated almost as a public policy. The reason is simple. Love for your country and for its people will be beneficial to both you and them now and in the future. This will be very instrumental first of all, in removing a lot of stress from your mind. Love is the most powerful force in the universe. It will change the way you see people, change the way you see yourself, and it will certainly change the way you treat others and the way they react to you. It will change things around you, and this will be for the better. Many people have gone on to great things because someone showed them love. And, many people have become criminals because there was no love for them even in their own homes. One of the reasons America has such a great crime problem from its Black population is because they are so soundly hated there. I watched a movie about a serial killer who became that because as a child he was hated. He killed women mostly but he met one who was very tender to him. Interestingly, he did not kill her. I know this was just a movie, but in real life we are kindest to those who treat us the best.

If you love your country it will make you proud to be a part of it and will even help you to want to contribute to its well-being. Remember always that what you do affects your life, sometimes as equally as what is done to you.

The human spirit, even yours, can survive any onslaught if you will only give it the chance to do so. When you love your country you will respect its other citizens. You will be courteous and kind to them. You won't kill them, harm them, drug them, nor rape them. You won't seek to wreak vengeance on its innocent citizens of any colour because someone else did you wrong. Love even your enemies, they are humans too with imperfections just like you.

To show your love for your country, start with your neighbourhood. Keep it as clean as you can from physical and moral pollution. Don't litter its streets and don't encourage wrong acts of behaviour. Do your best to keep out those who dare to make your neighbourhood a place for the free flow of drugs, and those who come in to draft your young neighbours into criminal activity. Even if you live in the projects, do your part to keep it in proper condition. It is where you live. Be proud of it. A lot of us are known for being untidy and it is unfortunately very true. It is part of why our neighbourhoods are so ignored by city fathers and planners, and it is because of our lack of cleanliness that some Whites don't like when we move into their neighbourhoods. They see their property values going down because of the lack of housekeeping skills with some of us. It is a foregone conclusion that our Black skin is legendary for certain kinds of expectations from others. These expectations are usually not good, and as Blacks we have to start doing something that will change the way others think of us. This might take a few generation to accomplish, so we must begin immediately. We should start showing some civic pride, among other very important things, which others see as obvious delinquencies.

Remember that you will never reach a higher standard than the one you have set for yourself. So set your mark high, and step by step, even though it is by painful effort, by self-denial and sacrifice, ascend the whole length of the ladder of progress. Let nothing hinder you. Fate has not woven its meshes of encumberance about any human being so firmly that he or she needs to remain helpless and in uncertainty. Opposing circumstances should create a firm determination to overcome them. The breaking down of one barrier will give greater impetus to break down even bigger ones and gives courage to go forward. Press with determination in the right direction, and circumstances will be your helpers, not your hindrance. Let no one enslave your mind.

CONCLUSION

I have been questioned about why I would write a book like this and has been called racist a number of times by some people because of it. I hope I am not racist and I hope I will not be seen as one. However, I am not afraid of the word discretionary because everyone I know has the right to be. However, we must stay within the bounds of human decency even as we express our views, or as we mould our opinions and conclusions. We have to ensure that we give each other space, respect, and consideration for the fact that we share the planet on which we have been collectively placed by powers over which we have no control.

While I've had to speak frankly and sometimes very harshly in this book about the evils that racism has brought on to the Black race, let us be reminded also that in spite of the racial imbalances of the past, some of the members of the White race, have proven time and again to be the best friend of the Black race. They have indeed come to our rescue very many times when others would have completely destroyed us. They have given of their jobs, have supported our little businesses, fought some of our battles and social issues for us, and in many cases have ensured our survival under very difficult circumstances. The English defended Blacks in South Africa against the Boers who were also White but who would have viciously enslaved and annihilated Black Africans. The White nations of England and France brought pressure on the Arab Muslims to free Blacks from their cruel and mindless enslavement of us. Whites fought for the abolition of slavery, even though it financially benefitted them and their country, and some even gave their lives to protect and help us. No other group has done as much for us as they. So when all is said and done, let us show our gratitude to them for their help and support instead of always hating, and in some cases, unjustly killing them by our criminal activities.

I have said harsh things against Blacks too when we are found to be gullible, lazy, untidy, crime inclined and unmotivated. But I have been congratulatory and supportive when we succeed and when we improve ourselves. Though some of you, White, Black, Brown, or Yellow might exercise strong opposition to some of the contents of this book, I am also hoping that some of its contents will change some minds for the better.

Finally:

* Let us bear in mind that one day, ready or not, it will all come to an end. There will be for us no more sunrises, no minutes, hours, or days. All the

things collected, whether treasured or forgotten, will pass to someone else. Wealth, fame, and temporal power will shrivel to irrelevance. It will not matter what you were owed. Your grudges, resentments, frustrations, and jealousies will finally disappear, so too your hopes and ambitions. Even your to-do lists will expire. The wins and losses that once seemed so important will fade away. It won't matter where you came from, or on what side of the tracks you lived. It won't matter if you were beautiful or brilliant. Even your gender and skin colour will be irrelevant.

So what will matter? How will the value of your days be measured?

What will matter is not what you bought, but what you built, not what you got but what you gave. What will matter is not your success, but your significance. What will matter is not what you learned, but what you taught. What will matter is every act of integrity, compassion, courage or sacrifice that enriched, empowered or inspired others to emulate your example. What will matter is not your competence, but your character. What will matter is not how many people you knew, but how many will feel a lasting loss because you're gone. What will matter are not your memories but the memories that live in those who loved you. What will matter is how long you will be remembered, by whom and for what.

Living a life that matters doesn't happen by accident. It's not a matter of circumstance. It is a deliberate choice. Choose to live a life that matters!

* The above nugget was given to me by a friend. She read it to a group of people among whom I was present, and I asked her for a copy. I don't know who the author is.

Made in the USA